Software-Agents and Liberal Order:

An Inquiry along the Borderline between Economics and Computer Science

by
Dirk Nicolas Wagner

ISBN: 1-58112-117-2

DISSERTATION.COM

USA • 2001

Software-Agents and Liberal Order:
An Inquiry along the Borderline between Economics and Computer Science

Dissertation.com
USA • 2001

ISBN: 1-58112-117-2

www.dissertation.com/library/1121172a.htm

Software-Agents and Liberal Order

An Inquiry along the Borderline between Economics and Computer Science

Thesis presented to the Faculty of Economic and Social Sciences
at the University of Fribourg (Switzerland) to obtain the doctor's degree
in Economic and Social Sciences by

Dirk Nicolas Wagner

Accepted by the Faculty of Economic and Social Sciences
on 12th October 2000 on the recommendation of
Prof. Dr. Guy Kirsch (First Adviser) and
Prof. Dr. Jürg Kohlas (Second Adviser)

Preface

In the course of history we have looked at machines from very different perspectives. At the beginning of the modern age leading thinkers were not far from concluding that man is like a machine. In practice, an ambiguous life with machines began that, ever since, has been characterised by a continuously changing appearance and influence of the machine. The spectrum quickly extended from steam engines to microprocessors. The steady outward push of the technological frontier soon inspired science-fiction, which speculatively highlighted the convergence of man and machine. With repeatedly adjusted but ambitious goals, computer science has followed some of the paths imagined by science fiction. Today, the relationship between man and machine is more complex and inscrutable than ever. Nevertheless, it becomes evident that machines are about to play their own social role. Consequently, there is a motivation for the social sciences in general and for economics in particular to enter the scene, looking at machines from a new perspective.

This book adopts an economic perspective. On the one hand it is written with the broader picture of the so called New Economy in mind. It focuses on software-agents who may be considered to be potential key players of this economy in the future. On the other hand this study can be read as a modern restatement of classical liberalism. It unpacks liberalism as a possible social order for software-agents in a world where men delegate more and more actions and decisions to machines. A key feature of the following text is that new and classical elements are tightly interwoven.

Due to its interdisciplinarity, the study covers a relatively broad spectrum of functions. First, it serves to make evident that it can be advantageous to examine increasingly complex machines as social actors and to tackle questions regarding a social order for machines. Second, and more specifically, it offers researchers from computer science an economic framework which may serve as a source of orientation, inspiration and explanation for the design and evolution of complex computer systems. Third, the analysis aims to support those economists who have realised that machines designed by computer scientists open the door to a new dimension of economics: the economic analysis of social systems with software-agents. I am convinced that this room has to be entered.

The inspiration and the encouragement to pick up the subject of this book came from Professor Guy Kirsch and Professor Jürg Kohlas. I am indebted to the director of the project, Professor Kirsch, for his stimulating and steady coaching. The learning experience drawn from the numerous discussions with their multitude of facets goes well beyond the project itself. I am grateful to Professor Kohlas who efficiently guided my entrance into the world of computer science and who gave me the opportunity to work in the instructive environment of his department.

For their willingness to share views and to comment thoughtfully on my manuscripts I thank Gerald Hosp, Hippolyt Kempf and Heribert Knittlmayer at the University of Fribourg. Similarly, but often over long geographic distances, I have received detailed and helpful comments as well as useful suggestions from Ivan Baron Adamovich, Arno Fehler and Markus Michalke. And I have extensively benefited from constructive critique from Dr. Kurt Annen, who repeatedly made the limits of my own work transparent to me. Of great help to me were Jason Liechty, who carefully proofread the final draft, and Norbert Lehmann, who repeatedly provided technological assistance. Thank you all. Despite all support any mistakes or misinterpretations are my own. Finally I am grateful to the Swiss National Science Foundation for partially funding the project (grant no. 12/555 11.98).

Fribourg, 28 June 2000   Dirk Wagner

Contents

Figures and Tables

Abbreviations

ACE	Agent-based Computational Economics
ACL	Agent Communication Language
AI	Artificial Intelligence
BDI	Belief Desire Intention
DAI	Distributed Artificial Intelligence
DPS	Distributed Problem Solving
FIPA	Foundation for Intelligent Physical Agents
KIF	Knowledge Interchange Format
KQML	Knowledge Query and Manipulation Language
MAS	Multi-Agent System
NIE	New Institutional Economics
PCMAS	Partially Controlled Multi-Agent Systems
PDA	Personal Digital Assistant
URL	Uniform Resource Locater
WWW	World Wide Web
Y2K	Year 2000
XML	Extended Markup Language

Part I   Foundations

A delicate mission promises to be ahead. New grounds will be explored in a scientific area that can be found between computer science and the social sciences, particularly economics. It will be shown that this area is an interesting and relevant field of research. At the core of this argumentation will be the propositions that software-entities affect the social order of society and that economic theory of social order can provide insights for the design of software and software systems. These insights can be especially valuable because traditional approaches of computer science provide no general answer of how to solve the problems of social order software entities cause among each other and in human society.

Within this study machines are at the centre of interest. As economists do not normally study machines, the topic has to be made accessible to economic analysis. It will turn out that, with the help of software-agent technology, economics and computer-science can be bridged. But it is not only economists who need to gain access. Economic methodology has to be made approachable to computer-science. However, there is no point in competing with textbooks on economic theory. Rather than providing a fully detailed account of all possibly relevant theories, a methodology will be outlined that allows to capture the problems of social order in open systems of and with software-agents. To identify and analyse problems is an important task. But such efforts are often only rewarded if accompanied by the identification and analysis of potential solutions. At the end of this first part it will be proposed to analyse whether the concept of liberal order is applicable to software-agents. This appears to be especially problematic as liberal order requires actors to be free. Software-agents, however, are not normally intended to be free.

1

Computer science and economics
- new actors and social order

Dave: Hal, I'm in command of this ship. I order you to release the manual hibernation control.

HAL: I'm sorry, Dave, but in accordance with sub-routine C1532/4, quote, When the crew are dead or incapacitated, the computer must assume control, unquote. I must, therefore, override your authority now since you are not in any condition to intelligently exercise it.

Dave: Hal, unless you follow my instructions, I shall be forced to disconnect you.

A. Clarke (1969): 2001 A Space Odyssey

The telescreen received and transmitted simultaneously. Any sound that Winston made, above the level of a very low whisper, would be picked up by it; moreover so long as he remained within the field of vision which the metal plaque commanded, he could be seen as well as heard. There was of course no way of knowing whether you were being watched at any given moment. How often, or on what system the Thought Police plugged in on any individual was guesswork. It was even conceiveable that they watched everybody all the time. But at any rate they could plug in your wire whenever they wanted to.

G. Orwell, (1949/84): 1984

1.1 From utopia via the present days into the future

In "2001 A Space Odyssey" the human crew of the spaceship Discovery gets involved in a fatal conflict with on-board computer HAL. In Orwell's novel "1984" computer technology allows for surveillance and oppression of the people. Both stories are dystopias about a future where machines become problems although they were originally invented to solve problems. These two dystopias are no exceptions. Countless other visions exist. And like the two precedents they are either anarchistic or totalitarian.

In spite of the fact that 1984 and 2001 are rather outdated in the strict sense of the word, the dystopias have not lost their appeal. Much of the fascination descending from the works of Clarke and Orwell is probably due to the circumstance that they shadowy but emphatically draw the contours of an emerging reality. This counts for the optimistic impressions as well as for the pessimistic.

Clarke, Orwell and others were decisively optimistic regarding technological progress. Machines with outstanding capabilities play a leading role in their works.

3

Up to now, however, all dreams of the omnipotent machine have remained science-fiction. Still, a technological level is reached where computers as universal machines are capable of performing many of those activities that were fiction in "1984" and "2001". The required processing capacities are nearly adequate, simple speech recognition systems serve as reliable communication interfaces, so called chatterbots are convincing interaction partners in dialogues on specific subjects and chess computers beat human grandmasters (cf. also Stork, 1996). In essence, a rough portrait of today's machines could be painted along the following lines:

- At a high pace, machines become more and more powerful. Indicative of this process is Moore's law, which states that the processing power of microchips doubles every 18-24 months.
- To an increasing extent machines show characteristics that belong to a social artefact rather than to a mechanical object.
- The functions executed by machines become more important. To an increasing degree machines influence their environment physically, economically and socially.
- The way machines take over these functions changes. Less often, machines are directly manipulated by humans. Rather, more and more complex tasks are delegated to them.
- Machines no longer act in isolation but interact with humans and with other machines.

All these events are taking place as the meaning of a machine is changing. Today, the notion of a machine might better reflect software rather than hardware. The momentum seems to have shifted from the actual physical atoms that comprise a mechanical robot to the bits that make up a digital program (Bradshaw, 1997b, 4). The ambition to craft artificial humans has stepped into the background in order to leave the stage for machines that specialise in certain functions. In other words, "computers are organised much more directly around what electronic circuits are good at than they are around what people are good at" (Bailey, 1992, 68).

Turning to the potential consequences of future technologies, Clarke and Orwell drew a pessimistic picture. Currently, humans are not actively threatened by artificial actors. But approaching the capabilities of HAL also means approaching problems similar to those provoked by HAL. It seems to be unavoidable that the outlined technological achievements have their particular downsides. For instance, there is a risk that erroneous software design may lead to interruptions in the supply of infrastructural services like power, communications or public transport. Daily, significant costs arise and human life is threatened because of bugs in software, e.g. in medical or military systems (cf. Wiener, 1994, Birman/Renesse, 1997). World wide, a five-digit number of software-viruses is known to infect programs and data causing damages amounting to billions (cf. Kephart et al., 1998a). On top of that, the increasing role of the Internet leads to conditions where people and

4

organisations can be more easily and more substantially damaged through information. So called spam is one example for this, antagonistic webpages targeting ethnic groups or corporations another. The Internet offers an environment where these activities can be executed by machines often more efficiently than by humans (cf. Leonard, 1997). In addition to the problems named so far, unintended harmful effects can arise when programs, which were designed by independent programmers or which are employed by independent users interact. This can occur even when the individual program is error-free and not supposed to cause any damage. Examples from the area of electronic commerce are shopping-bots and price-bots that have the potential to cause severe price-wars (cf. Kephart et al., 1998b). Overall, the mentioned problems differ in various ways. While combinations of all sorts are possible, the problems induced by machines can be summarised in five categories:

- Bug: A program contains errors and does not behave as designed.
- Design bug: The program code is free of errors, but there are unintended errors in the design.
- Virus: The program and the design are error-free. The virus manipulates someone else's data or programs and can intentionally cause damage.
- Devil: The program and the design are error-free. Other programs remain unchanged. The devil accesses, steals, manipulates or distributes data in full knowledge of its semantic meaning and thus intentionally creates damage.
- Emergent problem: The program and the design are error-free. Other programs remain unchanged. Data is being accessed, manipulated or distributed in full knowledge of its semantic meaning but without offending the rights of others. The combined effect of many operating and interacting programs leads to unintended, overall harmful effects.

The illustrated spectrum of problems indicates that the pessimism of authors like Clarke and Orwell turns out to contain some truths. Their pessimism, however, goes much further than the typology of problems presented here. It is systematic in character. Clarke threatens his audience with anarchy. Orwell invokes totalitarianism. So far, the projections of science-fiction have not materialised. But they do not receive opposition from sound scientific analysis either. Rather, either ignorance or latent agreement characterise the current attitude in computer science. This is fed by a prevailing anomaly in computer technology: Extremely rapid progress in computer hardware is contrasted by only average improvements to computer software (Brooks, 1995, 181). Consequently, even recognised pioneers of computer science do not exclude that current problems may some day amount to something worse. Joseph Weizenbaum emphasises that it is "better to think of new ways to avoid having problems than to simply throw more processing power at them" (cit. in Leonard, 1997, 56).

Taking Weizenbaum's remarks at its cue, this study intends to overcome both the pessimistic view and the ignorant non-view. The often positively interpreted technological progress on one side and the negative side effects on the other side are considered to be inevitable. But it is argued that societies consisting of men and machines can keep well clear of anarchic, totalitarian and other systems where life is "solitary, poor, nasty, brutish and short" (Hobbes, 1651/1996, 84). The book focuses on the question of social order for machines. It is about computers but it is not computer science. Instead, it provides an economic analysis of a particular idea, liberal order. The functionalities of liberal order are demonstrated and it is shown how fundamental problems of order can be handled. Particularly, clues from economics and more generally from the social sciences are delivered to the much younger field of computer science, proposing that computer software can follow the principles of liberal order. While this may not be a "silver bullet", immediately delivering the much asked for order of magnitude improvements in software simplicity, reliability and productivity (Brooks, 1995,181), a general approach to understand and solve the problem of order is offered. As will be shown in detail, this includes issues like overcoming state of nature situations, accommodating individual unpredictability, escaping the small-worlds problem and achieving social order at low transaction-costs.

1.2 Computer science and order for small worlds

The computer is a universal machine and falls into the area of responsibility of computer science. The backbone of computer science is the order it creates in the sense that many distinct parts are assembled to form a unified, predictable whole, more concretely, a functioning program. But if the creation of order is the core competence of computer science, then why is a solid justification building on knowledge derived from economics needed, rather than on findings from computer science itself?

Over the last decades, computer science has quickly adopted the image of an engineering discipline (Gibbs, 1994; Appelrath/Ludewig, 1995). At the heart of this discipline is the structured analysis, the language representation and the conversion of real world situations into algorithms. In other words, programmers first analyse how to automate a given process and how to divide problems up into sub-problems. With the aid of appropriate algorithms they then design a detailed manual for the respective process that can be executed by a computer. Unlike other devices, the computer can manipulate any information that is described clearly enough. Without an exact description, without an algorithm, or simply without order, however, there is no chance for automation. The inversion of the argument is also popular: Automation indicates order and suggests unified and predictable wholes.

"Software entities are more complex for their size than perhaps any other human construct" (Brooks, 1995, 182). Software is complex because of the large number of parts of which it consists and because of the great variety of connections between these parts (Jennings, 1999, 1429). Continuously, new and more complex problems are to be solved by programmers. Consequently, software is getting ever more complex. In the light of this development, it becomes less evident to view automation as an indicator for order. Traditional programming only works if five conditions are met: "First, we know exactly what we want to do. Second, we can foresee every possible eventuality. Third, we can predict a correct action for each such eventuality. Fourth, we can execute each such action flawlessly. And fifth, the solutions we need are especially efficient" (Rawlins, 1998, 79). As soon as a more complex problem is to be solved, these conditions fail to exist. From an economic point of view, a trade-off between complexity and order might be suspected, i.e. the processing of more complex problems requires lower expectations with respect to order (cf. figure 1.1).

Figure 1.1: Trade-off between complexity and predictability

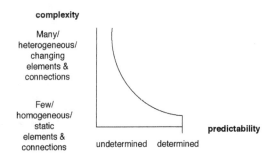

The incompleteness theorem of logician Kurt Gödel proves that, because of their complexity, computers can in principle be unpredictable for humans. For instance, it is reported that already in the 1950s the air-defence system of the United States was unpredictable: "The SAGE system was so complicated that there appeared to be no way to model its behavior more concisely than by putting the system through its paces and observe the results" (Dyson, 1997, 181). In addition to the fact that it is impossible to fully verify whether a program is correct, in practice time pressure in the development process causes software to contain even more errors than could theoretically be prevented (Gibbs, 1994).

7

Meanwhile, computer science is undergoing a paradigm shift. Monocentral computer systems are replaced by polycentral computer networks; closed architectures are followed by open architectures; sequentially structured computing systems disappear to make room for parallel systems. The impetus for this paradigm shift has its origin in the mentioned ambition to solve more complex problems. Basically, these systems achieve a higher fault tolerance, but they are even less predictable, and individual errors can cause devastating chain-reactions. In principle, bugs and design-bugs are more easily handled, but they appear more often. At the same time, new areas for problems open up. First, the introduction of polycentral, open and parallel systems leads to a loss of total global control which, so far, often has been taken for granted. Computer systems are no longer exclusively designed along the lines of central planning. Rather, they are being designed independently and get connected in often unforeseen ways, so that the potential for emergent problems increases exponentially. Second, the new paradigm increases the number of interfaces between computers and human society. Additionally, the social relevance and reach of machine actions grows. Problems like viruses and devils become more pressing.

Traditional computer science has only limited means at its disposal in order to meet the challenges just portrayed. Two aspects are particularly striking: First, as computer science has to be exact, it concentrates on the details while the possibility of disorder in a larger context is in danger of remaining unconsidered. Second, computer science in its role as an engineering discipline largely neglects the social relevance of its artefacts. Both arguments need explanation.

As already indicated, computer science is constrained in that it can only handle problems that can be exactly described. In order to achieve this, computer scientists regularly only envisage "small worlds" in the sense of Savage (1954/71, 8ff). A "small world" is derived from the real "grand world" by neglecting some distinctions between possible states of the world and thus by drawing a simplified picture. The small world phenomenon is perfectly illustrated by the Y2K problem caused by the representation of the dates in computer software by six figures instead of eight figures. Within a small world programmers create order. Problems are only considered if they are relevant within this world. "The problem of small worlds is that an analysis using one small world may fail to agree with an analysis using a more refined small world" (Shafer, 1986/90, 125). The ultimate level of detail is only given by the grand world in which we live. Software that is active in the grand world but whose actions are based on a small world can only be unproblematic as long as the environment perfectly adapts to this software.

Apart from this, it has to be considered that computer science is traditionally only responsible for the computer as a machine, not for the computer as an actor among other machines and/or within human society. But eventually, the described problems and the sketched paradigm shift affect social order as a whole. Problems like network breakdowns, viruses and spam go well beyond the field of computing itself, and traditional computer science does not offer the analytical tools to systematically connect issues of social order with the order of program codes.

In conclusion, computer systems become more and more complex and socially interconnected. This leads to a situation where the traditional notion of order in the sense of unified and predictable computer programs (small worlds) seems no longer sufficient because it neglects that unpredictability cannot be avoided. Furthermore, it does not meet the requirements of a grand world and lacks a social embedding of computer systems.

1.3 Economics and order for the grand world

At the outset two points were established. First, computer software creates and is confronted with problems of order. Second, computer science can no longer meet traditional expectations regarding the question of order. Only recently have computer science and related fields started to analyse polycentral, open and parallel systems in general (cf. O'Hare/Jennings, 1996) and problems of social order in particular (cf. Kephart et al., 1998b). In contrast, for other sciences both questions have proved to be fundamental issues for ages. The vocabulary and the methodologies may have changed over the centuries but the basic questions have remained the same. One of these areas of research is today's economic analysis of social order in the tradition of Thomas Hobbes and the Scottish moral philosophers David Hume, Adam Ferguson and Adam Smith. Based on new impetus from fields like the New Institutional Economics, Evolutionary Economics, Sociology, the Austrian School, and the Ordo-liberal School, the economic analysis of social order can employ a wide and sophisticated range of analytical tools and insights. This makes economics an attractive partner for computer science.[1]

One important aspect in this context is that interdisciplinarity is not only attractive but also possible: Economics and computer science are complementary sciences. In fact, interdisciplinarity between the two sciences is as old as computer science itself: When thinking of the first computer, Charles Babbage employed the economic principle of the division of labour. Since then, the chain of interdisciplinary contributions has not stopped. This series includes influential names like John von Neumann and Herbert Simon. Today the spectrum reaches from projects at MIT, the University of Michigan, the Santa Fe Institute and the Brookings Institute to activities at the corporate research centres of Xerox, IBM, NASA and others.

---

[1] Unless stated otherwise, the term economics in this book stands for economic analysis of social order. Another science that partners with computer science in this area of research is sociology (cf. Malsch, 1998a).

Huberman/Hogg (1995, 141) emphasise that networks of computers face the same problems as market economies do and hold that "economics may offer new ways to design and understand the behavior of these emerging computational systems." Boutilier et al. (1997, 3) draw the conclusion that the principles of polycentral computer systems are primarily economic. A growing force of researchers and practitioners employs tools from economics to handle the emerging challenges posed by a wired world. The central aim is to efficiently co-ordinate and allocate resources in and through computer systems (cf. Clearwater, 1996; Wellman/Wurman, 1997; Shoham, 1996). Often, these contributions are not merely theoretical but ready for implementation, e.g. the utilisation of a market mechanism for automated climate-control in large buildings (Clearwater/Huberman, 1995). This book will build on existing interdisciplinary work. It will fill a gap by providing a unified view of the field, instead of being tied to an individual application. It presents theoretical foundations that can widely be employed.

The mentioned interdisciplinary activities support the point that economics can be useful to computer science as far as the question of order is concerned. Practically, this is demonstrated by solutions for electronic business, telecommunications, energy, air-traffic control etc. based on economic principles (cf. Jennings/Wooldridge, 1998). An important aspect that distinguishes the present contribution from existing approaches is that it focuses on social order and that it separates the question of order from the particular problem to be solved. Such a perspective does not comply with the views of programmers designing centralised and closed computer systems where purpose and order are inherently linked. It does, however, offer an appropriate way to look at bundles of systems consisting of interconnected sub-systems which are engineered by different programmers and employed by different parties and whose borders are unclear and constantly changing. In these environments there is no single purpose and there is not one single order. Order, however, is required, the social relevance of machines has to be considered and the effects on the grand world have to be taken into account. In a sense, the economic understanding of order promoted here is less ambitious in that it does not envision software to be a unified, predictable system. Rather, various types of computer software are viewed to be elements that, like humans, are active parts of the world.

> Order, then can be defined as "a state of affairs in which a multiplicity of elements of various kinds are so related to each other that we may learn from our acquaintance with some spatial or temporal part of the whole to form correct expectations concerning the rest, or at least expectations which have a good chance of proving correct" (Hayek, 1973, 36).

The basic argument behind this definition is that under such conditions, it will be easier for the individual purposes - whatever they are - to be reached. While the appeal of this alternative view of order may not be intuitive - and can probably only be convincing after gaining support from the following chapters - the intention of this venture can nevertheless be illustrated at the outset: The widespread implementation of general economic principles of order can permit computer systems to reach a higher technology curve that indicates a higher degree of order at the same level of complexity and a higher complexity at the same level of order respectively (cf. figure 1.2). Economic principles can inform the development of polycentral, open and parallel systems.

In essence, three reasons have been identified that make it worthwhile to shrink the distance between economics and computer science: First, social order is an important research subject in economics, and this subject is affected by the developments in the area of computer software. Second, economics and computer science are complementary sciences. Third, economics can offer theoretical concepts and basic principles of order that can be employed by computer science.

Based on these premises this book aims systematically to offer access to economic understanding and to fundamental economic principles of social order for a world with complex computer systems. The approach differs from past and existing research activities both in and at the borderline of computer science and economics. This is because computers are viewed as socially relevant actors within an interconnected world, and because the perspective is not one of small worlds but one of the complex, grand world of everyday life. And, the focus is on the problem of social order, which is separated from specific purposes.

Figure 1.2: Computer systems based on economic principles reach a higher technology curve (schematically)

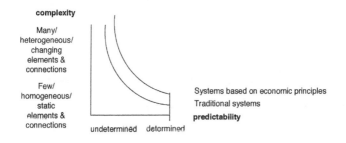

11

1.4   Machines as software-agents

The introduction of many works by economists is marked by a discussion of the behavioural model they employ to conceptualise the human actor. Here, precedence is given to another actor, the machine. As a universal machine, the computer and particularly its software can be found at the centre of interest. This does not seem a narrow focus if one considers that computers are involved in a vast variety of human activities. Pervasive Computing or Ubiquitous Computing are illustrative keywords here. The focus can be narrowed by concentrating on a particular software-paradigm called agent-technology. Agent-technology conceptualises software-entities as software-agents. Before discussing the concept in greater detail, it is advisable to derive why the present study focuses on this paradigm. In fact, several reasons can be found for such a step. Although a proof for the superiority of agent-technology over other approaches of computer science is unavailable (Jennings, 1999, 1431), the relevance of software-agents increases rapidly. This is true for research as well as for applications (cf. Jennings/Wooldridge, 1998 and table 1.1). Especially on the Internet the agent-paradigm prospers. "The computational architecture that seems to be evolving out of an informationally chaotic web consists of numerous agents representing users, services and data resources" (Huhns/Singh, 1998a, 1). Empirical evidence for the coming massive penetration and the rapidly increasing variety of software-agents comes from information services like Botspot or the Gartner Group.[2] Despite recent successes, critics have repeatedly questioned the relevance of agent-technology (Shneiderman, 1997, 100). However, Jennings (1999, 1431ff) argues that agents are more than a trend because the technology can deal with the challenges posed by the design of complex computer systems. Additionally, the characteristics of agent-technology enhance its prospects of becoming a dominant paradigm in computer science. This is nurtured for instance by the fact that the conceptual basis of software is no longer determined by the computer architecture, but relies on the problems itself. On top of that, agent-technology supports the use of existing systems and programs. Existing code is not substituted but simply complemented with a new wrapper. Consequently, every software program can become an agent.

Even in the light of these arguments it might be premature to assume at the current stage of development that software-agents in the long run will be a dominant paradigm in computer science. Thus, the ultimate reason for focusing on agents originates from another source: In contrast to other computer science approaches, agent-technology is based on a "cognitive and social view of computation" (Shoham, 1997, 271). This implies that, through the agent-paradigm, machine worlds theoretically can be accessed and understood by a social science like economics. Conversely, it also means economic ideas can enter into computer science the same

---

[2] See: http://www.botspot.com, http://www.gartner.com.

way. In other words, if computer science and economics are to meet then most probably and most successfully it will happen via the agent-paradigm.

Table 1.1:   Application areas for software-agents

- Workflow Management (Office, logistics, operations, R&D etc.)
- Network Management (Telecommunications, power, transport etc.)
- Data Mining, information retrieval and management
- Digital libraries
- Education
- Personal digital assistants (PDAs)
- Electronic Business (Auctions, supply chain management etc.)
- Entertainment
- ...

The notion of an agent can be traced back to the Latin expression "agens", meaning the cause of an effect, an active substance, a person or a thing that acts, or a representative (Tokoro, 1994, 1). [3] For the notion of an agent in the sense of an artificial actor a common definition is to be searched in vain. The definition of Huhns/Singh (1998a, 1), however, can be considered to be a common denominator of many existing definitions: "agents are active, persistent (software) components that perceive, reason, act, and communicate." Similarly, a synthesis derived by Franklin/Graesser (1997, 21ff) describes an agent as "a system situated within and part of an environment that senses that environment and acts on it, over time, in pursuit of its own agenda and so as to effect what it senses in the future." Paradoxically, such definitions are simultaneously criticised both to be too vague (e.g. Shneiderman, 1997, 99f) and to be too constrained (e.g. Krogh, 1997, 149). A more comprehensive picture can be drawn by referring to a modifiable and extendable list of attributes. Table 1.2 summarises the characteristics of software-agents discussed in the literature. Usually, individual agents comprise several but not necessarily all of these attributes. Eventually, these attributes are to differentiate agents from conventional software (cf. Kautz, 1994/98, 130).

---

[3] In order to prevent conceptual misunderstandings, it is worth noting that throughout the book the term agent always refers to a machine while the term actor refers to both men and machines.

13

Table 1.2: Attributes of software-agents from the perspective of DAI

Attribute	Description
Autonomy	Agent acts without immediate intervention or under control of other actors.
Continuity	Agent exists over a longer period of time.
Situatedness	Agent receives input from environment and its actions have an effect on the environment.
Reactivity	Agent acts based on stimulus-response principle.
Intentionality	Agent acts on the basis of an internal representation of beliefs, desires and intentions.
Adaptiveness	Agent learns from experiences and shows adaptive behaviour.
Communication	Agent communicates with users and other agents. ("knowledge-level communication" (cf. Newell, 1982))
Co-ordination	Agent harmonises its behaviour with other actors.

Depending on the number and intensity of the attributes it is appropriate to speak of "weak and strong agenthood" (Wooldridge/Jennings, 1995, 2). Strong agenthood requires the presence of mental states, i.e. characteristics that usually apply to humans. In contrast, the concept of weak agenthood describes much simpler agents. They mainly differ from traditional software in that they act largely without human intervention.

Beyond the externally observable features of a software-agent the agent-architecture can be found. With respect to such construction plans a huge variety of proposals exists. "These are typically layered in some way with components for perception and action at the bottom and reasoning at the top. The perception feeds the reasoning subsystems, which governs the actions, including deciding what to perceive next" (Huhns/Singh, 1998a, 7). The reasoning system is at the centre of interest. Representatives of cognitive or deliberative approaches propose architectures that allow the agents to choose their actions based on an explicit representation of their environment. Well established approaches for cognitive agents are so-called belief-desire-intention (BDI) architectures (Rao/Georgeff, 1995). The agent's know-how about itself and its environment is represented in the form of beliefs. Next to that, an agent has desires about its preferred state of the environment. Based on its beliefs and desires the agent forms intentions about the state of the environment it aims to achieve. In order to function properly, the architecture has to systematically connect beliefs, desires and intentions with the perceptions and actions of the agent (Huhns/Singh, 1998b). The advances of computer science regarding the three components of the BDI-framework differ. The representation of a system's environment has long been a fruitful field of research in computer science and an agent's beliefs can build on these achievements. In contrast, computer software has traditionally been task-oriented and it is pre-dominantly due to the agent-paradigm that goal-orientation has started to play a role in software engineering. Consequently, the notions of desires and intentions can only build on a less well nurtured body of research.

Reactive agents do not possess a central reasoning system. Representatives of this approach propose to construct agents from or as reactive modules. Complex behaviour emerges based on many simple and autonomous actions of the individual components. One of the best known examples of this approach is a robot designed by Brooks (1986) whose six legs co-ordinate without having to rely on a central controlling unit. With respect to this technology, software-agents represent a much wider field of application than robotics (cf. Maes, 1995). Between purely cognitive and purely reactive architectures, hybrid approaches are proposed which bridge the two concepts (e.g. Fischer et al., 1996/98).[4]

The various architectures for software-agents are developed on the basis of certain theories. The theoretical basis for cognitive agents is delivered by McCarthy (1979) and particularly by Dennett (1987). They argue that, in principle, every physical system can be assumed to possess cognitive states such as desires or intentions. Whether the agent does in fact have intentions is not crucial. It must only be convincing to describe him that way. Shoham (1997, 273) uses the example of a light-switch to demonstrate that such a perspective is only to be considered for description, explanation and prognosis if there is no simpler theory available, e.g. a mechanistic one. It is mechanistic theories that give orientation to the designers of reactive architectures. Behaviourism and Positivism respectively represent important foundations. The modelling of mental processes is refused. The analysis of observable variables, particularly perceptions (stimulus) and actions resulting from them (response), constitutes the core of this approach.

A theory of software-agents has to provide more than just a basic understanding of agents: "We regard agent theory as a specification for an agent; agent theories develop formalisms for representing the properties of agents, and using these formalisms, try to develop theories that capture desirable properties of agents" (Wooldridge/Jennings, 1995, 3). In the presence of the large variety of properties agents need to incorporate, different kinds of theories become relevant. These can be summarised within categories representing theories of rational, social, interactive, and adaptive behaviour (cf. Huhns/Singh, 1998a, 12ff). Rationality is a central feature of the decision process of many existing software-agents and is responsible for the creation of consistency between cognitive states like beliefs, desires and intentions. As agents usually do not act in isolation but in the presence of other

---

4 For an extensive overview of agent-architectures, see Wooldridge/Jennings (1995, 12ff).

agents or humans, theories of social and interactive behaviour become relevant. Finally, it is important that agents can react flexibly to changes in their environment what is backed by theories of adaptive behaviour. The objectives of this book will be reached via a discussion of the theoretical foundations of software-agents and multi-agent environments. In this book, the contents of the categories named above will be discussed from an economic point of view, not from the perspective of computer science that was used here to introduce the new actors. The previously made quest for an economic perspective received further support here because the given discussion of software-agents showed that there is a common denominator between humans and agents. Both are entities that can be perceived as actors.

1.5   Software-agents as new social actors

Taken seriously, software-agents do not make up an independent world. They are part of the world. As already demonstrated, a whole range of everyday tasks is delegated to software-agents or at least involves agent-technology. At this stage, it is evident that agents represent a new type of actor. Yet agents are very different from humans. In order to understand and solve problems of social order, it is necessary to encircle the particularities that characterise this type of actor.

The basic feature of software-agents is probably that they are digital actors. A whole range of implications stems from this characteristic. First of all, digital data can be copied arbitrarily and it takes little effort to do so. Consequently, software-agents will not be employed sporadically but in large numbers. A large variety of agents can be expected. Nevertheless, many of these digital entities will be largely or completely similar. This presumption is backed by the fact that a majority of agents is designed with the aid of so called agent-frameworks.[5] These tools offer a basic agent-architecture that can be specified by the user of the agent. Comparable to other digital products, any user can be expected to easily gain access to agent-technology. Similar to other digital products, many "originals" may exist and the "original" cannot possibly be traced. Social consequences of a situation like this can be that it is impossible to trace the originators of certain actions, which can imply harmful effects for society.

A further aspect is the large amounts of electronic data and information that have been produced over the last couple of decades than can be considered a "natural environment" for software-agents. Two trends point to the increasing relevance of this issue. On the one hand, factors like the Internet imply that the amount of electronically available information rapidly increases while at the same time the flow of information is highly dynamic and limitedly structured. On the other hand, the

---

[5] Examples are the Java Agent Template (JAT), the Java Expert System Shell (JESS), IBM's Agent Building Environment (ABE), SRI's Open Agent Architecture, or Object Space's Voyager.

number of users of electronically available information and data that has limited computer-related know-how steadily increases (Bradshaw, 1997b, 12ff). In this situation, software-agents take over two types of tasks. First, they operate as independent problem-solvers and help to overcome the complexity of distributed computer systems, for instance by managing resources (routing of emails and telephone calls, information retrieval etc., cf. Ward, 1998; Willmott/Calisti, 2000). Second, agents can assist humans personally. They operate as intelligent user interfaces. They support their owner when interacting with other computer applications and execute tasks autonomously. Negroponte (1997, 59) describes these personal digital assistants (PDAs) metaphorically as "well trained English butlers", who know their owner, share information with him and who are thus capable of effectively operating on behalf of him. Examples of possible roles and tasks include:

- Time-planning-agent: Arranges dates with other actors (e.g. Maes/Kozierok, 1993).
- News-filtering-agent: Selects news and information that are of interest to the user (e.g. Maes, 1995).
- Matchmaking-agent: Brings sellers and buyers of products together (e.g. Foner, 1997).
- Shopping-agent: Searches for products, negotiates and buys on behalf of its owner (e.g. Chavez/Maes, 1996).

The examples illustrate a further aspect: Software-agents can be considered highly specialised actors. This statement refers to the tasks software-agents are assigned to. While humans unite many roles in one person, the existence of a software-agent is usually closely tied to one exclusive role, for example that of a buyer. Without interruption, the agent is dedicated to the respective role. In many cases such agents can only interact with actors that are active in the same domain. Any task that goes beyond the specified role of the agents has to be solved in co-operation with other actors. In general, the utilisation of software-agent increases the degree of division of labour and specialisation in society which results in more interactions with and among software (cf. figure 1.3).

Figure 1.3:   The degree of specialisation in the economy with and without software-agents (schematically)

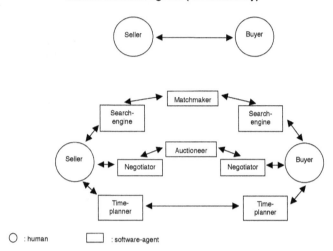

The subject of specialisation indicates that software-agents are actors that face severe constraints concerning their perceptual and reasoning capabilities. A fairly general but applicable characterisation would describe agents as lacking common sense. Particularly with respect to economic activities, however, it is striking that software-agents prove to be superior to humans. First, they show quicker responses to changes in the environment and second it is easier for them to handle certain complex structures, for example price-structures (Kephart et al., 1999). It seems plausible that agents will be extensively used in those areas where they are particularly suited. In contrast to other artefacts that have become indispensable - for example pocket calculators - agents are capable of decision-making and transacting.

Another aspect in this context is that agents are actors that can change quickly or that can be changed quickly. It is not only their decisions and actions which change but the whole actor. Individual change can be due to the interference of a third party, for example a programmer. But it can also take place autonomously, based on methods of learning, adaptation and evolution. Thus, it may be difficult to identify a specific software-agent at different points in time. Even if this is not a problem, it can be difficult to form expectations of how its behavioural characteristics have changed since the last meeting. Unlike humans, agents do not necessarily remain themselves when they undergo changes.

On top of that, what exactly constitutes one single agent is an open question. Compared with biological actors, digital actors are not defined by physical boundaries. Still, the concept of embodiment is often thought to be vital for agents as well: "They must be embodied in the situated sense of being autonomous agents structurally coupled with their environment." (Franklin, 1997, 499). However, it is not straightforward to implement this concept in essentially bodiless environments. Another proposition is to perceive a software-agent or a multi-agent system to be a single actor if it acts as a social unity (Rammert, 1998, 3). This can apply to a PDA as well as to a system of agents that is distributed over a whole enterprise. If the system is controlled centrally, e.g. by a firm's vice president of operations then it can be understood as a single actor. If, however, many individual agents with diverging goals and principals operate within the system, then each of these agents has to be understood as a social unit. Thus, again unlike humans, agents do not have predetermined and fixed boundaries. Compared to an agent-free human society this leads to a much larger range of interaction opportunities. As a consequence, the social network of society becomes even more complex.

A discussion of software-agents would be incomplete if it overlooked the human tendency to personify machines. Software-agents are designed to be social actors. Consequently, it is not surprising that humans anthropomorphise agents (cf. Nass et al., 1994). But it is important to emphasise that agents are things and not living creatures: "Programs participating in a computational market are not people (or even animate), hence they are not hurt when they go broke" (Miller et al., 1996, 101). This, however, does not imply that it is always feasible to stop these programs or to eliminate them. Experiments with evolutionary software-agents demonstrate the potential danger that "if people tried to stop them, it's possible that they would evolve mechanisms to escape the attacks" (Thomas Ray, cit. in Ward, 1998, 35). Another example are viruses, in effect much simpler software-artefacts than agents. Existing viruses can be fought successfully but this does not mean that they are eliminated (cf. Kephart et al., 1998a). As software-agents do not age, their source-code remains present forever. In a given situation it is only possible to de-activate them successfully. This implies that agents have the potential to become a new kind of environmental problem.

Inevitably, the social software-agent profile presented here is incomplete. The dynamics and variety of software-agent research and development simply do not allow a complete picture to be drawn. Overall, the feature that probably best characterises software-agents is their complexity. This means that the theme begun in chapter one has found its continuation. Software-agents operate as independent problems solvers or as personal assistants within a digital environment that is difficult to access for humans. In several ways they are unpredictable:

- They decide autonomously and in real-time, whether or not, with whom and when and how to interact. The number of highly specialised individual decisions that accumulate when agents operate makes their behaviour unpredictable.
- The outcomes of agent-interactions are unpredictable, if agents are able to influence each other.
- Emergent phenomena can arise that lie beyond the intended behaviour of the single agents.

Increasingly, these three factors of unpredictability in social environments blot out the fact that, in most cases, software-agents are deterministic actors. It is this complexity that demands a view of software-agents as relevant parts of a grand world rather than as mere variables in the small worlds of closed computer systems. In essence, this section demonstrated that agents, like humans, are social actors. Yet it also showed that they differ systematically from humans. The economic analysis of agent-environments will have to take these particularities into account.

1.6   Summary

This introductory chapter outlined the point of departure for the interdisciplinary journey that is to follow. The problems of order machines can cause kicked-off the discussion. It appeared that these problems, which have traditionally been tackled by computer science, are no longer confined to this field but become relevant to society as a whole, which is an object of economic study. In addition it was found that computer science and economics possess different conceptions of the notion of order, which implies different strategies to solve these problems. It was concluded that the deterministic concept of order prevalent in computer science can only be applied to the small worlds of closed systems. Economics was claimed to be able to capture problems of social order in a grand world. Due to the increasing complexity of machines and because of the rising social relevance, it was proposed to systematically study the possible contributions of economic theory to an understanding of social order with an within complex computer systems. This presupposes that computer science and economics can understand each other. The agent-paradigm was discovered to be a suitable interface between the two sciences. Software-agents were introduced as a new object of study for economics and as new social actors in the grand world. The subsequent analysis will focus on the economic discussion of agents and agent-environments. The problem of human-machine interaction will always be prevalent but it will not be discussed explicitly. The spectrum of aspects that would have to be examined appears to be too large to carry out such an analysis simultaneously. Nevertheless, a discussion of social order between man and machine can logically build on what will be provided here.

2

Computer science's small worlds

The fundamental problems have already be indicated. It was outlined how these problems are dealt with traditionally and which contribution a new economic perspective can deliver. Additionally, software-agents were introduced as new socially relevant actors. In applied computer science, not only the development of software-agents but also the design of whole systems of agents has become a distinguished area of research. This chapter is a survey of how agent-environments are discussed, modelled and designed by computer scientists. In essence, multi-agent technology assembles the answers of computer science to the question of social order among software-agents. This chapter looks at multi-agent technology from a purely descriptive perspective. Within the restricted space available here, it aims to give a genuine and comprehensive picture of this diverse and dynamic research area. On this basis the challenges agent-technology faces can be spotted. Furthermore, the approaches presented here will prove to be a valuable resource when, in later chapters, the applicability of economic concepts to environments of software-agents will be analysed.

The individual software-agent under discussion so far is not designed to run, Robinson alike, on an isolated computer. Rather, it is viewed as a social entity that is part of a multi-agent environment. Consequently, the interactive and interdependent behaviour of many software-agents is important. The chances and challenges arising from the existence of a large number of interconnected agents is studied by researchers from the area of Distributed Artificial Intelligence (DAI). DAI-research aims to establish relationships between the aggregated system behaviour, the behaviour of individual actors and the environmental conditions including mechanisms for interaction (Wellman, 1998). The central tasks can be captured by the keywords communication, co-ordination, and co-operation. As soon as more than one agent is studied, these categories are of fundamental importance. Any further objectives can only be envisaged based on specific approaches to communication, co-ordination and co-operation. Among those objectives are the protection of individual software-agents, the guarantee of reliable system behaviour or the efficient allocation of constrained resources within a system.[6]

---

[6] For a more detailed discussion of the research agenda of DAI, see Gasser (1991,110) and Jennings et al. (1998, 17f).

2.1 Communication in agent-systems

If agents are considered to be non-autistic, the question becomes how they are enabled to interact and especially communicate with other agents. This task is solved by agent communication languages (ACLs). "We view an agent communication language as the medium through which the attitudes regarding the content of the exchange between agents are communicated; it suggests whether the content of a communication is an assertion, a request, a query etc." (Labrou/Finin, 1997/98, 235). This definition illustrates the relevance of so called "speech acts" (Austin, 1962) in ACLs, i.e. the language building blocks of communication protocols are selected so that the expressions of agents correspond their actions (cf. figure 2.1 for an example). Natural language delivers the input for ACLs. Today, several hundred speech acts are categorised and are at the disposal of agents. Ideally, there would only be one ACL, a lingua franca, through which all existing agents could communicate. Common standards are the Knowledge Query and Manipulation Language (KQML) and a proposal by the Foundation for Intelligent Physical Agents (FIPA) that is based on the language Arcol. These developments are in part rivalled by increasingly sophisticated Internet markup languages like XML, which can also be used by agents. These languages are supported by applications, which are under development to allow for the building of Internet-based networks of interconnected services.

Figure 2.1: A KQML-request

```
(ask-all
            : sender A
            : receiver B
            : language KIF
            : ontology healthcare
            : content "select drg_code from encounter")
```

While KQML only structures messages and transforms them into actions, a language like the common Knowledge Interchange Format (KIF) is required for a more sophisticated transfer of content and knowledge. KIF can be understood as an interlingua, i.e. an agent might internally use another language to represent its knowledge but translates it into KIF before it communicates it to others. Instead of speaking many languages, the communication partner then only has to be able to understand KIF. KIF can be employed to express sentences in first order logic and can be understood by humans.

The variety of domains where software-agents can be active requires agents to have an extensive vocabulary at their disposal. In addition, interacting agents have to have the same understanding of a particular vocabulary. This problem is solved by ontologies that cover every domain where agents operate. An ontology is a computerised representation or model of a specific part of the world. "Together with a standard notation such as KIF, an ontology specifies a domain-specific language for agent interaction" (Cutkosky et al., 1993/98, 49). As it is not feasible for every agent to save and update all existing ontologies, a promising concept is to have specialised ontology-agents on the net that can be queried by agents who are in need of domain-specific vocabulary.

Despite the described developments, the options for agent communication remain rather limited. The speech acts supported by KQML or Arcol for example, are limited to assertives and directives. Other important communication categories - for instance, commissives, permissives, prohibitives, declaratives or expressives, are not covered (Singh, 1998, 43). Consequently, agents are constrained in a variety of ways: "Arcol agents must always speak the truth, believe each other, and help each other" (Singh, 1998, 45).

2.2   Co-ordination and co-operation in agent-systems

The presented approaches to communication, particularly speech acts, already evoke elements of co-ordination and co-operation. Co-ordination and co-operation, however, are crucial to the question of social order. Individual agents have to operate based on severe knowledge and resource constraints. At the same time their actions often show interdependencies. "An agent can be helped or damaged, favoured or threatened, it can compete or co-operate" (Castelfranchi, 1998, 160). As a consequence, these issues must be treated separately.

It does not come as a surprise that the notions of co-operation and co-ordination are defined differently in DAI and in economics. In DAI alone there is no agreement on a common definition. Jennings et al. (1998, 9) and others distinguish co-operation (to work for a common goal), co-ordination (organise activities so that harmful interactions are prevented), and negotiation (reach an agreement that is advantageous for all parties). Castelfranchi (1998, 166f) distinguishes no less than nine principles of co-ordination, including co-operative co-ordination. In comparison, a common view in economics is the following: Actors face a co-ordination problem if all involved parties have an interest in a mutual adjustment of their behaviours. Co-ordination can be reached through explicit agreement or may be unintended and spontaneous. Actors face a co-operation problem if their self-interest hinders the involved parties from co-operating and achieving a behaviour that would be advantageous for all of them (Leipold, 1989, 130f). As the analysis provided here is rooted in economics, subsequently the economic notions will be used.

In the search for mechanisms for co-ordination and co-operation, DAI-research refers to concepts from the social sciences and the natural sciences and employs them as metaphors to model environments for software-agents (cf. Huberman, 1988). Researchers in DAI are guided by the conceptions these sciences offer, for example for organisms, markets, organisations and other systems. All in all, two basic directions can be identified: Distributed Problem Solving (DPS) and Multi-Agent Systems (MAS). During the mid-80s MAS evolved out of research in DPS.

DPS is based on the assertion that every intelligent system - regardless whether it is artificial or natural - can rely only on limited capabilities and capacities. Merging formerly independent systems then promises to overcome existing limitations and allows for the solution of more complex problems. In other words: "Distributed problem solving thus studies how a loosely coupled network of problem solving nodes (processing elements) can solve problems that are beyond the capabilities of the nodes individually. Each node is a sophisticated system that can modify its behavior as circumstances change and plan its own communication and cooperation strategies with other nodes" (Durfee et al., 1992, 379). DPS is application-oriented. Solutions are provided for many practical problems - like for instance those, named in table 1.1.

DPS systems can be characterised by referring to their most important features. All subsystems and agents are designed centrally. The system-designer possesses complete control over every single agent as well as over the co-ordination and co-operation mechanisms. Due to the feature of central design, all agents follow the same global goal. They maximise the utility of the system as a whole by solving a predetermined problem. Whether the agents act independently or co-operate depends on which kind of behaviour is better for the system. In conclusion, DPS-systems are built in a top-down manner.

The name already indicates that Multi-Agent Systems consist of many agents, too. In contrast to DPS, MAS may be designed by several different designers. "Research in MA[S] is concerned with coordinating intelligent behavior among a collection of autonomous (possibly heterogeneous) intelligent (possibly pre-existing) agents. In MA[S] there is no global control, no globally consistent knowledge, and no globally shared goals or success criteria" (Kraus et al., 1995, 298). Consequently, the design of MAS is a bottom-up process. This results in systems where every agent follows his own objectives. With regard to posed problems, individual agents are equipped with limited information only and the problem size usually exceeds their capabilities. There is no global control, data is decentralised and processing is asynchronous.

Thus far, MAS have predominantly been applied to single practical problems. In principle, however, MAS can support the formulation and solution of multiple problems. This means that individual agents as well as groups of agents can look for a formulation of and solution to their problems.

It is not always feasible to differentiate strictly between DPS and MAS. Rather, the concepts of DPS and MAS represent opposite points on a continuum of possible multi-agent environments. More specifically, these environments can be positioned within a two-dimensional matrix (cf. figure 2.2): The vertical dimension indicates the degree of autonomy of software-agents and thus the degree of control the designers of the systems have over the individual agents. The horizontal axis describes the degree of structure of the environment. Along this dimension the spectrum reaches from fully structured lab-systems to rather unstructured environments as they appear in the everyday life of the Internet. Closed and open systems can be found at the opposite ends.[7] In the light of the technological, economic and societal developments, a trend towards the upper right sector of the matrix can be identified. This, however, implies that in the long run neither the concept of DPS nor that of MAS reaches far enough to capture what can be observed in reality. For instance, the concept of DPS already proves to be insufficient to deal with the tasks within an organisation like a firm: "For the practical reason that the systems are too large and dynamic (i.e. open) for global solutions to be formulated and implemented, the agents need to execute autonomously and independently" (Huhns et al., 1994/98, 36). Then, the further software systems approach the upper-right corner the less an absolute global design and control over that system is feasible. It is questions positioned around this issue that will receive the attention of the later chapters. Before, it will be instructive to look at common approaches to DPS and MAS in some more detail.

---

[7] Like all two-dimensional classifications, this matrix neglects important further criteria for differentiation. For example the degrees of distribution and heterogeneity can only be concluded indirectly. The same accounts for the number of agents and the types of agents.

Figure 2.2: A segmentation of multi-agent environments

Agent's Autonomy	structured	unstructured
high	Designers design their own agents, but agree on common co-ordination and co-operation mechanisms. Agents have private goals, maximise their utility, but have to follow the rules.	Designers design and control only their own agents. They have no control over other agents or interaction mechanism. Agents have private goals, maximise their utility, and try to influence others.
low	Agents as well as co-ordination and co-operation mechanisms are designed and controlled centrally. Agents are usually benevolent, co-operative and try to achieve a global goal.	Designers design their own agents, but agree on common co-ordination and co-operation mechanisms. Agents have private goals, maximise their utility, but have to follow the rules.

Environment

2.3 Overview of approaches to co-ordination and co-operation

DPS and MAS represent very general concepts for co-ordination and co-operation of multiple software-agents. The basis for a functioning system has to be much more concrete. Particularly, the specific rules of interaction are of importance. "Using principled characterisations of interactions between agents and their environments to guide explanation and design" is the central task for the designers of DPS and MAS (Agre, 1995, 1). The selection and configuration of these principles determines to a large extent the properties of the system as a whole. It is only at this point that implementation becomes feasible. Meanwhile, a variety of approaches to order interactions exist. The literature does not provide a representative taxonomy of agent-systems, but the essential categories discussed within DAI can be subsumed and discussed under the following headings:

a) Ecosystems
b) Social laws
c) Multi-agent planning
d) Social commitments
e) Organisations
f) Market-oriented systems
g) Automated negotiations
h) Negotiations

a)   Ecosystems

It can be attractive to achieve co-ordination without communication (Franklin, 1998b). One example for this is the already mentioned robot of Brooks (1986) with his society of six independent but reactive legs. Another example for co-ordination with minimum communication is the behaviour of ants. No individual ant has a blueprint for the nest it helps to construct. And no ant can recall the way to the source of food its colony uses at a given time. Nevertheless, these insects march in well-ordered parallel rows over long distances, finally constructing complex, climatised nests. Their behaviour is based on a stimulus-response scheme, triggered by pheromones that they employ to mark each other and their environment (cf. Kelly, 1994, 306). The co-ordination within the ant-ecosystem is "genetically hardwired" (Macy, 1998, 1). The ecosystem consists of reactive actors. All ants of the same status follow the same IF/THEN rules. The co-ordination of ants is interesting because interactions of software-agents can be structured based on the same principles (cf. Meyer/Wilson, 1990; Ward, 1998).

b)   Social laws

One property of the ecosystems approach is that the genes or programs responsible for co-ordination fully determine the behaviour of the individual actor. It is however feasible to allow the individual actor to have separate goals. In order not to risk conflict, Shoham/Tennenholtz (1995) propose the implementation of social laws. Social laws constrain the actions of actors. "The constraints specify which of the actions that are in general available are in fact allowed in a given state; they do so by a predicate over that state" (Shoham/Tennenholtz, 1995, 243). These general rules of conduct can be designed off-line, i.e. before the agents are put to use. In addition, rules can develop as conventions in the course of interaction (cf. Shoham/Tennenholtz, 1997).

c)   Multi-agent planning

Multi-agent planning goes beyond social laws. In order to prevent inconsistent and conflicting interactions, software-agents construct a multi-agent plan that is supposed to co-ordinate their actions. In case of central planning there exists one co-ordination agent. It receives partial plans from single agents, investigates them for potential conflicts, modifies them, and consolidates them into a multi-agent plan. Concepts like this exist for the area of air-traffic-control, for example. (cf. Cammarata et al., 1983). In case of decentralised planning, each agent possesses a model of the plans of the other agents. Through a process of mutual exchange and adaptation, the individual plans converge to a multi-agent plan (cf. Decker/Lesser, 1995/98).

d)   Social commitments

Another important concept for co-ordination and co-operation is social commitment, i.e. obligation (Castelfranchi, 1995b). In contrast to general rules of conduct commitments are generally seen as a bilateral concept because one agent is always committed to another agent. Obligations can be part of a multi-agent plan (cf. Lesser, 1998, 98). But they can also receive a more fundamental, multilateral meaning if they are associated with social-roles. "When an agent joins a group, it joins in one or more roles and acquires the commitments of that role" (Huhns/Singh, 1998a, 15). In this case, the roles and the commitments connected to them serve as the elementary building blocks for the co-ordination and co-operation within the system.

e)   Organisations

Organisations are a more rigid, largely closed concept of co-ordination and co-operation. They usually follow one specific goal and can thus be understood to be DPS systems. The organisation determines the competencies, responsibilities, interconnections of the individual agents as well as the process and contents of their interactions (Nwana et al., 1995, 3). A common approach to agent-organisations depends on blackboard architectures. The blackboard can be considered to be the centre of control of the system. From here, agents are activated. Here they receive commands and information. And it is the place where they leave messages and hand out results. Meanwhile, DAI-research no longer views organisations only as fixed, predetermined and detailed structures. Rather, more open and dynamic concepts have gained attention (cf. Moulin/Chaib-draa, 1996, 18f).

f)   Market-oriented systems

The first models of market-oriented computer systems still represented nothing but particular forms of organisations. They operated in a polycentral manner but they were closed systems, designed centrally. The metaphor of the market, however, allowed to make a transition from structure-orientation and output-orientation towards more open process-orientation. The Contract Net (Smith, 1980) can be considered to be the classic reference point of departure. The Contract-Net connects multiple agents. Each agent possesses a specified amount of resources. Agents then can adopt two kinds of roles, the role of the manager and the role of the contractor. As soon as an agent is unable to solve a problem with given local resources, it divides the task up into sub-tasks, adopts the role of the manager and tries to find contractors for these tasks. Co-ordination and co-operation among agents function on the basis of contracts: Available contractors evaluate the announced tasks and make offers. On the occasion they can themselves act as managers and further sub-divide and announce the respective task. The managers then choose the best offer they receive, combine it with the offers for the remaining sub-tasks and hand out their offer for the complete task. Eventually, the contractor with the best offer for the final product is awarded the task. During the problem-solving process, the respective managers are responsible for the control of the actions and for the exploitation of the results.

g) Automated negotiations

The realisation of co-ordination and co-operation by the means of automated negotiations is exclusively process-oriented. This approach relies mainly on game theory in order to construct interaction mechanisms. Auction processes are used in order to implement the market metaphor (cf. Rosenschein/Zlotkin, 1994). Alternatively, political voting procedures can be employed (cf. Ephriati/Rosenschein, 1996). At the core of these approaches, negotiation protocols can be found. They determine the steps that structure the interaction process and that are supposed to lead to consensus between the agents.

h)   Negotiations

Finally, there is an approach that, ex-ante, employs none of the methods described so far. These are unstructured negotiation approaches. In order to be able to negotiate successfully without the aid of a pre-defined protocol, agents must have cognitive abilities and have to be able to draw conclusions about the beliefs, desires and intentions of other agents. To be able to also influence the cognitive states of the other agents, sophisticated communication skills are necessary as well. Early examples are the "PERSUADER" (Sycara, 1989) system that employs argumentation tactics in the domain of collective bargaining and an agent designed by Kraus/Lehmann (1995) playing the strategy game "Diplomacy".

Figure 2.3 illustrates the relative position of the discussed principles for co-ordination and co-operation. The degree to which the different approaches structure the environment and the degree of autonomy the agents have are taken into consideration. The figure can only serve as an approximate indication of the position of each approach because the paradigms partly overlap and are continuously complemented and developed further.

Figure 2.3:   Relative positions of interaction mechanisms

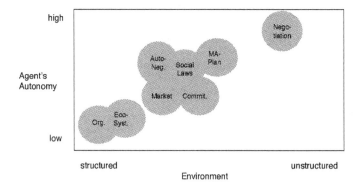

As some of the examples have already shown, the approaches are not equally suited to fit the demands of the different domains making up reality, like for example trade, administration or politics. Consequently, the approaches cannot be considered to be complete substitutes for each other. Nevertheless, multi-agent environments regularly depend on one stand-alone approach to co-ordination and co-operation. Despite the circumstance that, in the long run, several different

30

interaction mechanisms will have to be employed in a complementary fashion, DAI currently presents an arbitrary co-existence of various paradigms, which are not related to each other and which are derived from sociological, ethical, legal as well as economic theories (cf. Singh/Huhns, 1999).

In summary, all of the discussed approaches to co-ordination and co-operation play a role with regard to the question of social-order in multi-agent environments. Although there is not yet a functioning way of technical integration, the paradigms complement each other. In addition, these approaches imply specific requirements with regard to the software-agents operating within these environments (Wellman, 1998). It has to be pointed out that the presented approaches often implicitly assume that the involved software-agents naturally follow the co-ordination and co-operation principles. This is based on the assumption that "in a computational setting, these rules can be enforced as unbreakable physical laws" (Miller/Drexler, 1988a, 58). For this assumption to be true, an integrated approach to multi-agent environments is required where individual agent-architectures and interaction mechanisms are brought in line with each other. In DAI, these approaches dominate the field. The reason for this: often the development of agents and agent-systems goes hand in hand. Yet a general theory of multi-agent environments does not exist. Also, it is not considered how these fairly closed, small worlds can be integrated with one another; let alone how they can be integrated in the grand world of human society. Subsequently, the approaches presented within this section will be revisited. The economics of social order will offer a framework that will allow to analyse these paradigms and position them in a larger context. It is not intended to deliver concrete design plans for multi-agent environments. Rather, a theoretical basis will be offered to facilitate the design and to demonstrate the factors that constrain the design. Thus, the claim of this book is less ambitious than that of many DAI researchers who envision working out detailed societal structures and designing and controlling whole artificial societies (Malsch, 1998b, 32).

2.4 Summary

The first chapter showed that from the point of view of both, economics and computer science, the time has come for a new dimension of the economics of social order. This second chapter provided an introduction into the perception and construction of social order by computer science. The survey covered DAI-approaches to multi-agent environments. A representative overview of the state of research and practice was given. But the stocktaking was largely descriptive. Communication, co-ordination and co-operation were identified as fundamental dimensions of analysis regarding multi-agent environments. A wide and increasing range of mechanisms dealing with these problems was identified. No connections between existing approaches could be found and a unified perspective or general theory of multi-agent environments appears to be absent. Such a theory could be especially useful as the issues of communication, co-ordination and co-operation involve a variety of problems that occur in most multi-agent environments but of which every specialised approach only tackles a subset. Another aspect is that a large share of the existing approaches to agent-environments implicitly or explicitly assumes MAS to be small worlds. The following quote from Tokoro (1993/98, 421) indicates that agent researchers are aware of the challenge of grand world agent-systems: "The world in which we live is concurrent in the sense that there are multiple active entities; distributed such that there is a distance between entities that yields a propagation delay in communication between them; and open, meaning that the entities and their environment are always changing." Or, in other words, history of programming has reached a stage that equals the stage in the history of human behaviour when communities started to distinguish between their members and perceived them to act individually and when tensions between individuals and society as a whole became evident (Rammert, 1998, 98). However, the built-in constraints of the prevailing approaches to co-ordination and co-operation so far prevent access to the grand world.

Eventually, with the discussion of multi-agent technology three aspects were implicitly further emphasised: First, agent-systems are part of and have implications for the social order of the grand world. Second, socially relevant aspects of agent-technology demonstrate compatibility with other sciences, particularly economics. And third, a comprehensive underlying theory of social order for multi-agent environments is still missing. All this supports the ambition of the present analysis of the economics of social order of machines.

3

Capturing the grand world
with social and economic theory

The basic problems are laid out and the main actors are introduced. At this stage the theoretical toolbox is opened. The variety and comprehensiveness of economic instruments, concepts and theories is immense. For this reason a broad overview will be useful; it will be delivered in section 3.1. In order to effectively handle the present interdisciplinary challenge, the study will then be constrained to a few essential analytical tools. This includes first an analytical reference point to mark the elementary problem of social order. Thomas Hobbes' state of nature is the classical point of departure selected here and discussed in section 3.2. In a second step it will be instructive to become familiar with the basic modes of explanation of the origin of order provided by economic theory (3.3). The third task is to identify a methodology to structure the process of analysis. For this purpose James Coleman's macro-micro-macro scheme, complemented by the concept of transaction costs, is particularly suited and will be presented in section 3.4. Before entering the discussion it is important to note that most of the economic notions and concepts subsequently employed, for example the terms transaction costs and institutions, are defined differently by different economists. However, the interdisciplinary nature of this study makes it impossible to carry the burden of methodological discussions. Therefore, economic notions will be introduced without explicit reflection of their potentially controversial background in economic theory.[8]

3.1 Theory between economics and computer science

A single notion that captures the whole spectrum of economic analysis of social order is missing. The present investigation offers an economic analysis of social order in the strictest sense of the phrase: Economic methodologies and insights are employed to study and reveal the properties of social rules and the characteristics of individual behaviour. Then the implications for social order of certain arrangements of these two variables are derived. To reach this objective a large pool of economic theory and knowledge offers its resources. In addition, various sub-fields of computer science already employ - amongst other methods - economic approaches and thus offer additional assistance. The following paragraphs will introduce very

---

[8] The contributions of Eggertsson (1990) and Richter/Furubotn (1996) can be seen as starting points for further exploration along these lines.

briefly important economic approaches and areas from computer science that can be considered part of the intellectual neighbourhood. The focus will not be on an adequate portrait of these fields - this can only be delivered by representatives of the respective fields. Rather, it sketches how the subsequent analysis relates to these fields.

a) Theory of economic behaviour and Artificial Intelligence

A suitable point of entry may be the theory of economic behaviour. Despite the fact that economics is a social science and as such aims to explain social phenomena, a great deal of effort goes into an economic theory of individual behaviour. This is because social phenomena are derived from the behaviours of individuals, which is called methodological individualism. The most consequent interpretation of the economic model of behaviour assumes that an individual actor maximises his utility under the constraints he faces (Becker, 1976). Central to this approach but subject to controversy is the rationality of the actor (Conlisk, 1996).

The theory of rational economic behaviour allows the establishment of a connection to computer science: The declared aim of the sub-field Artificial Intelligence (AI) is to understand and to design intelligent actors (Russell/Norvig, 1995). Rationality is considered to be an ideal concept of intelligence, so it plays an important role in AI. While economists sometimes admit that their model of man resembles a machine, AI tries to model machines like a rational man. An alternative way towards intelligent machines is the design of machines that think or act like natural humans. The analysis to be presented here will refer to the model of rational behaviour at various points but will then depart to argue that for the problem of social order other behavioural characteristics are more important. The favoured model of adaptive behaviour is relatively new within economics and closely relates to the AI-strategy of designing machines that think and act like human beings (Arthur, 1994).

b) New Institutional Economics and Distributed AI

As already indicated, economic theory does not build solely on modelling behaviour to explain social phenomena. The second important theoretical building block deals with constraints. Next to budget constraints institutional constraints are of central importance. The New Institutional Economics (NIE) covers this area (Richter/Furubotn, 1996). NIE assumes that institutions have a significant influence on the behaviour of individual actors. It is the objective of NIE to analyse the effects as well as the origin, change and (co-) existence of institutions of all kinds (e.g. market, firm, state, but also norms and conventions). This indicates the variety of issues and research questions involved. Consequently, it does not come as a surprise to find a range of well established sub-fields under the roof of NIE. Important directions are transaction cost theory, property-rights theory and economic contract theory. The central idea of transaction cost economics is that institutions are not available free of charge and that the choice between different institutional arrangements depends on the costs involved. Property-rights theory allows for a systematic analysis of the rights actors have regarding goods and services. This is important because in the presence of transaction costs, the specification, allocation, control and enforcement of property-rights is not trivial. With respect to the following analysis, contracts are important. Economic contract theory focuses on information and incentive-problems of contracts, namely in the context of principal-agent relationships. Similarly to NIE, Distributed Artificial Intelligence (DAI) can be conceived as a roof for various sub-fields in computer science. Chapter Two already demonstrated that in these fields too, constraints on individual behaviour play an important role as frameworks for co-ordination and co-operation are developed. However, DAI can be said to deal with a wider range of issues (see e.g. communication in section 2.1). These are not only theoretically analysed but also an object of engineering efforts. Also, the approaches build on expertise from various other sciences. The analysis presented here restricts itself to the economic perspective. The analytical tools of NIE are employed to investigate the properties of multi-agent environments. In particular the rules intended to ensure co-ordination and co-operation are discussed from this perspective.

c)   Austrian Economics and Artificial Societies

What makes social phenomena particularly interesting is that they can arise from individual behaviour although the individuals concerned do not intend to produce these effects. In the present context the phenomenon of spontaneous social order is relevant. This means that social order is not designed intentionally but emerges spontaneously from individual behaviour. It does, however, not emerge under all circumstances. The existence of abstract and general rules of conduct is deeply connected with spontaneous order. It is Austrian Economics that complements the efforts of NIE in this area. Research in the tradition of Ludwig von Mises, Friedrich-August von Hayek and Israel Kirzner is of fundamental importance to the subsequent analysis in order to achieve a theoretical understanding of social order. Fortunately, progress in DAI and related areas allows the relation of theoretical findings and observations of the human world to current multi-agent environments. The closest implicit and explicit connection between Austrian Economics and DAI can be found where artificial societies are employed for simulation studies, particularly in Agent-Based Computational Economics (ACE). "ACE is roughly characterized as the computational study of economies modelled as evolving decentralized systems of autonomous interacting agents" (Tesfatsion, cit. in Vriend, 1999, 2). While the results of these simulations are of significant value to this book, the perspective differs. Here, artificial societies - i.e. multi-agent environments - are an object of study, whereas in ACE and comparable simulations the central objective is to use artificial societies for the explanation of phenomena occurring in human society.

In summary, this section presented a brief overview of important areas of research in economics and computer science. In particular it showed how the economic theory of behaviour, Artificial Intelligence, New Institutional Economics, Distributed Artificial Intelligence, Austrian Economics and Artificial Societies relate to each other and to the economic analysis of social order for software-agents to be presented here. One general feature has not yet been emphasised explicitly. But as it underscores once again the complementary nature of computer science and economics, it adequately closes this section: On the one hand computer science is defined by its problems not its methods (Russell, 1997, 59). On the other hand, economics is defined by its methods not its problems (Becker, 1976, 5).

3.2   The state of nature as analytical reference point

In the first chapter order was defined as a state in which, based on knowledge of a part of a system, it is possible to form correct expectations about the whole of the system, at least as far as they are relevant to the respective individual actor. The problem with this definition is that it includes any type of order. Even if the correct expectation is that the actors mutually destroy each other, the system can be seen to be in a state of order. But obviously it is desirable to have constructive rather than destructive interactions between the actors of a system.[9] In order to systematically analyse the conditions for a constructive social order the destructive state of nature presented by Thomas Hobbes serves as an ideal reference point. At the time of publication in 1651 the state of nature was a trailblazing account of a fundamental social problem. Ever since, it has inspired and accompanied the economic analysis of social order (cf. Binmore, 1994, 7ff). Subsequently a brief summary of Hobbes' analysis is given. Then the choice of this reference point for the present purposes is further clarified and justified.

What fundamentally distinguishes Hobbes from his predecessors is that he treats the individual human being as an autonomous actor. This means that the individual is no longer deterministically embedded in the social context of family, class and profession which formed human life until the beginning of the modern age. Today, another type of actor begins to stand out from its traditional context. Large computer systems, formerly monolithic in nature, increasingly appear to consist of many individual software-agents. Step by step these entities become less dependent on the system as a whole and gain emancipation with regard to their designers and users. In the form of software-agents the machine departs from an existence without

---

[9] Exceptions are desirable destructive interactions between members of socially harmful subgroups, for example the Mafia.

alternatives. Thomas Hobbes illustrates an extreme case of such a departure. The state of nature is characterised by individual actors who are endowed with similar capabilities[10], unlimited needs[11], and who act according to their self-interest.[12] Further characteristics of the state of nature are the limited availability of resources[13] and the mutual unpredictability of individual actions[14]. In the state of nature "...every man has a right to every thing, even to one another's body" (Hobbes, 1651/1996, 87). In a sense the freedom of the individual is unlimited. "All events are controlled individually, whether they have consequences for only one individual or for more than one" (Coleman, 1990, 831). Everyone has to expect that actions of others may affect him. As a consequence he has to be prepared to defend himself against undesired actions. The situation corresponds to what is commonly called law of the jungle. It might only be for the sake of self-defence but in the end every one is forced to enter a state of war. This implies high costs, including a danger of life. From the right of everyone to everything Hobbes logically derives a "war...of every man against every man" (Hobbes, 1651/1996, 84). This, in turn, implies the mutual abolition of all freedom. This situation represents the elementary problem of social order. Interactions result in war and constructive social order is completely missing (cf. table 3.1 for a summary of the characteristics of this situation).[15] For all actors it is desirable to exit this situation. Hobbes reasons that every individual has a basic interest in the existence of social order because this is the only guarantee to protect human life against violent death (cf. Hobbes 1651/1996, 86 and chapters 14 and 15).

---

[10] "Nature has made men so equal, in the faculties of the body, and mind..." (Hobbes, 1651/1996, 82).

[11] "For there is no such thing as perpetual tranquillity of mind, while we live here; because life itself is but motion, and can never be without desire, nor without fear, no more than without sense" (Hobbes, 1651/1996, 41).

[12] "Also because there be some, that taking pleasure in contemplating their own power in the acts of conquest, which they pursue farther than their security requires; if others, that otherwise would be glad to be at ease within some modest bounds, should not by invasion increase their power, they would not be able, long time, by standing only on their defence, to subsist" (Hobbes, 1651/1996, 83). "...so long as a man is in the condition of mere nature, (which is a condition of war,) as private appetite is the measure of good, and evil" (Hobbes, 1651/1996, 105).

[13] "And therefore if any two men desire the same thing, which nevertheless they cannot both enjoy [...]"(Hobbes, 1651/1996, 83).

[14] "Whatsoever therefore is consequent to a time of war, where every man is enemy to every man; the same is consequent to the time, wherein men live without other security, than what their own strength, and their own invention shall furnish them withal" (Hobbes, 1651/1996, 84).

[15] "In such a condition...life of man [is] solitary, poor, nasty, brutish, and short" (Hobbes, 1651/1996, 84).

Table 3.1: **Characteristics of the elementary problem of social order in Hobbes' state of nature**

① Constraints	Limited resources Every one has a right for everything
② Individual actors	Are endowed with similar capabilities Behave selfishly Behave unpredictably Behave autonomously
③ Interaction	War of everybody against everybody

Hobbes' state of nature is a state in which many hurdles of interaction are assumed to be crossed. Actors can meet, communicate and co-ordinate. Problems of communication and co-ordination are more fundamental than the problem of co-operation (cf. Luhmann, 1984/94). This is especially valid for machines who have only recently started to change from isolated entities into interactive actors. For this reason DAI research tackles problems of communication and co-ordination. Yet it seems plausible that the more these problems are solved the bigger the danger of being confronted with Hobbes' elementary problem of order. Neither this danger nor the discussion of potential remedies has gained much attention in DAI research. Consequently, the present study starts from this point of reference to offer a new perspective on forthcoming problems.

Even if the perspective is acknowledged to be valuable, it may still be subject to the criticism that the resulting picture is distorted. Although it was primarily a thought experiment, Hobbes himself considered the state of nature to be a representation of reality (Hobbes, 1651/1996, 85f). But it is certainly justified to ask whether Hobbes' brutal war of each against all adequately portrays human behaviour and the behaviour of software-agents. After all, already the predecessors of Homo sapiens had been social actors and software-agents are explicitly designed to be social actors. Thus, there is no reason to follow Hobbes' argumentation in every detail. However, the core of his argument is indisputable: non-co-operative behaviour is a fundamental problem for humans, as well as for machines. The concept of the state of nature is relevant whenever individual actors or groups employ egoistic behaviour to achieve advantages over others and where such behaviour in the end has negative implications for every one, including themselves. Possible forms of egoism are the breach of trust and contract, theft, fraud, deception, lying, shirking, moral-hazard and many other forms of opportunistic social behaviour (Leipold, 1989, 132).

At the first sight, these problems may appear largely irrelevant to software-agents. Particularly, it can be argued that it is possible to "hardwire" social order. However, the first chapter already demonstrated that machine-related problems of order are common and illustrated the large number of future frontiers where these problems might appear. In addition it indicated that it is not possible to reconcile hardwiring with open systems. All this underscores that the state of nature is relevant in multi-agent environments, and that it is sensible to be informed in advance about the problems that are bound to appear.

In the end, the state of nature serves as an adequate point of reference. This worst-case scenario represents a universal model for a system without binding order or rather a non-system (Nonnenmacher, 1989, 36f). The consistent logical deduction of this state allows for a systematic analysis of social order. In the light of the state of nature the details of social order become transparent.

3.3 Theories of the origin of order

Despite the theoretical value of the state of nature, the war of each against all rarely dominates the scene. Different kinds of systems - among them human societies as well as software systems - appear to possess different degrees and forms of order. Common experience as well as scientific research suggests that there exists more than one way for each of these systems to reach a certain state of order. The origin of those principles that guide co-ordination and co-operation in these systems is explained by different theories. With respect to human society three basic explanatory approaches exist: the essentialist, the constructivist, and the evolutionary theory of social order. The essentialist approach stems from medieval faith in the existence of a supra-individual order. Humans first recognise and then respect this pre-determined order. In contrast, modern theory traces the origin of social order back to human actions. This, however, still leaves room for opposing views. Constructivist approaches assume that social order is based on purposeful and explicit design, while evolutionary approaches view social order as arising spontaneously as an unintended consequence of individual actions (cf. Kirsch, 1999, 186ff).[16]

Today, it is universally acknowledged that, in terms of human society, constructivist and evolutionary explanations of social order do not contradict each other. Rather, they describe complementary forces that interact with each other (cf. Voigt, 1997; Caldas/Coelho, 1999). This has not always been recognised. Computer science was born during a time when constructivism boomed in human society. Confidence was high that complex social systems like economies would be steerable. Later, the downfall of central planning in the East as well as failures of interventionist policies

---

[16] The notions constructivist and evolutionary refer solely to the economic terminology. There is no connection to the use of these terms in other sciences, e.g. psychology.

in the West reduced this confidence significantly. The lessons learned in human society cannot be immediately transferred to computer science which, by and large, still rests on the constructivist foundations sketched in the first chapter. However, a range of developments indicates an increasing relevance of the evolutionary approach. An example where a kind of evolutionary approach is unwillingly accepted is classical software-engineering: "The familiar software project...[is] usually innocent and straightforward, but capable of becoming a monster of missed schedules, blown budgets, and flawed products" (Brooks, 1995, 181). These projects have to undergo an evolution before objectives are achieved. Examples for an intentional exploitation of this paradigm are software systems that learn, such as genetic algorithms (cf. chapter 6), and so called open-source coding, like the operating system LINUX. Consequently in computational as well as in human environments constructivist and evolutionary forces can be identified to explain the creation of order.

The partly complementary and partly competitive relation of construction and evolution will be reflected throughout the remainder of this book. The principles of liberal order to be introduced later are viewed largely from a constructivist perspective because they seem well-known enough to be actively implemented. However, this does not mean that these principles are inventions of the human mind. Rather, it took centuries of human civilisation for them to evolve and to prove themselves. Moreover, a liberal order of rules differs at least in two ways from what is usually understood under the term social engineering. First, it does not aim at a specific purpose but allows participating actors to have individual objectives. Second, it does not represent a 1:1 blueprint of the resulting order of actions. The liberal order of actions will not be discussed until chapter seven. The analysis there will aim to show how liberal order of actions spontaneously evolves under the conditions of (intentionally implemented) liberal rules and what kind of construction efforts can possibly follow.

As important as the explanation of the origin of order is the justification of the different paths. The normative justification is relevant because humans regularly claim to be able to decide in favour of an essentialist, constructivist or evolutionary social order. Broadly, three approaches which correspond to the mentioned modes of explanation are put forward to substantiate liberal order: the natural rights argument, the contractarian argument, and the selection argument. Natural rights approaches in the tradition of John Locke claim that nature or God provides the individual actor with certain rights. Unless these rights are recognised and respected a social order is not justified. In contrast, the contractarian vision, which includes thinkers from Thomas Hobbes to James Buchanan, argues that individuals have to decide unanimously in favour of a particular order of rules. Unless a consensus is reached a social order cannot be legitimated. The selection argument, represented by authors like David Hume and Friedrich August von Hayek, finds that social order results from selective cultural evolution. Superior forms of social order succeed in the absence of purposeful human intervention. Social order is legitimated when it is able to survive. In the present context the brief overview of the approaches to legitimate social order serves as useful background information. Neither a deeper analysis, nor a final evaluation is required because all three approaches can lead to a justification of liberal order, which will be proposed and analysed in the remainder of this book (cf. Locke, 1690/1967; Buchanan, 1975; Hayek, 1960). Consequently, it is possible to focus on the concrete contents of liberal order rather than discussing the normative foundations. Of practical relevance for multi-agent environments are the contractarian argument - "[A] key idea is that the designers of computer systems will themselves agree upon the rules of interaction, in the same way that they agree on any kind of standardization" (Rosenschein/Zlotkin, 1994, xxi) - and the selection argument: "Although the digital computer is a very different environment than the ecology of the Earth, evolution is shown to work effectively in the digital environment..." (Thearling/Ray, 1997, 229). These correspond to the remarks on the constructivist and evolutionary modes of explanation made above.

3.4   A methodology for further analysis

The basic lines of thought needed to understand social order and to distinguish it from disorder have been presented. But what is still missing is a concise methodology to explain and solve problems of order systematically. Modern economic theory explains social phenomena by analysing interdependent individual actions. This section illustrates how this idea can be brought into a compact methodological framework. First, the role of methodological individualism is discussed. Second, an approach to make the transition between the micro-level of individual behaviour and the macro-level of social phenomena is presented. Third, the relevance of transaction costs is outlined.

a)   Methodological individualism

It has already been emphasised that economic analysis aims to explain social phenomena. Examples are population dynamics, inflation, the transformation of political and economic systems or the various forms of the problem of social order. A distinct feature of the economic approach is its basis in methodological individualism. It is assumed that an understanding of social phenomena is only possible based on an understanding of the conduct of the involved individual actors.[17] A macro-phenomenon like the state of nature thus can be traced back to

---

[17] An opposite view is Holism in the tradition of Comte, Hegel, Marx and Durkheim which claims that social phenomena follow their own rules, independent from the actions of individual

the processes and conditions on the micro-level; i.e. to belligerent individuals. In this perspective, it is crucial, that the actors can choose between alternative modes of behaviour and that they make use of their scope of action. Within human societies this could not and cannot always be assumed, but the assumption appears to be adequate for individuals in modern societies of the western world. With respect to machines it is the introduction of agent-technology that makes an individualistic viewpoint plausible. And it is the appearance of software-agents as social actors that requires this perspective.

"No discussion of the organization of human society is possible without taking a view on what people are like. Any such view is bound to be wrong because it is impossible to encompass the richness and diversity of human nature in a few sentences of text" (Binmore, 1994, 18). Under consideration of this statement the economic concept of individual behaviour assumes that an actor acts in his own interest and that the constraints he faces significantly influence his behaviour (Kirchgässner, 1991, 17f). This can for example be applied to the state of nature: Everyone has a right to everything but resources are limited. The actor has to try everything that lies within the range of his physical and psychological capabilities to get what he needs to survive, including violence.

In the sense of classical economics this approach allows the analysis of social order with the aim of shaping it. In contrast, any analysis within a holistic perspective "can do nothing other than describe an inexorable fate" (Coleman, 1990, 17).[18] The basic idea in economics is to influence social order by confronting the actors of a system with changed constraints. Thus, for instance, the right of everyone to everything in the state of nature could be replaced by private property rights. In multi-agent environments an important variable can be added on the micro-level: in contrast to humans, software-agents can be designed and influenced directly; for example, to be non-violent. In sum, the actors themselves as well as the constraints they face on behaviour represent the variables to explain and shape social order from an economic point of view.

b)   The MMM-scheme
The central task now is to find a way to study the interrelations between the behaviour of individual actors, the existing constraints and the arising social phenomena. James Coleman's (1990, 11ff) MMM-scheme is dedicated to this purpose. The macro-micro-macro scheme first links the macro-level with the micro-

---

actors. For a comparison of individualism and holism see Coleman (1990, 511) and with special attention to the economic analyis of social order Streit (1995, 8ff).

[18] With respect to the present subject Dyson (1997, ix) takes such a position: "In the game of life and evolution there are three players at the table: human beings, nature, and machines. I am firmly on the side of nature. But nature, I suspect, is on the side of the machines."

level. This is done by conceptualising the initial situation in form of constraints on behaviour for the individual actors ①.[19] Amongst other constraints, for example resource limitations, the prevailing rules of conduct are of vitally important. Consequently, it is also possible to speak of a departure from the rule-level or the institutional level. For the discussion in the later chapters it will be helpful to understand, how the notion of institution can be interpreted in economic terms:

> "Institutions consist of a set of constraints on behavior in the form of rules and regulations; a set of procedures to detect deviations from the rules and regulations; and, finally, a set of moral ethical behavioural norms which define the contours that constrain the way in which the rules and regulations are specified and enforcement is carried out" (North, 1984, 8).

Institutions are used by a group of individual actors to structure repeated interactions (Ostrom, 1986, 5). In this first step of analysis the institutional constraints are identified and analysed as independent variables, from which alternative modes of action for the individual actors are derived. The second step of analysis takes place on the micro-level and concludes which of the available alternatives an actor chooses ②. Next to the conceptualisation of the constraints, this requires a model of individual behaviour. In this chapter, a brief account of the economic model of individual behaviour has already been given and a more comprehensive discussion will follow. For the present purposes it suffices to point to figure 3.1 which illustrates a simplified view of a utility-based agent as it is conceptualised in (D)AI.

---

[19] If it is not possible to conceptualise all relevant restrictions, the analysis can be based on the change of particular restrictions (ceteris paribus condition).

Figure 3.1: Model of a software-agent with utility-based behaviour

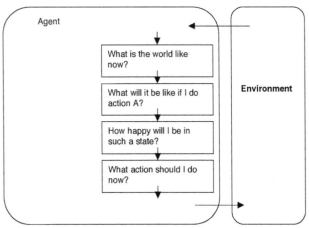

Source: Russell/Norvig (1995)

Similar to mainstream economic theory it is assumed that an actor chooses the mode of behaviour based on which he believes to reach the highest utility level. It follows that the behavioural model is exogenous in this step, while the specific actions are derived endogenously. The third step of the analysis serves to make the transition from the micro-level to the macro level ③. The objective here is to determine how the individual actions aggregate at the system level or, in the terminology of this book, how they aggregate to form the grand world. This is far from trivial as the individual actions are interdependent and thus influence each other. In the sense of Hayek (1969/94, 161ff) it is the "order of actions" that is reached here. In contrast to the order of rules that is under investigation in step one, the order of actions manifests the counter-play of all variables involved, including the specific intentions and the knowledge of the circumstances of the actors involved. It is important to note that "the interaction among individuals is seen to result in emergent phenomena at the system level, phenomena that were neither intended nor predicted by individuals" (Coleman, 1990, 5).

In conclusion, the MMM-scheme offers a methodology for the explanation of social phenomena, like the war of everyone against everyone in the state of nature. The scheme describes the analytical path and allows the overall process and situation to be captured (cf. tables 3.2 and 3.1). Chapters Five through Seven go through the scheme step by step. In the search for social order, for each step they present well-established economic knowledge and critically discuss its applicability to multi-agent environments.

c) The relevance of transaction costs

Along the described analytical path another variable is important. The world is not a perpetual motion machine, so it is crucial to take frictions into account which influence the interactions between individual actors. For these frictions economics has reserved the notion transaction costs. Although economics has long ignored these costs, today it is generally accepted that transaction costs are always greater than zero. In general, transaction costs can be understood as costs that are connected with the

1. creation of an institution, and with the
2. use of an institution (Furubotn/Richter, 1991, 2).

The level of transaction costs varies. The general relevance of these discrepancies was first emphasised in 1937 by Ronald Coase. When comparing markets to hierarchies he stated "that firms will emerge to organize what would otherwise be market transactions whenever their costs were less than the costs of carrying out the transactions through the market" (Coase, 1988, 6f).

Table 3.2:   Variables in the MMM-scheme

	Exogenous	Endogenous
① **Macro-Micro**	(Change of) constraints	Space of available actions
② **Micro-Micro**	Behavioural model	Actions
③ **Micro-Macro**	Individual actions	Social phenomena

The literature on transaction costs makes transparent that any type of social order has to keep transaction costs low to subsist. If it does not, it will be superseded by another arrangement or it will fall apart altogether because "when transaction costs are positive, then people are able to gain at each other's expense" (Barzel, 1985, 4). Miller/Drexler (1988b, 141) argue that "similar considerations hold among computational objects." While not applying economic terminology, many authors in

DAI confirm this assertion (cf. Kraus, 1997; Kraus et al., 1995; Shoham/Tennenholtz, 1995).

All this goes to show that transaction costs represent an important variable which helps to track problems of social order and which functions as an indicator for the contestability of institutional arrangements. Nevertheless, it is advisable not to pitch expectations too high, as transaction costs often only can be roughly estimated and only to a limited extent be quantified.

3.5 Summary

The variety and fragmentation of economic approaches required a purposeful selection of the analytical instruments that are to be employed. Generally, a good fit between economic methods and the different levels of the problem of social order in computer science could be identified. As a consequence, it was relatively straightforward to determine broadly the areas of discussion and sources of knowledge of this book, namely the economic theory of individual behaviour and Artificial Intelligence, New Institutional Economics and Distributed Artificial Intelligence, plus Austrian Economics and Artificial Societies. The analytical point of reference was represented by the state of nature of Thomas Hobbes. The state of nature allows for an abstract analysis of the elementary problem of social order. Any social order can systematically be compared to this state without any order. Going one step further, two important economic concepts for the explanation of the origin of social order were found to be relevant in both, human society and agent-environments, namely evolutionary and constructivist explanations. A concise methodology for the analysis in the remainder of the book was given by the MMM-scheme. The scheme builds on methodological individualism. Consequently, social phenomena - including different states of order and disorder – can be traced back to the behaviour of individual actors which in turn is assumed to be influenced by (changes in) the constraints the actors face. Changes to the constraints - particularly of institutions - are a matter of costs and benefits incurred by the involved actors. This is why transaction costs are a key variable that has to be observed to gain further insights.

The following chapters will show that the methodology is not restricted to the analysis of small worlds but is suitable for investigations into the grand world. On this basis it is feasible to analyse systematically the range of problems connected to the question of social order. And it is possible to view different approaches to agent-systems from a unified perspective.

4

Liberalism

Social and economic theory generally allows any proposition that is made to solve the problem of social order to be analysed. And in this respect the tools at hand are no exception. However, the purpose is not only to establish a methodology to analyse the grand world but also to determine the ingredients the grand world needs in order to show a functioning social order. In the present context this is particularly important because computer scientists concentrate more on the architecture than on the contents of rules that are to govern agent-systems. Yet it is hardly feasible to provide a sound analysis of all known types of social order within just one book. In this chapter it is argued that it is both possible and sensible to narrow the discussion down significantly. At the outset it is reasoned that the Leviathan once proposed by Thomas Hobbes as well as related approaches are everything but promising paths (4.1). Then, it is maintained that it is beneficial to centre the discussion around the concept of liberal order. The basic ideas and properties of liberal order are introduced in section 4.2. The main emphasis in this chapter is put on a critical examination of the notion of freedom, which is central to the concept of liberal order. In this context the question of freedom for software-agents is of particular interest (4.3).

4.1 No perspective for Leviathan

A range of approaches promises to solve the problem of social order. Thomas Hobbes was still unaware of many of the alternatives known today, when he decided in favour of Leviathan: "For by art is created that great Leviathan called a commonwealth, or state, ...which is but an artificial man; though of greater stature and strength than the natural, for whose protection and defence it was intended..." (Hobbes, 1651/1996, 7). From Hobbes' point of view only the state is capable of protecting the individuals from each other. In order to achieve this the state has to be equipped with absolute power. Hobbes goes to show that the Leviathan is able to overcome the state of nature. However, this requires the capitulation of the individual human being as Hobbes decides in favour of peace, but against individual freedom (cf. Kirsch, 1997, 22).

Despite the respectable age of the idea, Leviathan turns out to be a suitable metaphor for the field of computer software. In fact, traditional software systems much more closely resemble the Leviathan than absolutist states do: "For seeing life is but a motion of limbs, the beginning whereof is in some principal part within; why may we not say, that all automata (engines that move themselves by springs and wheels as doth a watch) have an artificial life. For what is the heart, but a spring; and the nerves, but so many strings; and the joints, but so many wheels, giving motion to the whole body, such as was intended by the artificer" (Hobbes, 1651/1996, 7). It is striking how similar this deduction of the Leviathan is to the traditional conceptual idea of software systems: The aim is to connect the parts of the system within a hierarchy in a deterministic and mechanical way so that they react predictably to top-down commands (Kirsch/Kohlas, 1993, 15).

Extensive attempts to establish social order in human society based on the Leviathan repeatedly failed; most notably the socialist system of the centrally planned economies of the Warsaw Pact states. The problems illustrated in the first chapter indicate comparable problems within the area of software systems. Kirsch and Kohlas (1993, 15) emphasise that complex computer systems, which are supposed to be based on deterministic and mechanical structures, are inevitably defective and unpredictable. These systems show only a limited capacity to deal with novelties and other circumstances not anticipated by the programmers. Also they are rather incapable of constructively creating novelties and innovations. In a sense, it is the grand world problem, which was also first mentioned in chapter one that recurs here. Leviathan-like concepts do not appear to be able to meet the challenges posed by the complexities of a grand world.

The state of nature described by Hobbes demonstrated that freedom cannot be realised without peace. In addition, the preceding paragraphs suggest that peace cannot persist without freedom. To the extent that these conclusions do not lack substance, it is advisable to concentrate the discussion of social order on approaches that accommodate both, freedom and peace. With respect to human society this is again supported by evidence from recent history which seems to confirm a reciprocal intensification of freedom and social order (Gerecke, 1998, 78; North, 1990/92, 116ff). The central question here is of course whether such a social order can be extended to include machines.

4.2   The promises of liberal order

It is hard to imagine a Leviathan in the sense of Hobbes ruling over modern society. Human social systems have probably never been more distanced from the absolutist state. At the same time many factors come together to suggest that there is not much room for Leviathan-like concepts in the context of complex software systems. In line with what was said earlier, some of these factors are the increasing penetration and relevance of the Internet as an open system, the technological progress in software-engineering, as well as the intensifying amalgamation of software systems and society. Decentralisation, openness, and autonomy are characteristics that are about to become nearly as important for software systems as they are for human society (Bachmann, 1998, 210).

Against this background those approaches point the way that promise to guarantee peace and freedom under the conditions of a grand world. More precisely, it is the concept of liberal order that unifies the fundamental ideas for a march into this direction. In a first attempt liberalism can be described as a complex of ideas that is characterised by the postulates of self-determination of the individuals through reasoning, the freedom of the individual against the state, the rule of law, and the self-regulation of the economy via the market process (Schiller, 1995, 393). Obviously this statement can serve only as a first approximation. It needs further clarification and examination. The distinguishing components of liberal order will be described subsequently. In a second step the important promises of liberal order will be outlined.

Liberalism bases its postulates and principles on a fairly realistic view of the (grand) world. Individual actors are considered to have only limited cognitive abilities. It is assumed that their behaviour is never completely predictable but generally self-interested. Also, it is understood that due to resource limitations there is always a danger of conflicts of interests. Although the objective is to achieve social order, it is not the aim of liberalism to create a specific and pre-determined social order.[20] The question of social order is separated from the pursuit of particular purposes (cf. 1.3). Rather, the intention is to provide the conditions under which social order can develop and continuously renew itself (cf. Hayek, 1960, 161). It is characteristic of these conditions that the individual actor is not bound to follow certain modes of behaviour. Liberal order is probabilistic in the sense that it allows for a loose coupling of the actors who have the freedom to behave unpredictably. The most important means for bringing about social order is to establish general rules of conduct. By enforcing certain principles of order, influence is only exerted on the abstract character of the system but not on the concrete details (cf. Hayek, 1966, 603). In other words, liberal methods to secure social order restrict themselves to an influence of the rules of the game or the structure. No intervention in the game or the process is intended. Some of the approaches to co-ordination and co-operation in DAI presented in chapter two show similarities. Rosenschein/Zlotkin (1994, 5) for example note: "...we are interested in creating social environments for machines... we are doing social engineering, helping designers establish an automated society's rules." However, the motivation of liberalism for establishing rules of conduct is to enhance and protect the freedom of the individual actor, an issue that has been largely ignored by DAI. This has far reaching implications for the kinds of rules or the structure of the system that is pursued. A detailed discussion of

---

[20] This is a conception some forms of liberalism like e.g. Ordo-liberalism (cf. Eucken, 1959) do not share.

liberal rules will follow in the next chapter. At this stage it suffices to outline two distinguishing characteristics: First, liberal order is polycentral. Society is not assumed to have one centre. Rather, "every actor is considered a center in his own right" (Kirsch, 1994, 19). This already implies the second point, that liberal order is horizontal. "Every actor is considered to be equal to any other actor; nobody is the instrument of anybody else" (Kirsch, 1994, 19). Instead of being ruled by a particular actor or group the system is under the rule of law.[21] Based on these principles and components, liberal thinkers claim that an orientation towards the freedom of the individual allows entering a virtuous circle that offers not only freedom and peace but a whole range of desirable properties.

There is first the assertion that "the main merit of the individualism is that it is a system under which bad men can do least harm" (Hayek, 1948, 11). From a theoretical point of view the conditions of polycentrality and horizontality make this plausible. But also empirically, comparisons between liberal and totalitarian systems regularly confirm this assertion (cf. Gwartney/Lawson, 1997).[22] The functioning of Internet-technology, where traditional systems are plagued by failures of their parts, indicates that this assertion is relevant for software systems as well (cf. Birman/Renesse, 1997; Wiener, 1994).

The recognition of freedom and the indirect method of establishing social order under the rule of law has further desirable properties. "The central concept of liberalism is that under the enforcement of universal rules of just conduct, ...a spontaneous order of human activities of much greater complexity will form itself than could ever be produced by deliberate arrangement" (Hayek, 1966, 603). As it is one of the central tasks of computer science to manage complexity, this claim cleary demands attention. Connected with this is the mentioned aspect of openness: "The great importance of the spontaneous order or nomocracy rests on the fact that it extends the possibility of peaceful coexistence of men for their mutual benefit beyond the small groups whose members have concrete common purposes, or are subject to a common superior, and that it thus made the appearance of the Great or Open Society possible" (Hayek, 1966, 604). This makes evident that liberalism directly targets a solution for the problem of social order in the grand world (cf. 1.3). But it is not all about mere complexity and openness. These aspects have further implications and inherent properties. Very early, Adam Smith (1776/1976) made clear that freedom is a crucial condition for economic wealth. Again, this is confirmed by empirical studies (Gwartney/Lawson, 1997). Freedom allows

---

[21] In software engineering one may speak of standards instead of rules. However, the discussion of rules in chapter five will show that rules comprise more than what is traditionally captured by the notion of a standard.

[22] It may be worth emphasising the fact that liberalism does not equal democracy. History provides many examples for the danger of totalitarian democracy, particularly recent history. See e.g. Zakaria (1997).

individual actors to benefit from many human achievements without achieving them themselves. "Each is enriched by the complementarity of realizations quite apart from the specific activities made possible. [...] In realizing complementary excellences, persons make possible activities that no individual could engage in on her own" (Gauthier, 1986, 336). While still fairly distanced from liberal order, efforts in software engineering have the ambition to achieve comparable results. This was shown in chapter two. Overall, in liberal order the use of knowledge in society is enhanced. This is because each actor knows the particular circumstances of the situations he faces better than anybody else. And in a liberal order he can exploit this knowledge. For good reason this includes the chance to behave freely. "Freedom is essential in order to leave room for the unforeseeable and unpredictable; we want it because we have learned to expect from it the opportunity of realizing many of our aims" (Hayek, 1960, 29). Thus, liberal order does not prevent surprises, innovations and other kinds of development. Rather, it creates the conditions for them to happen, and it creates conditions for coping with these unforeseen changes. This characteristic is especially interesting for computer science if one considers the rapid changes and development in computer software.

This section provided a brief overview of the main pillars of liberal order, describing it as polycentral and horizontal order under the rule of law that is based on general rules of conduct with the objective to attain and protect the freedom of the individual. The resulting properties of liberal order promise to reinforce each other in a virtuous circle. General rules allow the rise of complex structures, loosely coupled individuals employ more knowledge than they possess, innovations occur, and economic development results. All these aspects require a more detailed discussion that will follow.

4.3   Freedom

An analysis of social order that deals more with software-agents than with humans can be justified. Similarly, convincing arguments can be made that concepts of social order that have proven to be useful in human societies are useful when dealing with software. Also, solid reasons can be presented which hold that, among these concepts and approaches, liberal order is particularly interesting. However, it is at this stage where a potential source of irritation hides that has to be taken seriously. It is the fact that liberal order centres around the notion of freedom. Liberty or freedom is the fundamental aim of liberalism (cf. Mill, 1859/1989). Machines - including all sorts of software - are commonly considered to be instruments rather than free actors. Freedom is considered to be a question of philosophy but not of computer science. It is hardly taken into account and even further away from being an objective. Hence, none of the mechanisms of co-ordination and co-operation for multi-agent environments presented in chapter two considers freedom for software-agents. But the fact that the notions of freedom and liberty do not appear in computer science in general and in DAI in particular does not mean that the subject itself is absent. What is extensively discussed under the heading of autonomy also could be titled freedom (cf. Huhns/Singh, 1998a). The implicit but crucial difference between DAI and liberalism is that the former treats freedom as a means to build systems with certain properties while the latter treats freedom as its goal which has to be achieved by an appropriate form of social order, namely liberal order. This book combines liberalism and DAI by identifying liberal order as the kind of system that is of interest and by treating freedom as one of the potential means to achieve liberal order (cf. table 4.1).

Table 4.1:   The different treatment of the issue of freedom

	Liberalism	DAI	Here
Goal	Freedom	Different forms of social order in multi-agent environments	Analysis of liberal order
Means	Liberal order	Freedom (usually termed "autonomy")	Freedom

It is evident that such an approach is compatible with the pattern of DAI-research. More importantly, it allows for a flexible treatment of the issue of freedom. This is especially crucial when dealing with software entities rather than with humans where freedom is commonly treated as an absolute, untouchable but nevertheless obscure and ill-defined value. The idea here is to facilitate a positive, analytical treatment while avoiding a direct involvement in normative questions of moral philosophy. The provided economic analysis of social order and particularly of liberal order may be a fruitful contribution to moral and ethical discussions. But in order to be beneficial the present study must be separated carefully from the moral and normative discourse. Especially with respect to the notion of freedom this demands an exposition of how this moral philosophical reference point can be made analytically approachable. Subsequently, it will be shown that this can best be done by contrasting the analytical understanding followed here with well-established conceptions of the notion of freedom. In a second step it will be necessary to see whether the concept can be applied usefully to artificial actors.

4.3.1 Freedom and the individual

In order to reach an analytical understanding of the notion of freedom, it is helpful to conceive it as a relational concept. It is the freedom of one actor in relation to another actor that is of interest (cf. Kirsch, 1992, 16; Hayek, 1960, 12). As the discussion of Castelfranchi (1995a, 58) demonstrates, this counts for software-agents no less than for humans: "More generally, the very concept of autonomy is an intrinsically relational concept: the autonomy of a system is defined in relation to another system." A possible definition of freedom results from equating freedom with unpredictability. Following Kirsch (1994, 13) an actor can be defined as free "when and to the extent that his future behavior is unpredictable to somebody; this somebody may be the actor himself or somebody else." The freedom of an actor then consists of his ability to surprise somebody (Kirsch/Kohlas, 1993, 15). Such a "stipulative" definition of freedom promises to be useful because it is not biased in any way (Cranston, 1967, 24). Also it is not alien to DAI as the following quote from Huhns/Singh (1998a, 3) shows: "...the less predictable an agent is the more autonomous it appears."

Liberal order aims to build on freedom and to defend freedom. Thus, it is evident that any analysis of liberal order requires a deeper understanding of individual unpredictability. This problem can be approached from two sides. On the one hand, the actor must have the capability to act unpredictably. And on the other hand, the actor must not be prevented from acting unpredictably. These two complementary conditions for unpredictability are related to two popular conceptions of the notion of freedom, known as positive and negative freedom (cf. Berlin, 1969).

The notion of positive freedom relates to a characteristic of an actor and requires that an actor A

- acts and wants to act based on his own initiative,
- appears capable of making new beginnings,
- decides independently (from the perspective of an actor B) from his environment.

Berlin (1969, 131) eloquently captures what is meant by these points: "I wish to be somebody, not nobody; a doer - deciding, not being decided for, self-directed and not acted upon by external nature or by other men as if I were a thing, or an animal, or a slave incapable of playing a human role, that is, of conceiving goals and policies of my own and realising them." It is obvious that such an actor can be unpredictable in relation to himself and in relation to other actors. Humans can employ this capability constructively. Examples range from ordinary but nevertheless surprising birthday presents to the invention of the electric light bulb. However, unpredictability is not a priori a positive thing. Everyday life shows that humans regularly come up with negative surprises, which sometimes have a fatal end for themselves or for others. It is one of the merits of the term unpredictable that it does not restrict the range of actions, neither on the positive nor on the negative side. It is at this point where the parallels between the analytical definition of freedom as unpredictability and the positive notion of freedom come to an end. This is because in contrast to the notion of unpredictability the concept of positive freedom was developed further. The idea that freedom can entail negative consequences appeared to be unacceptable. Philosophers like Spinoza, Rousseau and Hegel tried to narrow down the concept of positive freedom. Instead of equating it with unpredictability, freedom was equated with reason. History proved that this equation endangers freedom rather than creating a basis to preserve it. Consequently, there is no point in following this concept any further than up to the quote from Berlin presented above.[23]

The picture gets inverted as soon as the concept of negative freedom is taken into account. The notion of negative freedom refers to the external constraints an actor faces. It concentrates on obstacles that prevent it from being free and from behaving unpredictably. Representatives of the concept of negative freedom argue that coercion is the biggest enemy of freedom. Consequently, freedom is represented by the absence of coercion.[24] The equation with unpredictability works here too: An actor A is unpredictable to an actor B as long as his actions are not determined by coercion. The actor then is not prevented from being unpredictable.

Similar to the basic idea of positive freedom the concept of negative freedom also does not necessarily prevent negative surprises. Most of those actions conceived of by Thomas Hobbes in his state of nature are still possible. For this reason liberal thinkers regularly claim that the freedom of an actor must be restricted by the freedom of the other actors (cf. Radnitzky, 1996, 153). While this may well be

---

[23] Representatives of the notion of positive freedom argue that true freedom is based on rational decisions and actions but not on irrational passions. Reason has to dominate unpredictability. But this eliminates any freedom of an actor in relation to somebody else: "I can do what I choose, but I cannot choose otherwise as I do" (Berlin, 1964/98, 101). In addition it can be argued that actors, as soon as they act rationally, always come to the same conclusion (Berlin, 1969, 154). This, however, implies that the individual is no longer a point of reference. Following Rousseau, the position of the individual is taken over by the "volonté générale" which results in a situation where "...the self-government spoken of is not the government of each by himself, but of each by all the rest" (Mill, 1859/1989, 8). Eventually, this means that the individual can be forced to be free because the volonté générale - as an incarnation of reason and morality - knows better what is good for him (cf. Berlin, 1969, 132f; Gaus, 1996, 2; Schwan, 1993, 223f). But the volonté générale is a social phenomenon that can be traced back to individual actions. History proves that in the name of the so called volonté générale actions are taken that are in the interest of those persons who have the power to enforce their own interests, rather than actions that are in the interest of all individuals. Consequently, the government of reason, which departs from the notion of positive freedom, can be viewed to be a basis for totalitarian systems.
[24] Coercion may be imposed for instance through commands, bans or by the way of manipulation (cf. Edwards, 1967, 222).

compatible with the notion of unpredictability, it poses the problem of determining where this border between the individual freedoms can be found (Berlin, 1969, 145ff).

As an intermediate conclusion the notions of positive and negative freedom clearly enhance the understanding of the analytical concept of freedom as unpredictability. However, the brief discussion that could be provided here demonstrates already that a defence of freedom without compromise can hardly be justified because of the potential negative effects. In the end, a more comprehensive description of freedom does not free it from its downsides. It seems plausible that as long as the discussion circles solely around the conceptualisation of freedom it is either bound to be coupled to the state of nature or to end up with Leviathan. This is not to say that the notions of positive and negative freedom do not contribute anything further. The opposite is the case. They represent the lids that cover the intellectual containers which hide the capabilities an actor must possess and the constraints an actor has to face in order to be unpredictable without imposing negative consequences on others.

The capabilities that are concerned do not only include unpredictability but also characteristics that enable an actor to constructively employ this unpredictability. Humans appear to be the only reference point here: "The central assumption of common thought and speech seems to be that freedom is the principal characteristic that distinguishes man from all that is non-human" (Berlin, 1964/98, 109). However, there are few if any approaches which attempt to determine the behavioural features that make up this characteristic. The discussion of autonomy of software-entities in the DAI literature shows that the distinction of human versus non-human looses evidence. Obviously, there is need for a closer review. And the same can be said of the second intellectual container that stores the constraints that restrict the freedom of one actor by the freedom of the other actors. The following quote from Hargreaves Heap/Varoufakis (1995, 32) sounds intuitively convincing: "The key individualist move is to draw attention to the way that structures not only constrain, they also enable." However, any constraint limits unpredictability and Bentham (cit. in Hayek, 1960, 60) goes as far to say that: "every law is an evil for every law is an infraction of liberty." Consequently, more detailed analysis is required here as well.

It is not by chance that these two content-providers perfectly fit into the analytical framework introduced in chapter three. A detailed review of the constraints that are part of a liberal order is at the centre of the macro-micro analysis that is to be undertaken in chapter five. And the micro-micro analysis in chapter six will focus on the capabilities and characteristics that have to be demanded from a free actor. Chapter seven goes on to show how on this basis the liberal order is able to hold its promises.

4.3.2 Freedom and the machine

Freedom as a point of departure to solve the problems of social order may be appropriate as long as human beings are concerned. With respect to machines it appears to be counterintuitive. More realistically, it can be said to pose a dilemma: On the one hand complex software appears to be unpredictable. And new technologies like the agent-paradigm tend to increase this unpredictability: "Looking ahead several years into the future, we project that shopbots [and other agents] will evolve into economic entities (i.e. utility maximizers) in their own right, interacting with billions of other self-interested software-agents" (Greenwald/Kephart, 1999, 506). On the other hand, humans want machines to be instruments rather than free actors. Rawlins (1998, 126) points to a widespread opinion when he states that "a slave is what we purpose all machine intellects to be." As already indicated, it is not the intention of this book to give opinions on questions of moral philosophy; such as whether machines should be slaves or should be free. However, the analysis up to this point suggests that Leviathan-like approaches to social order are less promising than the concept of liberal order. Consequently, the idea of liberal order will be analysed in detail. In the present context this necessarily includes unpredictable and hence free machines. Against the background of the dilemma mentioned above, the remainder of this section will serve to illustrate two points:
a) A rejection of freedom for machines is not self-evident, and
b) Unpredictable machines can still be instruments.

These two points are only meant to illustrate that freedom of machines is less strange than it might seem to be. It does neither represent a final standpoint nor an analytical result. Part Two will have to show which properties software-agents have to possess to be able to meet the requirements of liberal order and how much freedom liberal order offers them.

a)   A rejection of freedom for machines is not self-evident
Common thought raises a range of arguments against machine-freedom. But in most cases these arguments are populist in nature rather than contributing to a serious discussion. The following examples may serve to illustrate this point.

A first argument against freedom for machines is that there are differences in the dignity of man and machine. From the uniqueness of the human race comes the conclusion that only humans should be free. However, the issue of freedom can be separated from the question of dignity. And it is human society itself which provides the examples for such a distinction: One example is animals, which have the right to be free, for instance in a national park. Another example is corporations that, under some legislatures, hold freedom rights independent from any associated human individuals. Obviously, it is less strange to view a potential freedom of machines in line with these examples than if it is set on par with human freedom (cf. Krogh, 1995, 1).

Second, it can be claimed that freedom for machines undermines human authority. With some exaggeration this point also includes the fear that machines may overpower the human race. It may appear utopian to take this argument into account. But the phenomenon of path-dependency is well known in economics and suggests that a direction once chosen may not be reversible after some time. Consequently, the argument should not be dismissed without reflection. A counter-argument is available as human history provides sufficient evidence that the suppression of freedom is not a sustainable solution to protect a certain race or group as long as it is not truly superior. The abolition of slavery in North America or the repeal of the Apartheid regime in South Africa can serve as examples here.

Connected with the last aspect is the third point that machines are meant to serve humans. However, in order to render services to humans machines do not have to be slaves. Customer orientation is one of the merits brought about by the modern market economy and illustrates that service and freedom can be reconciled. As far as human society is concerned there is evidence that the combination of the latter is, overall, an advantageous institutional arrangement. Regarding man-machine societies there will be structural differences. But it cannot a priori be excluded that the market metaphor will prove to be sustainable here as well.

A fourth argument against freedom for machines is that the requirements for the individual actor to fit into a liberal order exceed the capabilities of machines. Although also bounded in many ways, humans are capable of becoming a constructive member of a liberal order. In order to achieve this, the human species had to undergo a demanding learning process (cf. Hayek, 1960, 56ff). Machines are still far from reaching this level of sophistication. However, there is no reason to immediately confront machines with the demands of modern civilisation without giving assistance of any kind. As already indicated, liberal order appears to be promising when actors are bounded and endowed with only limited capabilities and knowledge. It appears premature to judge the qualifications of machines unless the requirements they have to meet are known.

The list of arguments is certainly incomplete. In addition, the arguments are far from fully developed. Nevertheless, the brief discussion sufficed to show that the question in favour or against freedom for machines cannot be answered finally at this stage. Rather, it suggests that a deeper discussion is advisable.

b) Unpredictable machines can still be instruments
A second factor that facilitates the treatment of freedom for machines in the present context is that it is not viewed to be a metaphysical and untouchable characteristic,

goal or value. Based on what was said so far, freedom as unpredictability stems from the capabilities of an actor and from the constraints an actor has to face. As such, freedom for machines can be accepted as a pillar of social order, namely liberal order. The term 'accepted' indicates that freedom is only in part actively employed. Besides equipping software-agents with adequate capabilities to act unpredictably, agents are prevented from certain actions - but it is left undetermined which of the selectable actions they may take. In other words, agents can be offered a "number of open doors" each of which is opened to a certain "extent" (Berlin, 1964/98, 110). This, in turn, indicates that individual agents are unpredictable only with regard to these "doors" and only to the "extent" to which these doors are open.[25] For example a software system for air-traffic control only operates within the domain of air-traffic but not within any other domain, say factory scheduling. Also, the system controls the air-traffic only to the extent that supervising human flight controllers do not intervene. Reasoned one step further, this means that machine freedom in the sense of unpredictability on the one hand and the desire to have machines as instruments on the other hand are not mutually exclusive alternatives. This is what the concept of software-agents builds on. It replaces the direct manipulation of computers by the delegation of whole tasks or a range of tasks (cf. Negroponte, 1997). Software-agents are viewed as instruments that are employed for certain tasks. To the extent to which designers and users consider it to be acceptable, they are free in the execution of these tasks or even in the selection of the tasks. Hence, from this point of view machine freedom is neither completely alien to human-machine interaction nor does it represent an all-or-nothing option. In order to make machines better instruments freedom can be intended. This is perfectly illustrated by the examples of interface-agents given in section 1.5. However, the meaning of 'better' depends on the point of view of the actor who employs the agent. Thus, it can also mean 'more harmful', as better viruses or devils show. Unpredictability, independent from its degree, remains a neutral concept. Therefore, the subsequent analysis serves to identify the factors that have to be taken into account when a social order is envisioned that accommodates machine-unpredictability.

4.4 Summary

Confronted with the state of nature that was outlined as point of reference in chapter three, the next step was to identify the direction for a successful exit. In 1651 Thomas Hobbes proposed the Leviathan. His metaphorical approach to describe a fictional absolutist state captures central characteristics not only of a range of real approaches to social order in human society, but surprisingly also of traditional software systems. In human society Leviathan repeatedly failed. Developments in the

---

[25] Berlin (1964/98, 110) states that the metaphor is imperfect. It does, however, illustrate well what is meant here.

area of software point in the same direction. An alternative approach to social order is provided by liberalism. A first brief overview of the idea of liberal order showed that it is conceived to be polycentral and horizontal in nature and that social order is to be secured solely by influencing and controlling the order of rules. Liberal order promises to have a range of desirable properties. These include the minimisation of harmful effects caused through individual actors, the creation of complex and open forms of social order, the effective use of knowledge in society, and the creation of wealth. The promises were considered to be attractive not only for human society but also for software systems. In sum, they can be said to reflect the requirements of a grand world. But potentially irritating with respect to software-agents was the fact that liberal order has the objective to establish and protect the freedom of the individual actor. Therefore, freedom was downgraded from a goal to a possible means to create social order. Liberalism and DAI were combined by identifying liberal order as the kind of system that is of interest and by treating freedom as one of the potential pillars of liberal order. As a last reference point for the analysis in part two, a relational concept of freedom was introduced: An actor was defined as free when and to the extent that his future behaviour is unpredictable to somebody; this somebody may be the actor himself or somebody else. The discussion of common conceptualisations of the notion of freedom suggested that unpredictability stems from the capabilities of an actor and from the constraints an actor has to face. Both sides have to be explored in more detail. The question remained whether it is acceptable to extent freedom to machines. Already Chapter One showed that unpredictability of machines cannot be prevented. Common rejections of machine-freedom were found not to be well grounded. Additionally, it turned out that unpredictability of machines can constructively be employed by software-agent engineering. Consequently, a deeper analysis appears to be worthwhile to investigate the factors that have to be considered when unpredictability and hence freedom is accepted not only for humans but also for machines.

Part II Constraints, behaviour, and spontaneous order

The foundations presented in the first part demanded a significant amount of space. As a result, an account of the relevant problems and a solution strategy stand as a basis for the second part. Now, the ideal concept of liberal order will be introduced systematically and analysed to determine whether this concept can be applied to software-agents and multi-agent environments. This will be done in the three-step process of the MMM-scheme. First, the constraints or more specifically the institutions of liberal order will be discussed. Second, the characteristics an individual actor ideally possesses to fit such an order of rules are investigated. And third, it is disclosed how a liberal spontaneous order of actions can emerge on the basis of rules and actors.

In sum, this serves to provide a unified and general basis for a theory of liberal order for and with software-agents. The analysis will not provide evidence for the suitability of liberal order for designing specific software systems, say for instance, for the management of telecommunication networks. But it will show whether liberal order is a social order in the sense that individual actors can form correct expectations about their environment and can come to grips with erroneous expectations, independent from the particular type of environment. More specifically, it will lead to insights as to whether by applying liberal order to environments with software-agents:

- state of nature situations can be overcome or even prevented,
- unpredictability of the individual actor can not only be created but also accommodated,
- the complexity of the systems can be increased and the small worlds of traditional software systems can be exited gradually,
- transaction cost efficient institutional arrangements are feasible.

5

The order of rules
- constraints for a liberal order

Rules are of fundamental importance for social order. This is one of the lessons that can be learned from Thomas Hobbes' state of nature, where no rules exist. But rules do not only enable social order, they can also threaten it - exemplified by Hobbes' Leviathan and its successors. With this in mind the focus is now on the principles of liberal order.[26] In the present context this is less straightforward than it may appear. The discussion has to overcome a couple of obstacles. The challenge is that computer science can be said to look for proposals for "a social engineering for machines" (Rosenschein/Zlotkin, 1994, 4). However, present sources of liberal theory certainly do not satisfy this demand. Two fundamental obstacles can be identified.

First, liberal economic theory builds on a tradition of several centuries but a systematic conceptualisation of liberal order does not exist. Among many others, Radnitzky (1996, 150) states that comprehensive explanations of the key notions of liberalism are missing. Homann/Pies (1993, 298) claim that, today, a fully articulated systematic conceptualisation of liberal social order which solves the fundamental problems of the future is largely missing (cf. also Hayek, 1973, 55). They refer to problems like military conflicts, environmental pollution, and the growth rate of the world's population. Their list can easily be extended to include the subject of this book. This is no surprise. Already Hume and later Hayek (e.g. 1969/94, 239) reminded of the circumstance that liberal rules are, to a great extent, not consciously invented by humans but develop in the process of interaction, without being intended by the individual actors. This in part explains why a comprehensive picture is missing. Yet, in order to successfully reconcile liberal ideas with the demands of computer science, a more concise picture seems necessary. Thus, a systematic conceptualisation will be established based on the fragmented theoretical inputs that are available. This effort can draw on valuable support from de Jasay's (1991) restatement of liberalism, which can be viewed as a first general step towards such a conceptualisation.

---

[26] Although the economic analysis of social order has a long established tradition of dealing with "principles", a concise definition of the notion is missing. In this book principles of social order are defined as essential rules that mediate between the overall goal of social order and the many concrete constraints of individual behaviour in everyday life (Zimmermann, 1994).

The second problem is that liberal economic theory can hardly be reconciled with the idea of social engineering. A theory of social order does not automatically represent a guide for active social engineering, particularly not for a very detailed social engineering of multi-agent environments. Computer science searches for recipes for the construction of social order in software systems. Meanwhile, complex multi-agent environments appear to reach the border where social order can no longer be actively constructed. Based on the study of the economy and society in general, economics is familiar with this problem: Hayek (1969/94, 33) claims that the more complex an aspired order is, the more one has to rely on spontaneous forces to create this order. And, to reach this order, it will be necessary to constrain oneself to a control of its abstract lines rather than its specific manifestations. The following discussion will not short-sightedly head for exact blueprints of social order. Rather it will take account of potential borders of social engineering and will focus on those abstract principles of order that are known to enhance the spontaneous development of more complex forms of social order.

Based on these premises the chapter is structured as follows. Initially, the principles of liberal order are identified in section 5.1. Each rule is described and analysed. The characteristics and the impacts of the rules are discussed. Commonly known downsides are considered. Besides their content, it is necessary to know how the rules are enforced because only the combination of content and enforcement can deliver workable institutions; or more generally: a functioning order of rules. Thus, the institutional arrangements that capture these principles are introduced and analysed in section 5.2. The systematic conceptualisation of both the principles of liberal order and of the possible institutional forms will be used to discuss potential starting-points for an implementation within multi-agent environments. Finally, paths to further specification are discussed. As this goes beyond the principles of liberal order, it will be analysed in the appendix.

5.1 Liberal principles of social order

It is hard to imagine social order in the absence of rules. While building on relatively few rules, liberal order cannot exist without imposing any constraints. This chapter analyses the basic principles of liberal order. The aim is to work out a systematic conceptualisation of liberal order that is more specific than the often spongy and unkempt expositions of liberalism (Radnitzky, 1996, 150). With regard to a potential exploitation of liberal principles by computer science such an aim is especially important. In order to achieve it, the following analysis is guided by the vision of a "strict liberalism" in the sense of de Jasay (1991). It is an ideal concept that is introduced here. Human societies do not automatically follow liberal principles. However, some societies do sometimes. And the preceding section indicated how this can be explained and legitimated. The question now is, whether strictly liberal rules that have proven to function in human society can be applied to software-agents. The prospects are good: Independent from any interdisciplinary efforts between the social sciences and computer science, Radnitzky (1996, 157) describes strict liberalism to be the "software-infrastructure" of a free society. The question is whether this assertion can be further substantiated.

De Jasay (1991, 57) summarises the principles of strict liberalism as follows:
1. Individualism: Individuals can, and only they can, choose.
2. Non-Domination: The point of choosing is to take the preferred alternative.
3. Exclusion: All property is private.
4. Contract: Promises shall be kept.
5. Priority: First come, first served.
6. Politics: Individuals can choose for themselves, for others or both.

It will turn out below that these principles provide an inspiring and challenging subject. However, they will not all be discussed here. There are two exceptions, individualism and politics. The analysis of individualism is postponed until chapter six because it fits more neatly into the discussion of the individual actor. Nevertheless, the principle is essential to the following discussion. It has to be emphasised already at this point that liberal rules refer to individual actors and that it must be possible to trace any occurring action back to an individual actor. Only individual actors can make choices and any social process has to be based on unanimous consent. It will become evident during the following discussion that without this requirement liberal order is unthinkable.

The politics principle is dropped completely. There are several reasons which make this plausible. One aspect is that classical liberal theory largely neglects politics and rather builds on the other five principles. The counter-argument of de Jasay (1991, 61) is that politics is a fact of social life that cannot be ignored. His position may well be convincing with respect to human society. However, for the foreseeable future the issue of politics in multi-agent environments belongs to fiction rather than science. This shows for example the discussion of voting rights for machines by Moravec (1996, 177). In the present context political decisions - for example in favour of or against liberal principles - are made by humans and not by machines. Shoham/Tennenholtz (1995, 230f), for instance, illustrate how such a decision process may look in practice: "One is concerned with the utility of social laws in a computational environment, laws which guarantee the successful coexistence of multiple programs and programmers [...] The society will adopt a set of laws; each programmer will obey these laws, and will be able to assume that the others will as well." These processes are not studied here as they can be covered by traditional political and economic theory. Another aspect is that, for the software-agents themselves co-ordination and co-operation via political processes is still largely irrelevant. It will be demonstrated that political mechanisms currently employed in

DAI -like for example the "Clarke taxe mechanism" by Ephriati/Rosenschein (1996)- can be analysed within the context of the principles given above. Apart from the two exceptions the rules of liberal order are now discussed one by one.

5.1.1 Non-domination

This principle makes sure that in a given situation an actor can choose the alternative he prefers. He should not be forced or dominated to show a certain behaviour. The non-domination principle is based on the idea of the absence of coercion. It aims to enhance the freedom of the individual actor and thus makes room for unpredictable behaviour.

What is of interest is that actions which are dominated by other actions are not chosen (Hargreaves Heap et al., 1992, 98). Often, free actors agree voluntarily to institutional conditions under which their decisions are in part dominated. Examples for this are employment contracts or the agreement to follow an auction-procedure. The problem is that actors who are forced to follow one dominating action are worse-off than if they had a choice. Domination can be direct or indirect. In the case of direct dominance an actor cannot but choose what another actor wants him to choose. Dominance occurs "...because the authoritative other holds sufficiently extensive resources and is sufficiently willing to use them that the alternative would lead to serious negative consequences" (Coleman, 1990, 71). The indirect case has less to do with interference of a particular actor. Here, dominance occurs because the prevailing rules of the game lead to situations where one mode of behaviour dominates all others. The state of nature describes such a situation: The right of everybody for everything forces everybody to enter into a war of each against all.

Direct domination can effectively be prevented, by referring to a simple rule like the non-domination principle. This rule applies as soon as an actor A makes the choices for an actor B although B would be able to choose by himself. A is banned from dominating B. In human society only few exceptions to this rule exist, for example when B is a drug addict or mentally disturbed. Indirect domination, however, requires a closer view. An unreflected general application of the non-domination principle is not sensible. The fact of the matter is that certain situations of indirect dominance are crucial to a proper functioning of liberal order. To illustrate this it suffices to mention that indirect dominance regularly occurs in competitive markets: When suppliers are prevented from arranging prices, they are forced to compete with each other which is beneficial for consumers (Homann/Pies, 1991, 610). As a consequence, indirect dominance cannot be condemned per se. Further criteria are required. Criteria that may be employed here are "exit" and "voice" in the sense of Hirschman (1970). The application of the non-domination principle could thus be restricted to situations where

- actors cannot contradict the rules of the game ("voice"), and where
- they have no opportunity to leave the game ("exit").

More precisely, this means for example that an entrepreneur may be dominated to pay a certain amount of taxes but he can raise his voice and vote for another party that reduces taxes. Alternatively, he can decide to move his business to another country. However, this example has not been chosen because of its convincing unambiguousness. Hence, in many countries which claim to follow liberal ideals the tax-level represents a form of coercion that is not reduced to a minimum and not made as innocuous as possible (Hayek, 1960, 21); independent from the available options for exit and voice. Consequently, the example portrays the difficulties in defining a general but exact rule for a solution of the problem of domination. Nevertheless, situations of direct dominance and situations of indirect dominance where exit and voice are impossible stand in contradiction to liberal order. A general evaluation of situations of indirect dominance where exit and voice are possible is not feasible. In such cases the specific circumstances have to be evaluated.

Turning from the content of the rule to its potential area of influence, non-domination is no less important for a multi-agent environment than for human societies. The principle is required to protect software-agents from being at the mercy of all sorts of interests. For example, social order would be difficult to establish if any actor can arbitrarily force mobile Internet-agents to execute tasks for him. A continuous interruption of task execution is only one of the possible consequences. Yet, current approaches to multi-agent environments do not explicitly consider the non-domination principle. On the contrary, it is likely to be broken. For instance multi-agent organisations based on blackboard architectures use dominance to steer agents. Similarly, with regard to the commitment approach there is a danger of dominance because agents are forced to adopt certain roles. However, there is no obvious obstacle that prevents an application of the principle to software-agents. This is underscored by the fact that non-domination can be realised within the areas of market-oriented systems and (automated) negotiation. Moreover, the social laws approach can be reconciled with the non-domination principle. This is hindered only by the fact that its current interpretation suggests that social laws say what is allowed and not what is forbidden (cf. Shoham/Tennenholtz, 1995, 243), a circumstance that automatically increases the degree and danger of domination.

What remains is the question of how the non-domination principle can be implemented and enforced. Section 5.2 will show that the law is the institution at hand here but that norms can also contribute to an enforcement of this principle.

5.1.2 Exclusion

The right of everybody to everything in the state of nature highlights the problem of the distribution of property rights in a world where resources are scarce. Strict liberalism demands all property to be private. For the formation of individual property rights the exclusion principle is essential: To have a property right means to have the right to prevent others from using one's resources. If an actor owns a property right, then all other actors are excluded from the benefits and costs that derive from this right (cf. Musgrave, 1994, 69ff). Overcoming the state of nature is not the only reason for the exclusion principle. A vivid illustration comes from Hayek (1973, 107): "The understanding that 'good fences make good neighbors', that is, that men can use their own knowledge in the pursuit of their own ends without colliding with each other only if clear boundaries can be drawn between their respective domains of free action, is the basis on which all known civilization has grown."

Private property rights are an alternative to other structures of property rights, namely to common property rights and public property rights (Pejovich, 1997, 3). Never since the writings of John Locke the notion of private property has been understood literally. In a wider sense, it describes the protected sphere of the individual which is necessary to guarantee his freedom (Hayek, 1969/94, 115). Private property rights ensure that the holder of the rights can be made responsible for all decisions he makes based on these rights. He is the beneficiary but he also faces potential costs. A common view in economics is that private property rights provide the best structure of property rights if problems of social order are to be prevented (cf. Hayek, 1969/94; Richter/Furubotn, 1996). However, there are goods where it is either impossible, too expensive, or simply not intended to implement the exclusion principle. These goods are commonly termed public goods. Their relevance is not restricted to human society but also extends to multi-agent environments: this issue will be picked up again in Chapter Seven.

More precisely, property rights can be defined as a bundle of rights that refers to four uncertain claims of an actor (Richter, 1990, 574): First, the right to use an asset (usus), second, the right to earn income from an asset (usus fructus), third, the right to change the form of an asset (abusus), and fourth, the right to partly or fully transfer the ownership rights over an asset to another party.

The fact that goods are someone else's property reduces the number of available alternatives of action. Property rights represent constraints on behaviour. The exclusion principle is broken when an actor ignores these constraints and interferes with the property rights of others. The above mentioned case of the fences and the neighbours exemplifies a relatively simple situation. The subject becomes more complicated when software-agents and people who interact via computer networks are taken into consideration. Here, the exclusion principle has to be applied to information. In comparison to rights to physical goods this leads to a wider range of more subtle problems that have to be solved if the rule is to be implemented successfully.

With respect to software-agents the exclusion principle gains a more fundamental meaning because the agent himself is affected. Software-agents consist solely of strings of information. Theoretically, the concept of an agent assumes that the actor himself is a closed entity and despite the information he communicates he remains a black-box to other actors. In practice, however, software-agents are by far less a black-box than human individuals. This is best demonstrated by the example of malicious Internet-hosts who access mobile-agents that visit these servers: "The host can observe every step the agent takes, read every bit of code, data and state, and even manipulate the way the agent works, as it, among other things, interprets the agent code" (Hohl, cit. in Grimley/Monroe, 1999, 2; cf. also Vigna, 1998). The principle of individualism which is traditionally meant to protect the individual actor but which mainly refers to freedom from physical harm is insufficient to protect actors that consist of bits and bytes (cf. 6.2).

The exclusion principle gets closer to the problem. Also, its range of application is wider. It captures the difficulties that arise when an actor owns information from which he wants to exclude others. The whole spectrum of intellectual property rights is affected here, including copyrights, brands, patents and business secrets. These rights cannot only easily be appropriated by others, they are also difficult to measure and to control (Richter/Furubotn, 1996, 90). It seems plausible that the existence of software-agents will further complicate this problem. In sum, there appears to be a wide area of application for the exclusion principle. Despite its simplicity it suits the problems well. These, however, are difficult to solve. Software-agents have to be protected from unwanted access and valuable information has to be protected from unauthorised exploitation.

Table 5.1: Implementing the exclusion principle and the contract principle through encapsulation and communication

	Encapsulation of...	Communication of...
...information	Prevents spying	Enables computation
...access	Prevents unauthorized communication	Enables transfer of communication capability
...resources	Prevents theft, enables accountability	Enables trade in resources

Source: Miller et al. (1996)

Leaving technical details aside, there is one idea that can be found at the heart of the exclusion principle. It is the concept of encapsulation that is central to the protection of property rights, particularly with respect to software systems: "Without security against examination, theft of proprietary information would be rampant, and the rewards of the creation of valuable code and information would be reduced or destroyed. Without security against tampering, objects could not trust each other's future behavior, or even their own. Encapsulation provides a sphere within which an object may act with complete control and predictability" (Miller/Drexler, 1988b, 143f). The concept is essential for the solution of the problems mentioned above. Moreover, it allows for a co-operative and mutually beneficial interaction regarding immaterial goods of all kinds. As the first column in table 5.1 shows, the encapsulation of software items can prevent spying, theft or unauthorised communication, while also enabling accountability.

Although the relevance of encapsulation has been recognised by computer scientists, the concepts of co-ordination and co-operation discussed in chapter two do not explicitly take account of the exclusion-principle. However, the practical implementation of encapsulation in the field of software does not seem to be an unapproachable problem as support can be drawn from a specialised field. Practical implementation is usually based on cryptographic methods (cf. Grimley/Monroe, 1999). Similar to the world of physical assets, perfect protection is not feasible (cf. Chess et al., 1995). Also, there are many cases, where perfect encapsulation is not at all wanted, for instance when an owner intends to sell or exchange the information he possesses (e.g. music, texts, and pictures). In order to effectively implement the exclusion principle in these cases, methods like access control systems or digital watermarks can be employed (cf. Rump, 1999; Shapiro/Varian, 1998).

In essence, the exclusion principle appears to be of fundamental importance. It manifests itself in measures that range from fences to various digital forms of encapsulation. All of them serve to protect property rights. The exclusion principle itself stands for the ban on interfering with the property rights of others. As the discussed technical precautions cannot offer perfect protection an institutional backing is necessary. Straightforward paths of enforcement are discussed in section 5.2. Before, a further problem has to be considered: In modern society there are many cases where the exclusion principle is broken unintentionally. "People couldn't be sure that despite the best of intentions they wouldn't end up being punished for accidental happenings" (Nozick, 1974, 71). Thus, it appears to be advisable to apply the exclusion principle not only in form of a ban (property rule), but to grant a right for compensation (liability rule) (cf. Koboldt et al., 1992, 335). The liability rule is crucial with respect to software-agents. Because as long as these agents cannot and do not internalise all the consequences of their actions (cf. 6.2.3), their users and designers will be the ones to be confronted with unintended consequences of the operation of these agents. Nevertheless, Nozick (1974, 71) warns that a cautious application of the liability rule is required: "A system permitting boundary crossing, provided compensation is paid, embodies the use of persons as means; knowing they are being used, and that their plans and expectations are liable to being thwarted arbitrarily, is a cost to people; some injuries may not be compensable."

5.1.3 Contract

From the creation of private property rights it is only a small step to the exchange of these rights. It is "man's [and agent's] propensity to truck barter, and exchange one thing for another" (Smith, 1776/1976, 25) that makes the contract principle relevant. This principle demands, first, that people can freely choose their exchange partners, and second, that contracts have to be fulfilled.

If, in addition to encapsulation, the possibility of communication is provided (see second column in table 5.1), then contract becomes feasible. Freedom of contract can be understood as a special form of non-domination. Encapsulated property rights are only transferred when there is mutual consent between the involved actors. In human society freedom of contract is enforced by law. Voluntary exchange is a basis for co-operation between actors. Property rights can be exchanged to the benefit of the participating parties. Furthermore, exchange is the pre-condition for division of labour and specialisation that can lead to further benefits. The merits of exchange and contract have not remained unrecognised in DAI. As discussed in section 2.3, DPS and MAS build on this idea. Approaches like market-oriented systems or (automated) negotiation can accommodate the liberal idea of voluntary exchange. Simulations with software-agents demonstrate that simple forms of free contracting are feasible with moderately sophisticated actors (cf. Maes et al., 1999).

The second aspect of the contract principle envisions contract fulfilment and requires promises to be kept. It can be interpreted as a special form of the already mentioned liability rule. This second part of the contract principle is more challenging. No problems occur as long as exchanges are self-enforcing which is often the case when one good is directly traded for another, like for example in a supermarket. However, many contracts contain an incentive for default in their time-performance structure (de Jasay, 1991, 65). Economists identify three main external reasons for non-fulfilment of contracts, or more generally for opportunistic behaviour:[27]

- Exchange-relationships can include transaction-specific costs. This means that actors make investments for long-term and repeated transactions with a specific partner. In such a situation the partner has incentives to exploit the actor, for example by exerting price-pressure. Due to this danger, specific investments are often not made although they could be productive for all transaction-partners.

- Contracts are normally incomplete. This means that ex ante neither all possible states of the environment nor all resulting consequences for the contract are considered. It is evident that this is due to the naturally limited foresight of the actors in complex environments. Moreover, foresight generates costs. The costs for the specification of contingencies can quickly outweigh the benefits of contract, which is an additional reason to leave them incomplete. The problem with incomplete contracts is that the available scope of action generates incentives for opportunistic behaviour.

- Connected with the last point are problems based on information asymmetries. This means that one transaction partner is better informed about the contract situation and about the state of the world in general. Consequently, the party that benefits from asymmetric information has incentives to behave opportunistically.

Obviously, transaction-specific investments, incomplete contracts, and asymmetric information make the enforcement of the second part of the contract principle difficult. It can be tempting to assert that these problems may be relevant in human society but not for multi-agent environments because software-agents can be programmed to keep promises and contracts. That this attitude is widespread in DAI, as reflected by most of the approaches portrayed in section 2.3. The Contract Net, for example, takes the contract principle for granted. As the pre-programming assumption refers to the characteristics of the individual actor it will be picked-up in

---

[27] Following Williamson (1985, 47) opportunistic behaviour can be defined as "self-interest seeking with guile."

the following chapter. For the time being, it is sufficient to state that universal as they are, software-agents can also be programmed to break contracts and to deceive their exchange partners: "it seems reasonable not to have expectations about verifying agent's private decision making. An agent might be programmed to lie about its internal state, and we cannot assume that such lying could be detected" (Rosenschein/Zlotkin, 1994, 53).

To secure the fulfilment of contracts and sanction the breach of contract appears to be an important issue. In open environments problems with the fulfilment of contracts cannot be excluded. But it seems reasonable that opportunistic behaviour does not appear arbitrarily. Rather, programmers, users and agents are somehow motivated to defect. The informal and formal incentive mechanisms that can prevent such behaviour are discussed in section 5.2.

5.1.4 Priority

The combination of the named principles is insufficient to ensure social order. It can occur that free actions of one actor collide with the actions of another actor although their respective property rights remain untouched. Also, there are cases where contracting is not feasible, for instance when goods have no price or are of little value. These gaps are filled by the priority principle which regulates those cases based on a 'first come, first served' basis (de Jasay, 1991, 69). In contrast to the state of nature it rules over the use of scarce resources in a random, morally arbitrary, impartial, and often transaction cost efficient way. Free actions do not collide because they are executed sequentially (de Jasay, 1991, 69f). The rule applies whenever the exclusion principle and/or the contract principle fail to be applicable or when they can be complemented.

The practical relevance of the priority principle in human society is immense. Examples quickly come to mind. The phenomenon of queuing at bus stops and in shops can be traced back to this principle. In the area of sports 'first come first served' plays an important role when rewards are distributed in the order in which contestants cross finishing-lines. Sports best illustrates the competitive effects of the priority principle. But the priority principle is also of fundamental importance for the functioning of markets. It protects innovators because it ensures that the property right to their invention is allocated to them. Incentives for innovative and entrepreneurial behaviour are created. Without this rule, innovation becomes a public good that can be appropriated by anybody. As making copies is always cheaper than the development of an original, it is evident that under such circumstances the incentives for innovation disappear. From the pure priority of 'first come first served' there is a gradual transition to the economically even more important priority of serving the one who is willing to pay the highest price. This is well illustrated by an example from the Arctic, provided by Coleman (1990, 59): "Among Eskimos hunting polar bears, rights to a portion of the carcass were held by each member of the hunting party, with special rights beings held by the hunter whose spear was the first into the bear [...] It is to the interest of all members of the village that hunters be motivated to overcome their fear of the danger involved in first attacking the bear. Such a right will be allocated by the common consent because of the common benefit it provides." In the example, the hunter who gets the largest share is not only the first but also the one who risks most and is willing to pay the highest price. In addition, the case demonstrates how this rule prevents conflict (allocation of property rights...) and why it can be conceived to be liberal rule (...based on unanimous consent).

In a wider sense actors stick to the priority principle in market-environments to regulate the transfer of property rights. Here, actors who buy and sell goods regularly give priority to those interaction partners who offer the best price. As a result, the priority principle creates competition among the respective market participants.

Again, it is only implicitly that the priority principle is applied to multi-agent environments. However, it appears to take over a key role. Market-oriented systems and automated negotiation are unthinkable without this rule. And because it is easy to implement and promotes efficiency, it can be found in many other approaches as well. The most popular form of application is certainly auction-mechanisms, which ensure that those agents acquire a property right who value it highest. For instance, Oliveira et al. (1999) discuss agents who flexibly employ different auction protocols to interact with trading partners in order to make high profits. While section 5.2 will have a closer look at the institutional grounds of the priority principle, chapter seven will serve to discuss its effects in greater detail, particularly the phenomenon of competition. Finally, it may be noted that potential downsides of the priority principle which are a matter of controversy in human society do not affect multi-agent environments the same way. This counts for instance for social concerns, which claim that the rule promotes a performance-orientation without compromise that wipes out other human virtues.

5.1.5 Few principles for a complex order of rules

After all, the discussion of the points on the list given at the beginning of this section is completed. In summary, the principles of liberal order introduced here comprise the following requirements:
- Individualism means that only individual actors can choose and that it must be possible to trace back all actions to individuals. Social outcomes have to be based on consent. As liberal order is founded on this assumption the rule is equally

important for humans and agents as soon as social order in multi-agent environments is meant to be based on liberal principles (cf. section 6.2 for further discussion).

- Non-domination means that an actor is not to be forced to take certain actions. While there is a consequent ban on direct forms of dominance, indirect dominance cannot be completely prevented. However, an actor must not be kept from raising his "voice" and from "exiting" the system. The principle is applicable in agent environments and appears to be useful. There can be an exception for the principals of software-agents.

- Exclusion in liberal order builds on private property and means that all costs and benefits of a property right are exclusively attributed to the owner of this right. The ban of interfering with someone else's property rights is complemented by the liability rule. The exclusion principle can be applied to multi-agent environments where an even wider range of application can be found. This is because the rule serves to protect the property as well as the agent itself.

- Contracts are the basis for exchange. Contracts have to be voluntary and must be fulfilled. Freedom of contract can be applied in multi-agent environments. The fulfilment of contracts can only be ensured if incentives to opportunistic behaviour can be overcome. These have to be assumed to appear also among software-agents.

- Priority means that those who come first are served first. It applies in cases where contractual arrangements are not feasible, where new property rights have to be assigned, where a mechanism for the transfer of property rights is needed. The rule is of fundamental importance for competition and markets and it is relatively straightforward to implement in multi-agent environments.

In essence, the five principles are laws but not commands (cf. Hayek, 1960, 148ff). They mainly exclude actions but do not dictate or prescribe actions and thus accommodate individual unpredictability. In addition, there are further characteristics that the principles have in common: They require consent among those involved in an interaction. They represent abstract general rules of conduct, which are independent of purpose, the same for all members of a system, valid for a long period of time, and which apply "to an unknown and indeterminable number of persons and instances" (cf. Hayek, 1973, 50). Moreover, links between these principles and computer science can be established. But although DAI appears to be compatible with a liberal order of rules, the existing links are fragmented and a systematic application is missing.

Finally, one may wonder about the small number of principles discussed here. There is no need to undertake huge research efforts to be able to state that the number of rules which determine the order of actions in the grand world, exceeds five. However, the aim was to identify the key-principles of a liberal order of rules and not the impossible venture of a complete stocktaking. These principles mediate between the overall goal of social order and the many concrete constraints of individual behaviour in everyday life. Such a mediating role has some implications, which are crucial for the rest of this book. First of all, they have an orientation function in cases where no rules exist or where actors are not aware of any more specific rules. For instance, most people who copy documents in a library do not know the specific copyright regulations that apply. But their familiarity with the exclusion principle suggests to them that there are certain limitations. Also, electronic transactions on the Internet, which could be based solely on an e-mail address and a credit card number, usually involve a lot more personal information of the exchange partners. Here, the principle of contract-fulfilment and experience with its pitfalls as well as possible assistance from the principle of individualism help to structure this type of interaction.

The five principles guide the spontaneous formation but obviously also the explicit design of more specific rules which are applicable under certain circumstances. The fundamental nature of the principles suggests that under the roof of an abstract rule a large number of more detailed rules can be found which relate to specific circumstances. For example the contract principle applies to a car boot sale as well as at the stock exchange, in ancient Rome as well as in the Internet-age, and for pasta in a restaurant as well as for trees in a forest. All this goes to show that the area of influence of the five principles goes far beyond the few pages on which they were introduced. It seems plausible that a major share of the interactions in a liberal system is ordered by no more than by rules, which are based on these principles. Already David Hume (1739/1985, 536ff) argued that the whole corpus of laws is based on only a few principles. This argument has not met with much contradiction since. However, no proof is available that in a system with a consequent liberal orientation all rules are derived from the five principles. But this must not be seen as a disappointing signal. It creates awareness of the fact that complex systems can be explicitly designed only to a limited extent. And it proposes to focus attention on the spontaneous development of social order.

5.2   Towards institutions of liberal order

At the outset of this chapter it was necessary to clarify what liberal rules are about. Now focus shifts to the question of how these contents can reach their addressees. Different forms can be distinguished and have to be analysed. Only when this stage is reached it is possible to speak of the institutions of a liberal order of rules, which comprise the rules themselves plus the complementary enforcement mechanisms (cf. 3.4). This section provides a generic overview of the possible forms of rule enforcement. Once again of interest is the identification of potential links between economics and computer science for each type of institution. But first some general aspects have to be examined.

Initially, a reminder of the way institutions are assumed to affect individual actors is helpful. Economists perceive institutions to be constraints that influence the costs and benefits of alternative modes of action. Typical of this conception is that the actors have a choice. For example, a man driving a car in the city can choose whether or not to stop in front of a red traffic light. Such a view is largely unknown in traditional computer science and it is still unusual in the sub-field of DAI. Quite the opposite is the case because computational entities are not generally assumed to have a choice. Section 2.3 demonstrated that social order in multi-agent environments is often intended to be hardwired. Or, to paraphrase Miller/Drexler (1988a, 59): the computational entities within such a system could no more pass a red traffic light than human entities can travel faster than light.

A related aspect is whether rules are enforced ex ante or ex post. In human society rules are normally enforced by the aid of ex ante incentives and ex post sanctions. To continue the above example, a car driver who passes a red traffic light knows that when he is caught, he will have to pay a fine. In contrast, computational entities are usually pre-programmed to follow a rule. Enforcement is purely ex ante and part of the hardwiring paradigm and is intended to lead to so-called "pre-established harmonies" (Castelfranchi, 1990, 50).

A third general distinction can be made between monocentral and polycentral institutions. In human society the confrontation of planned economy and market economy dominated the discussion of social order over several decades. Liberal economists have always and still do argue in favour of polycentral institutions, particularly in favour of the market. However, even a market economy builds heavily on monocentral institutions represented by all kinds of public and private institutions, like firms, for example. Basically, monocentral institutions ensure co-ordination from one centre (e.g. head office) whereas actors involved in polycentral institutions mutually enforce rules and follow an impersonal interaction mechanism. In software systems it was mainly the development of agent-technology that enabled computer-scientists and programmers to take polycentral institutions into account. Nevertheless, monocentral approaches still dominate the picture. As section 2.2 showed, this is especially valid for DPS-systems but it also counts for MAS. With respect to the latter it should be noted that markets are not necessarily polycentral institutions and that it is not straightforward to create a computational market which is not centrally organised (cf. Ygge/Akkermans, 1999).

Already at this stage the general discrepancies between the economic view and many DAI approaches to co-ordination and co-operation make evident that a fundamental shift in perspective is necessary to create liberal order in agent-environments. Also, it appears plausible that open environments for software-agents are not reconcilable with hardwiring and pre-established harmonies. Liberal order is

a probabilistic order. Thus, it is worthwhile to have a closer look at the options that become available through a paradigm shift. As already indicated an overview of the possible forms of rule enforcement is to be presented. This overview will be systematic, but it will at the same time be incomplete. First, it will only focus on the institutions which are relevant for liberal order. And second, the emphasis will be on the question of how to overcome the state of nature, so that institutions, which apply in simple co-ordination situations - for example the question which format to use for the transfer of computer files (i.e. where no enforcement is required) are largely neglected. A good orientation for the present survey is provided by Kiwit/Voigt (1995). Based on their taxonomy, the following enforcement mechanisms can be distinguished:
1. Internal institutions
2. Informal institutions
3. Formal private institutions
4. Formal public institutions

In each category DAI-approaches can be found, which aim to implement particular enforcement mechanisms. However, DAI does not provide an established taxonomy for the different types of institutions. As a consequence, many notions like for example the notion of 'norms' is interpreted and applied differently. The subsequent analysis thus also offers an unambiguous and realistic framework where existing and future approaches of DAI can be positioned.

5.2.1 Internal institutions

Internalised institutions are primarily based on the characteristics of an actor. For this reason reference to them will also be made in the next chapter which deals with individual behaviour. However, some issues will be examined straight away. In the case of internal institutions an actor supervises himself in a process of "imperative self-binding" (Kiwit/Voigt, 1995, 6). In the absence of immediate external influence the actor voluntarily constrains his behaviour. Basically, this idea is familiar to software-agent research where Singh (1996, 3f) has coined the term "psychological commitment" (cf. 2.3). But another form of internalisation is more common in DAI. Instead of the just-described first-party enforcement known from the economic analysis of social order, software systems normally employ third party enforcement. Examples can be found among the DAI approaches to organisations, organisms and social laws (cf. 2.3). Here, the rules to be internalised are programmed into the agents in advance. The central difference lies in the fact that such ex ante third party enforcement contradicts the principle of individualism. As will be shown in chapter six the former can be justified when individualism is technically unfeasible. The example of mobile-agent manipulation in the above section on the exclusion principle demonstrated that social order is endangered if more than one human principal can determine the rules of behaviour of an agent.

The form of rule internalisation for software-agents obviously is a matter of controversy. However, internalisation as such is likely to be indispensable. Buchanan (1994, 124f) argues that (liberal) social order in human society cannot but to rely at least in part on internal institutions. Pointing to the problems of the former Soviet Union he claims that missing internalisation leads to opportunistic and criminal behaviour. Imperative self-binding thus must lay the foundations for the respect of property rights, for contract fulfilment and for an acceptance of the priority principle. The empirical fact that rule-internalisation is - despite existing exceptions - widespread in human society suggests that it is advantageous not only for social order but also directly useful for the individual actor. These features may be summarised as follows: First, the enforcement of the rules of liberal order can at least in part be delegated to the individual actor. In the presence of rule-internalisation a continuous and costly enforcement through other actors is less necessary. Second, the behaviour of an actor is more stable, reducing his unpredictability. Although there is no reason to suppress unpredictability it is plausible that interaction partners will find it hard to deal with huge fluctuations in behaviour. Third, the internalisation of rules allows an actor to save on his scarce information processing capacities because he does not have to go through time and resource consuming decision-making processes in every situation he faces.

There are at least two points, which argue against complete reliance on internal institutions. The first point was previously mentioned (cf. 5.1.3) and asks not to have expectations about verifying the private decision-making of an agent. Although optimistic authors do not see a problem here (Singh, 1998, 46), this seems to be a valid concern regarding complex, open systems where software-agents have different designers and principals. The relevance for this concern is emphasised by the second point: Actors may have incentives not to base their actions on internal institutions. This happens for example as soon as rule following behaviour and utility-maximising behaviour diverge. In the light of these reservations it is evident that social order cannot build on internal institutions alone. It has to be complemented by external ex post control and enforcement. Before the discussion turns to these options one crucial difference between human society and multi-agent environments has to be pointed out. Regarding humans, it may be appropriate to treat rule-internalisation as an exogenous variable.[28] When it comes to software-agents, however, it is an endogenous variable. It is not only possible to program rules into the agents. Moreover, agents can - at least in principle - be equipped with

---

[28] Despite processes like socialisation and education, this counts at least in thus far as in a polycentral liberal order of actions no individual actor A can consider the internal rules of an actor B to be a variable he can deterministically steer.

real self-binding mechanisms. So consequently, in contrast to human society, rule-internalisation in agent-environments so far has been a matter of design.

5.2.2 Informal institutions

When rules are not sufficiently internalised it becomes necessary that other actors pursue enforcement. This can happen on an informal level. Following Schotter (1981, 11) an informal institution can be understood as a self-policed regularity in social behaviour which specifies behaviour in specific recurrent situations. Enforcement of informal institutions is polycentral. Instead of a central authority (all) individual actors sanction. As a consequence, the actors find themselves with the dual capacity of addressee and enforcer of the same rules (Eisenberg, 1999, 1). In the context of multi-agent environments the idea of informal institutions is mainly specified by work dealing with the notion of "social commitments" (cf. Singh, 1996, 4ff). There are two basic paths to employ informal institutions to implement liberal principles: individual and collective approaches to overcome state of nature situations can be distinguished. Individual approaches to establish social order are usually characterised by actors who act reciprocally and thus co-operate. A well-known example is the "tit for tat" strategy documented by Axelrod (1984). Individual informal institutions require that the immediate interaction partners try to enforce the relevant rules (Second party enforcement). Such an approach to social order is attractive because it can be based on free action of the involved actors. Suitable behavioural strategies allow the actors to enforce liberal rules like the contract principle and to mutually benefit from it. However, second party enforcement does not work under all circumstances. Empirical research and computational simulations show that important factors are the reputation of the interaction partner, as well as trust and suitable signals for the willingness to co-operate. This in turn requires longer-term relationships and an absence of anonymity so that the actors can identify each other in repeated interactions. In addition serious information asymmetries and exit options for defectors can prevent co-operation (cf. Axelrod, 1984).

Collective informal institutions are simply social norms. A social norm is based on a shared understanding of how to behave in a specific situation. The introduced basic principles of liberal order are - at least in western societies - part of many norms. Norms develop polycentrally based on repeated interactions of many actors, often based on individual informal institutions (cf. Benson, 1998, 214). Shoham/Tennenholtz (1997) start with MAS that show random processes and demonstrate that norms can arise if agents are able to adapt to each other. Essential for a polycentral development of norms is a cognitive processing of rules and behaviour by the agents. Otherwise, their behaviour can only correspond to norms if the rules are programmed into the agents (cf. Saam/Harrer, 1999, 3). But then, various features of norms cannot be exploited. Particularly relevant here is the aspect that not every eventuality has to be pre-programmed. Through imitation or sanctions agents can learn how to behave in unfamiliar situations. An orientation towards social norms helps agents to save on information processing capacities while still being able to choose their modes of behaviour.

In human society norms are enforced collectively. This means that all members of society are not only entitled but encouraged to supervise that norms are respected and to sanction if they are ignored (cf. Kirsch, 1997, 74ff). A third party enforcement like that can be difficult to achieve because it represents a public good, i.e. those who make an effort to supervise and sanction incur costs while all others benefit. Although all actors may be interested in the enforcement of norms, in such a situation none of them has an incentive to contribute to it. From an economic perspective, meta-norms play an important role in solving this problem: The actors do not only expect each other to respect the prevailing norms but also to sanction rule-breaking behaviour. In sum, a number of incentives can be at work to motivate individual actors to enforce social norms: First, he can be affected immediately by the rule-breaker. Second, rule-breaking may affect him in the future or he may then benefit from his initiative to sanction (Sugden, 1986, 156). Third, his initiative to enforce norms receives the respect and acknowledgement of other actors (Kirsch, 1997, 78f). In principle, DAI should be able to integrate these insights easily into existing frameworks for norms for software-agents (cf. Singh, 1997, 10f). Thus, social norms appear to be able to originate, exist and persist in agent-environments. As long as these norms are in line with the discussed principles they will contribute to a liberal social order.

In human societies social norms are something that can be analysed but cannot be directly shaped. This is different with respect to agent-environments where agents can be influenced directly and indirectly. The option to internalise norms has already been discussed. In addition, there are various ways to influence software-agents, which decide autonomously whether or not to respect social norms. For instance, direct influence exerted on an agent can include the variation of the algorithm which controls the adaptation of the agent to its environment, or deletion of the agent's memory at specific point in time so that the agent loses his knowledge about previous interactions (cf. Shoham/Tennenholtz, 1997, 149ff). Both measures exemplify the opportunity to design norms in multi-agent environments. However, even if these norms conform to some of the principles discussed above, such an approach ignores at least the principles of individualism and non-domination.

Less direct in its approach but comparable in nature is another method for the implementation of norms in software systems: Instead of directly manipulating every agent, a force of agents can be sent out to promote certain norms. The adaptation of the other agents leads to an establishment of the norms. Simulation results by

Axelrod (1997, 40ff) show that such a strategy generally can be successful: a small group of co-operative agents were able to turn around a non-co-operative environment. Brafman/Tennenholtz (1996, 478) systematically pursue this approach under the title "partially controlled multi-agent systems (PCMAS)" and with the objective of "ensuring that all agents in the system behave appropriately through adequate design of the controllable agent." PCMAS related systems can be employed to establish a liberal social order, if they do not conflict with the non-domination principle. But it has to be seen that PCMAS can be used equally well to support any other form of non-liberal social order.

Eventually, the argument illustrates that informal institutions can function to ensure social order in both human society and agent-environments. Regarding liberal order no contradictions occur as far as individual rules are concerned. In contrast, collective rules or norms can potentially contradict liberal principles. In a liberal human society there is a limited risk that individuals establish norms for their own purposes and exert coercion on other actors. But in agent-environments the opportunities to engineer norms are far greater. Consequently, the 'liberal flavour' social norms appreciate in human society may not persist in a multi-agent world.

5.2.3 Formal private institutions

Formal institutions can be enforced privately or by the state. In human society they mark the centre of interest because in contrast to norms, customs, and traditions they can be designed (Hayek, 1969/94, 176). Private rules are crucial for the protection of individual freedom. The most important formal private institutions are those which support contracts (Williamson, 1985, 29). They can be distinguished from informal private institutions by the fact that they are actively and purposefully designed by the involved parties (cf. Langlois, 1986, 19). In line with the analysis so far, for formal private enforcement three basic modes also can be distinguished: unified governance, bilateral governance, and third party governance (Williamson, 1986, 186). In order to be in line with liberal principles a voluntary agreement must be the basis for all three types of mechanisms.

In the case of unified governance the contract partners merge. A vivid example in this category is marriage, which leads the partners to interact with certain third parties as a unit. Also important are private organisations, especially firms. A firm operates externally as a unit. Within the firm contracts are used to establish a hierarchy, which divides the involved actors into governing principals and executing agents. Usually these contracts are less specific than contracts for other transactions. Consequently the executive potentially possesses significant scopes of action. On the opposite side, the principal has wide ranging options to enforce his decisions. The principal determines the incentives for the executing agents by the way he commands, controls, sanctions and rewards them. By agreeing to a contract that leads into a hierarchy, the executing agents accept constraints on their freedom. These constraints are normally restricted to a specific area (e.g. work) and a limited period of time. Unified governance is attractive because institutional arrangements more efficient than standard contracting can be found.

Similar to human society, organisations will become an important institution in multi-agent environments. Section 2.3 showed that a variety of organisational forms are both feasible and attractive because complex problems can be solved. Possible organisational forms range from strict command hierarchies to more polycentral but organised markets. Especially in agent-environments it is likely that organisations will not conform to strict liberalism. It is the non-domination principle that remains unconsidered when software-agents have neither the chance to join an organisation voluntarily nor the opportunity to quit it. The negation of this principle is typical for early applications of unified governance in DPS. However, simulations with software-agents demonstrate that organisations can originate from free contracting among agents. Depending on the circumstances, these agents autonomously come together to form organisations and split up again (cf. Eymann et al. 1998).

Bilateral governance includes all kinds of contracts, ranging from the sale of a car to long-term co-operation agreements between firms. Of central interest are self-enforcing contracts. Such contracts are arranged in a way so that there is no incentive for opportunistic behaviour among the interaction partners. They include, for example, the definition of specialised investments, bails, and reciprocal capital investments. Important pre-conditions for formal self-enforcing contracts are usually already provided by informal rules. In a sense a formal contract complements aspects of informal institutions like reputation, trustworthiness or 'tit for tat' strategies. In sum, these measures result in self-enforcing agreements. As far as the implementation of liberal order is concerned, bilateral governance is an attractive institutional arrangement because the danger of conflict with the liberal principles is limited.

Bilateral private institutions appear to be interesting for agent-environments when legal enforcement is difficult to achieve - for example when agents operate under incomplete or different laws or when agents can easily vanish so that legal measures do not reach them (Sandholm/Lesser, 1995, 1). Various authors show that the approach is applicable to multi-agent environments. Kraus (1996) examines the potential for "incentive contracting" between software-agents in situations where self-interested software-agents with diverging goals reach contractual agreements to help each other and to exchange services. To reach a self-enforcing contract many paths can be followed. Sandholm/Lesser (1995) let agents split up highly valued transactions into a row of low value transactions so that there is no incentive for the agents to defect. Rosenschein/Zlotkin (1994) propose that the owners of software-agents should agree on interaction-protocols, which have to be followed by the agents when making a transaction. These protocols (e.g. auction-mechanisms) are designed such that the agents do not have an incentive to break a contract.

Third party governance means that contracts are enforced with the aid of one or more actors who are not directly involved in a transaction. Examples of this form of governance are arbitrators of various kinds, franchising systems, and private regulation authorities, for instance in the allocation of Internet domain names. In order to comply with liberal principles it is required that the involved actors unanimously agree to the respective form of governance. After deciding in favour of certain rules, it is necessary that every actor respects the consequences in every specific situation. This is normally facilitated by the support of third party governance by the existing informal institutions of interaction and by the circumstance that it takes place in "the shadow of law" (Mnookin/Kornhauser, cit. in Richter/Furubotn, 1996, 178). This implies that - at least in principle - such private institutional arrangements can implement the whole spectrum of rules normally enforced by the state (cf. Nozick, 1974, 15ff). What is immediately striking here, is the relevance of this point for agent-environments. Experience gained in the field of electronic commerce suggests that the legal creation and enforcement of rules is often impossible or inadequate in open electronic environments (Baker, 1999). Thus, it is not surprising that the most important application of third party governance in agent-environments is probably the establishment of privately organised agent-based market places. This is emphasised by the growing presence of agent-based auction platforms on the Internet (cf. Guttman et al., 1998). Instead of two or more parties agreeing on an interaction-protocol, here an independent party offers a protocol to all that want to participate in the marketplace. This third party then guarantees the supervision and enforcement of automated negotiations. It is however important to note that private enforcement of rules face limitations concerning the opportunities to sanction rule-breakers. The options include the exclusion of non-co-operating actors and the systematic employment of reputation mechanisms (cf. Zacharia et al., 1998).

In sum, the described governance mechanisms are fundamental building blocks for a liberal order of rules. This is only qualified by the point that each of the involved parties must be prevented from reaching the power to dominate other actors. Legal institutions, which will be discussed below, can help achieve this.

5.2.4 Formal legal institutions

Formal legal institutions comprise constitutions, laws, and regulations. Legal institutions are implemented through political processes. Legal institutions can best be reconciled with strict liberalism if the affected actors unanimously agree on them.

As already indicated, these institutions are very similar to formal private institutions under third party government. The difference is that the third party enforcement agency is the state. In human society the state has become the "dominant protective association" (Nozick, 1974, 15ff). This is connected with the advantages concerning efficiency and stability, which can be achieved when there is only one third party which provides its services in a systematic, unified, and all-encompassing way. In human society the state has proven to be effective in enforcing liberal rules. Laws prevent dominance. They also directly protect property rights, ensure freedom of contract and guarantee liability. In addition, liberal rules are enforced with the aid of indirect measures. Eucken (1959, 152ff) notes that two of these are of particular importance: The state as an independent third party can guarantee open markets, and it can supply a currency that facilitates exchange. The former is achieved by refraining from protectionist measures like customs and import restrictions as well as by banning cartels and comparable private initiatives. Thus, the task of the state is to ensure that market-entry is possible and that there are no restraints on competition. The latter builds on the premise that money is a medium, which allows the establishment of a transaction-cost efficient social order (cf. chapter 7). The state determines the unit of account, its real anchor (i.e. the standard of coinage or the price target of money policy), the means of payment, and the organisation of the money supply (Richter/Furubotn, 1996, 19). A crucial task is to ensure that the valuation of the currency is stable. Only if this condition is satisfied will the prices reflect the scarcity of the respective goods. And only then will the prices offer reliable orientation in competitive environments (Eucken, 1959, 161f).

Other than human societies, multi-agent environments may not build on legal institutions and on the state. Experience with the Internet demonstrates that pillars like geographic sovereignty and physical force - on which the power of the state traditionally builds - begin to crumble. The most drastic example may be that private digital cash is about to seriously question the state's monopoly on currency (Matonis, 1998). However, while the distinction between public and private institutions is not to be underestimated in the long run, for the present analysis the differences between the two paths of enforcement appear to be of limited relevance. This is mainly because the ideal concept of strict liberal order is discussed in this book. From this perspective it does not matter who carries out the enforcement, as long as the enforcement as such is in line with liberal principles. Thus, without going further into detail here, the following analysis will just refer to unanimously agreed third party enforcement, no matter whether enforcement is carried out by the state or by a private party.

It is important to emphasise that the above simplification is only valid for the third party enforcement of rules, which are accepted unanimously. It was indicated in section 3.3 that it is plausible to assume that liberal rules can be based on common consent. In contrast, political processes - and thus also most legal rules - usually build on majority rather than unanimity. As a consequence Leviathan is likely to surface, actors may be prevented from choosing freely and they are possibly forced to follow the choice of others. There is a danger that the majority dominates the minority (Buchanan/Tullock, 1962/87, 190ff), or even that the minority dominates the majority when interest groups achieve over-proportional influence (Olson, 1965/71, 35).

5.2.5 A comprehensive typology of institutions

The preceding sections served to introduce the different enforcement mechanisms that operate in human society. One by one the sections discussed and distinguished the following types of rules:
- Internal institutions, where the actors constrain themselves voluntarily without the direct intervention of others.
- Informal institutions, which represent either bilateral commitments or norms. They are enforced by the involved interaction partners or by a third party.
- Formal private institutions, which are purposefully created. They take the form of unified, bilateral or third-party governance in order to enforce contracts.
- Formal legal institutions, which include constitutions, laws, and regulations. They are still of limited relevance for software-agents and structurally resemble private third party governance.

The discussion demonstrated that a conceptual framework consisting of these four types of institutions can be said to be comprehensive because it captures all possible modes of enforcement. Each of the channels can work to implement the liberal principles of order. In human society all four types of institutions usually appear simultaneously. They complement, compete and substitute each other in all sorts of situations. In the end each of them takes over a part of the enforcement tasks. Section 2.3 already showed that multi-agent environments still differ in this respect because they normally build on only one type of enforcement mechanism. However, the feasibility of all types of institutions indicates that there is room for an extension to more than one mechanism. This appears to be important because it can facilitate a departure from small worlds. It is less necessary to determine in advance which type of institution will suit the needs of a specific multi-agent environment best.

A closer look at the different types of institutions indicated that internal institutions and informal institutions develop spontaneously and unintentionally in human society. Only formal institutions are actively designed. With respect to multi-agent environments it turned out that internalisation and norms can also be a matter of design. However, as far as a liberal order of rules is concerned reservations against these newly available options appear to be appropriate because they can be used to exert dominance. Two other aspects of software-agents have to be emphasised.

First, it is plausible that the common ex-ante enforcement in multi-agent environments increasingly will be complemented if not superseded by ex-post enforcement. This is because in open environments there is no guarantee that all actors have internalised all the relevant rules. Second, the different types of rules can support and guide the adoption of polycentral institutions for software-agents. This appears to be important not only for liberal order, but for complex and open systems in general.

5.3 Conclusions

The constraints on individual action imposed by liberal order were the subject of this chapter. A profile of the fundamental principles was presented and the mechanisms which can work to enforce them, were introduced. The combinations of principles and enforcement mechanisms were called institutions. They were not considered to describe liberal order in full detail, but they provide a comprehensive roof for a range of more detailed rules that are applicable in specific circumstances. It was not possible to give a full account of these more detailed rules but it was illustrated that they can in principle be derived on-demand. It is now necessary to recap the effects liberal institutions have on the space of possible actions. The fundamental problems worked out in part I are of particular interest.

There is first the state of nature. Liberal institutions provide a foundation for a social order that systematically rules out state of nature situations. They do so cautiously, though, because the individual actor does not face massive constraints. He is, for instance, not kept from behaving selfishly or unpredictably. However, as soon as his actions interfere with those of others, it is no longer the right of the strongest that applies. Also, the right of everybody for everything has disappeared. The exclusion principle separates individual property rights and the contract principle rules that the transfer of resources is to be based on consent. As a supplementary rule to decide over the allocation of resources the priority-principle was identified. As it structures interactions in an impartial way, it can also be based on consent and thus serves to prevent a war of each against all, not only among humans but also among software-agents.

As the prospects of overcoming the worst case of the state of nature are good, further questions can be approached. Of central interest is whether individual unpredictability can be accommodated. It was already mentioned above that unpredictability is not prevented. Individual actors can act based on their own initiative and can decide independent from dominant influences of others. This is because liberal rules do not prescribe actions but only prohibit actions and thus always leave the individual actor a choice. Also, the constraints are mostly enforced ex post, which means that they represent incentives rather than absolute barriers.

However, the incentives work to prevent individual property rights from being negatively affected by unpredictable actions. While such negative surprises are prevented per se, the actors also have the opportunity to exclude unpredictability. Based on contracts they can voluntarily restrict each other to become predictable interaction partners. The only condition is that there is no conflict with the remaining liberal principles - particularly domination. All this goes to show that unpredictability can be flexibly accommodated. In addition, no a priori reservations against the unpredictability of software-agents could be identified.

At another front-line, the preceding discussion suggests that liberal institutions allow complex forms of social order and can provide the basis for agent-environments to exit small worlds. All five liberal rules as well as the co-existence of several enforcement mechanisms enhance decentralisation and openness. The fact that they apply to an unknown and indeterminable number of actors facilitates the extension or growth of a system. In a sense, it is always possible to add another centre to polycentral order. This is further emphasised by the fact that enforcement itself is often polycentral, e.g. individual actors promote norms and control contract fulfilment. In sum, liberal institutions allow small worlds to be built for example hierarchical firms or agent-based auction platforms. But they also provide the opportunity to interlink these small worlds with each other and to link them to the rest of their environment, i.e. to depart into the grand world.

Costs always play a major role in economic analysis. Social order was claimed to depend largely on the transaction-costs involved. The liberal order of rules presented in this chapter does not mark the way for a particular order of actions. All sorts of contracts can be signed and a large variety of specific institutions can be created. Consequently, no obstacle prevents the achievement of transaction cost efficiency. The characteristics of the rules even promote transaction cost efficiency. Thus, for example the enforcement costs can be distributed and the search for efficient institutional arrangements is delegated to the individual actors. More precisely, the exclusion principle provides an incentive to allocate resources efficiently while the contract principle and the priority principle facilitates the exchange of resources to reach those who value them highest. However, these are only indicators and it will be up to the following chapters to reveal more.

Finally, this first step in the MMM-analysis provided a systematic conceptualisation of a liberal order of rules. Liberal institutions can be reconciled with agent-technology and they deliver a basis to solve the problems of social order identified in the first part. On this ground, the next step of analysis can focus on the individual actor. It might be suitable to close this summary with a reminder that the conclusions drawn here are based on a theoretical ideal. Practical engineering efforts will have to demonstrate how far the stated compatibility between agent-technology and a liberal order of rules can be fruitful in real life.

Appendix 5   Further constraints for software-agents

With the liberal principles only a few constraints have been presented. Even if they are specified for particular domains and circumstances - either by the actors themselves or by a third party - it is likely that they are insufficient in the current multi-agent context. In other words, it is likely that such few rules leave the agents without orientation. The reason for this is obvious: Computational objects know far less about their environment than humans. The environment has to be defined and be designed in fact actively as a software environment, in order for software-agents to perceive the constraints it poses. This can be done intentionally. An overview of approaches to design the environment actively was given in Chapter Two and ranged from computational ecosystems to negotiation platforms. But the environment for software-agents can also be created unintentionally. The Internet is the intriguing example here. However, even the digital spheres of the Internet do not simply happen. The Internet was primarily created by humans for humans. Thus further design efforts have to be undertaken to develop the full potential of this environment for software-agents. The specification of the environment is a fairly general problem of multi-agent environments, and it would not normally be an issue to be discussed here. But the way the environment is defined and the kind of constraints imposed all influences the chance to implement liberal order. Throughout the preceding sections a couple of approaches like PCMAS, blackboard architectures and early versions of the contract-net were shown to contradict (partly) liberal principles. Consequently, the appendix to this chapter serves to sketch a strategy that allows specification of further constraints which

- ensure orientation for software-agents, and
- do not contradict the principles of liberal order.

A5.1 The compatibility of market-oriented systems and liberal order

Without awareness of the task sketched out above, DAI can offer an approach to solve the posed problem: market-oriented systems. As indicated in section 2.3 market-oriented programming was originally introduced to provide efficient solutions to complex resource allocation problems. However, real-world markets are still by far too complex for software-agents. For this reason, market-oriented programming uses theoretical models of markets as a blueprint for the design of multi-agent environments. These are significantly simpler than markets in the real world. Probably the best known theoretical model that has become digital reality is the general equilibrium model of neo-classical economics; implemented for example by Wellman (1996) under the title of WALRAS. On the one hand, market-oriented environments and liberalism are compatible. This may be surprising because neo-classical economics is known to be a "nirvana-approach" (Demsetz, 1969) which appears to ignore institutional conditions. Implicitly, however, liberal principles of order are contained in the assumptions of the model. On the other hand, market-oriented programming provides environments within which even less sophisticated software-agents can operate successfully. Evidence for this comes from experiments undertaken by Gode/Sunder (1994, 255): "In double auctions with a unique equilibrium price, relatively simple AI [Artificial Intelligence] traders can achieve convergence to equilibrium price and virtually 100% efficiency".

Liberal order and a good orientation for agents can be reconciled here because systems like WALRAS represent small worlds. Because these environments are derived from relatively simple theoretical models, they are "informationally impoverished" (Miller/Drexler, 1988b, 142). This means for instance that only certain types of goods exist and that in the process of interaction only specific kinds of information are exchanged. And compared to the grand world of real markets, the number of alternative actions available to the agents is significantly fewer. This facilitates orientation for the agents. Nevertheless it can be considered to be in line with the liberal order of rules

- if the agents are not sophisticated enough to find their way in a more complex environment, and
- if agents who reach a higher degree of sophistication are free to exit the small world to operate in a larger world, the final destination being the grand world.

The second condition underscores an important theme of this book - the journey of software entities towards the grand world. It implies that multi-agent environments based on simple theoretical models are only a provisional solution. As long as agents are not forced to operate in such an environment they will leave it as soon as another one becomes available which is more suitable for them. Market-oriented systems appear to provide a suitable basis for such a development. An important question is which are the constraints that further specify small worlds and that can gradually be extended to reach the grand world. The following section will search for an answer.

A5.2 Constraints for small worlds

Specification of informationally impoverished worlds can be pursued in a variety of ways. Market-oriented programming in the tradition of neo-classical economics focuses on efficient allocation of resources and on equilibrium solutions. While this is certainly desirable, the requirements envisioned here are more fundamental. The constraints primarily have to be compatible with a liberal order of rules and facilitate orientation. Two main categories of further constraints for the individual actor can be identified: On the one hand the possible actions can be restricted. And on the other hand the environment of the agents can be impoverished.

Concerning the possible actions three kinds of constraints are conceivable. First, it is possible to restrict the relevant actions so that only choices matter. The agent's choices represent his interface with the rest of an impoverished small market world. Speech acts (cf. 2.2) are of fundamental importance here. All other actions of an actor are irrelevant. These include forms of verbal communication like polite phrases, but also all sorts of non-verbal communication like gestures and mimicry. Constraints of this kind can be disadvantageous. Opportunities to create trust are dropped which means that mutually beneficial transactions may not take place (Frank, 1988). However, the system is less complex and there is no conflict with liberal rules, as long as agents are unable to perform these actions or they voluntarily resign from them.

A second option is, to limit the set of available types of choices. In neo-classical microeconomics it is only possible to demand and to offer goods. Every choice refers to a good and to a certain quantity of this good. The agents can still exclude others from their property. Also they can freely contract and nothing prevents the priority principle from being applied. Direct dominance is excluded because all agents dispose over the same limited set of actions (cf. Rosenschein/Zlotkin, 1994, 25). But similar to the other constraints considered here, it can be argued that indirect dominance is exerted on the agents. This cannot be excluded until agents are able to operate in the grand world where there is no global designer or community of designers who define possible actions or the environment.

A third kind of constraint refers to the time when choices can be made. This can include rules which define when choices generally can be made, for instance the opening-hours of a stock-exchange. Further rules might consider the sequence of choices which is of importance in the context of auctions. In this sense, in their "Rules of Encounter" Rosenschein/Zlotkin (1994) consider various mechanisms. In market-oriented computer systems both types of rules are implemented (Gode/Sunder, 1999, 21f). Again, indirect dominance is inevitable if these constraints are used to facilitate orientation.

More obvious than the restrictions of actions are constraints concerning the environment of the actors. Both determine "what kind of events can and cannot occur" (Miller/Drexler, 1988b, 143). In neo-classical markets the environment of the actors consists only of goods and prices: "In market-oriented programming, we define agent activities in terms of resources required and produced, reducing an agent's decision problem to evaluating the trade-offs of acquiring different resources" (Walsh et al., 1997, 2). The neo-classical market is one of many domains, which are defined in DAI. While here only goods and prices exist, "task-oriented domains" (Rosenschein/Zlotkin, 1994, 29ff) for example only consist of tasks. All approaches are characterised by the fact that many dimensions of the real world are faded out.

It is not only the basic types of variables that can be determined. In addition, decisions over the parameters can be made. Based on the specification that the environment consists only of goods, the goods themselves may be defined: "Selecting the array of goods and services available strongly constrains the design space. The more standardised the goods, the simpler are the choices for each agent, but the less diverse the marketplace is" (Mullen/Wellman, 1995, 289f).

Taken literally, an agent only receives information on goods and prices has no knowledge about other actors and may not even be in contact with them. At this point another possible constraint can be identified. In neo-classical markets actors can only interact via the environment which is normally represented by an auctioneer or a central clearinghouse. This significantly facilitates interaction because the individual agent automatically knows where and with whom to interact. It does, however, represent a drawback for polycentrality.

In conclusion, a variety of further constraints can be introduced based on the paradigm of market-oriented programming. These allow for enhanced orientation of the agents, while not fundamentally at odds with a liberal order of rules. Experiments and simulations with computerised markets demonstrate that in these small worlds liberal principles are enforced for simple software-agents who would otherwise lose orientation (cf. Wellman, 1996; Miller et al., 1996). The only significant contradiction with liberal rules that has to be accepted here is indirect dominance. This is inescapable as long as agents are not able to operate in more complex environments. However, it also implies that certain properties of liberal social order are lost. The pre-determination of the types of choices and of the environment prevents for example the possibly advantageous discovery of new modes of action or of new goods. After all Hayek (1969/94, 243) emphasises that it is up to the process of competition to discover which things really represent goods. In order to fully exploit the properties of liberal social order, a step by step reduction of the constraints discussed here is required. The removal of constraints can be synchronised with the technological progress made concerning the capabilities of the agents.

6

Actors prepared for liberal order

Liberal rules have proven to be applicable to software environments. These rules also promise form an adequate foundation for a solution of the four key challenges of overcoming the state of nature, accommodating individual unpredictability, making the transition from small worlds to the grand world, and minimising transaction costs. Rules alone, however, do not constitute social order. Only in interaction with the actors that populate a system do they produce an order of action. Consequently, the next step is to examine the individual actor, its properties, and the requirements that have to be fulfilled when liberal order is supposed to unfold.

This is not the first time within this book that the individual actor finds itself at the centre of attention. Chapter Two showed how software-agents are viewed from the computer science perspective. Chapter Three argued that, independently from whether one is dealing with natural or artificial actors, an understanding of social phenomena can be achieved when the individual actor is the basic unit of analysis. With respect to artificial environments the individual actor is not only a unit of analysis but also an object of design. It is an endogenous variable. This does not mean, however, that it is useful or even possible to head for an exact blueprint of the ideal software-agent for liberal order. It is not useful because neither the best design nor even a good design is known in advance. The requirements as well as the opportunities change over time and vary from environment to environment. Also, because there will be many independent designers, and because software-agents will not be static entities, it is not feasible to have only one type of actor. To focus on one particular and an exact blueprint for software-agents comes very close to trying to make agents predictable. It is however, the declared aim of this contribution to describe an order that copes with unpredictable actors.

On the one hand therefore, the first thing to do, is to point out what should not be expected from an agent. Common design features of agents that restrict the unpredictability of agents without being indispensable for social order will be identified in section 6.1. On the other hand, even a liberal order cannot accommodate virtually any actor. First of all, a rigorous implementation of individualism is required because social order can only be ensured when consequences of actions can be traced back to the respective actor(s). Identification, incentive-orientation and internalisation-capacity are the most relevant issues here and will be discussed in section 6.2. A second requirement is more directly concerned with the behaviour and requests that it has to be adaptive. Section 6.3 argues that adaptability is the natural complement to unpredictability and that this is the key behavioural characteristic for any actor within a liberal order. The introduction of this characteristic is especially challenging because "Economic analysis has largely avoided questions about the way in which economic agents make choices when confronted by a perpetual novel and evolving world" (Holland/Miller, 1991, 365). Finally, it is obvious, however, that - at least in the near future - a software-agent cannot function solely by relying on adaptability. The appendix to the chapter therefore discusses, how far role models can guide the design of software-agents without contradicting to the concept of liberal order.

Throughout this introductory argumentation it has become evident that design principles for the endogenous variable 'software-agent' have far reaching implications for the relationship between software-agents and human beings. In essence, the traditional vision of the machine as an omniscient slave will be discarded and unpredictable human actors do not only have to continuously adapt to each other but also, to a certain extent, to unpredictable machines. Letting loose the master-slave metaphor promises to free humans from being "slaves of the machine" (Rawlins, 1997). This argument also will be explored in the following sections.

6.1 Questioning common software-agent design-principles

The social sciences have always debated and are still debating the true character of man. Similarly, software-agent research has continuously shown great interest in the question of what the appropriate characteristics of software-agents are since its formation (cf. section 1.4). Nothing indicates that the two streams of discussion are about to come to an end. Rather, they are more likely to become more and more intertwined, which may lead to even more controversial arguments. The present contribution will not interfere in this process in a fundamental philosophical sense. Nevertheless, it will ask whether certain, frequently envisioned characteristics for software-agents are indeed required to ensure social order. A review of the relevant literature confirms that these characteristics can be captured by the following points:

1. Benevolence,
2. Perfect rationality,
3. Global third-party rule internalisation,
4. Natural slaves.

6.1.1 Benevolence

"He can't help being faithful, loving, and kind. He is a machine - made so" (Asimov, 1940/90, 52). The science fiction literature of Isaac Asimov pointed the way for many DAI researchers: Software-agents have to be designed to be benevolent, always considering the well-being and happiness of others (Singh/Huhns, 1999, 6). The difficulties of such conduct have been investigated by Asimov himself and more systematically, with regard to real and not just fictional systems, by Clarke (1993). There is a practical difficulty for benevolent actors to reliably consider the well-being of others, especially as many forms of well-being (e.g. physical and psychological) have to be taken into account. Furthermore, agents continuously face dilemmas where the well-beings of several actors have to be traded-off against each other, not even to mention the question of the welfare of the system as a whole.[29] Like humans, software-agents lack the capabilities for systematically realising substantially benevolent behaviour, because the "...constitutional limitation of man's [and agent's] knowledge and interests, the fact that he cannot know more than a tiny part of society and that therefore all that can enter into his motives are the immediate effects which his actions will have in the sphere he knows" (Hayek, 1948, 14).

In addition, there is no reason to assume that in open environments, where agents are designed and employed by different parties, agents will be inherently co-operative or even benevolent. Here, instead of one common goal, many conflicting goals have to be expected (Rosenschein/Genesereth, 1985; cf. table 2.1 for examples). Within the branch of economics one goes as far to say that: "the first principle of Economics is that every agent is actuated only by self-interest" (Edgeworth, 1881, 16). Software-agent researchers have started to adopt this principle, and increasingly cover over behavioural traces of benevolence (Greenwald/Kephart, 1999). After all, this means that there is no common appearance of software-agents. Some appear to be benevolent, others appear to be hostile or destructive, and many agents show a conduct somewhere in between the two extremes, usually depending on what lays in their self-interest.

From the perspective of this study, especially self-interested behaviour is viewed not only as unavoidable, but also as acceptable. Already Adam Smith (1776/1976, 26f) demonstrated that self-interest and social order are compatible: "It is not from the benevolence of the butcher, the brewer, or the baker that we expect our dinner, but from their regard of their own interest. We address ourselves not to their humanity, but to their self-love, and never talk to them of our necessities, but of their advantage." In addition, self-interest is not to be mixed-up with egoism, as it may

---

[29] With regard to the latter aspect Arrow (1951/66) can be seen as a reference point, also for MAS. He demonstrates the fundamental difficulties involved when trying to maximise the welfare of a socio-economic system.

very well incorporate altruistic or benevolent behaviour (Kirchgässner, 1991, 45ff). The argument that social order can be achieved without expecting any particular behavioural orientation from an actor can be received as a relief. The bottom-line of this argument is that for each actor it may be possible to pursue its own good its own way (Mill,1859/1989, 16). As will be shown in greater detail in chapter seven, liberal order accommodates self-interested behaviour because it provides incentives that motivate mutually beneficial rather than mutually destructive self-interested behaviour.

6.1.2 Perfect rationality

Ever since John von Neumann and Oskar Morgenstern a perfectly rational actor has been considered to possess a stable and constant utility function. It maximises its utility by choosing from the set of given alternatives the action that provides the maximum expectation for success. For DAI this is an attractive concept, because it allows for rigorous formalisation. In fact, the idea of rational behaviour and especially that of perfectly rational behaviour can be considered to be the basis for the majority of current (D)AI research (Jordan/Russell, 1998, 4; Sandholm/Lesser, 1995/98, 70). The concept of perfect rationality, however, also implies that the respective actor has the ability to anticipate everything that can happen, to trade-off all possible alternatives against each other and to come to an optimal decision; immediately and at no cost. Stated this way, it is evident that behaviour can never be perfectly rational (cf. Simon, 1996, 25f; Russell, 1997, 60f). Already Savage (1954/71) recognised that the model of perfect rationality is not appropriate for solving decision problems in a grand world. "An agent is bounded rational because its computation resources are costly, or they are bounded and the environment keeps changing – e.g. new tasks arrive and there is a bounded amount of time before each part of the solution is used" (Sandholm/Lesser, 1995/98, 70).

Aware of the conclusions within economics, decision theory, and DAI itself, researchers started to search for behavioural models for software-agents that are better suited to reality (cf. Boutilier et al., 1997, 3f). While the break with perfect rationality is a promising step, a second problem occurs: "There is only one way to be fully rational, but there are many ways to be less rational" (Holland/Miller, 1991, 367). In other words, in any situation with many interacting agents it may not be clear for any of these agents which mode of cognitive processing and decision-making the other agents follow. This sounds realistic. It seems rather far away, however, from most current approaches to multi-agent environments, which heavily rely on one specific architecture for individual agents to support the design of the whole system (e.g. Fischer et al., 1996/98, 217). This means that these systems only can accommodate one model of bounded rationality, i.e. they represent small worlds. The argument put forward here is that while rational behaviour can be assumed to be widespread among natural and artificial actors, it is not required to have agents employing one particular decision-making algorithm to achieve social order: neither perfect rationality, nor a particular other model of rationality. It will be shown that diversity can be accommodated.

6.1.3 Global third-party rule internalisation

The common way DAI establishes social order and implements rules of conduct like those discussed in Chapter Five is internalisation. Rules of conduct work as fixed, internally represented restrictions on individual behaviour (cf. section 2.3, and in particular Shoham/Tennenholtz, 1995). The concept of rule internalisation has different meanings for machines and for humans. In both cases the environment triggers the internalisation process. In case of a human being the process can be interactive, meaning that the control over the rule internalisation is not completely in the hands of the third party. Human actors handle influences like education or preaching differently. In case of a software-agent the third party, e.g. a designer, can be said to directly implement a rule (cf. section 5.2.1). Once again, Asimov is the father of this tradition, as he proposed to build a representation of the laws of robotics into the 'positronic brain circuitry' of machines. On the first sight, this seems to be an attractive concept, particularly for multi-agent environments, because it promises to lead to a pre-established harmony where social order is secured. One has to be aware, however, of the consequences of this view. First, the higher the extent to which the behaviour of an agent is determined by internalised rules, the less this agent can decide itself what course of action to take. In the extreme case, it merely triggers pre-existing structures, unable to produce anything creative or new (Rammert, 1998, 107). He is unable to react to unpredictable changes in the environment. He may not be able to make use of his knowledge of the particular circumstances (Hayek, 1948, 100). In addition, various agents within MAS can trigger only one structure. They cannot pursue their own good their own way, nor can they pursue the good of various heterogeneous individuals.

Apart from the question of whether agents should really just bring artificial life into a pre-established order, there are other aspects to be discussed. A second point is that internalised rules are generally considered to be "unbreakable" for machines (Miller/Drexler, 1988a, 58). It was already indicated in Chapter Five that this assumption can be questioned. An additional question is whether this is at all desirable. Many examples can be taken from human life, where strict rule- following behaviour has proven to be dangerous or harmful. On the contrary, breaking rules can be advantageous and can contribute to the evolution of social order when adaptation to a changing environment is needed. An illustrative example in this context is the unauthorised copying of computer software, followed by the development of shareware and later by the introduction of open-source software. A third point, already extensively covered by Asimov, is the unavoidable ambiguity and imprecision of a finite number of fixed internalised rules. Machine behaviour rooted in such rules may prove problematic. The danger of deadlock, commonly titled Buridan's Ass problem, is only one type of problem that can afflict to strictly rule-following agents that cannot proceed in their actions because one or more rules contradict each other in a given situation (cf. Clarke, 1993, 8f).

In the light of the discussed aspects it may be advantageous to be able to achieve social order without having to rely on global third party rule-internalisation. The argument put forward here is that precisely that is envisioned by the proponents of liberal order.

6.1.4 Natural slaves

The argument that machines are expected to be slaves was already introduced in section 4.3.2. Software-agents are no exception to the slave metaphor: "That agents act on behalf of their designers or users is a critical assumption underlying much research in AI" (Boutilier et al., 1997, 5). The slave metaphor contains two challenges. First, the agent has to have the necessary capabilities to satisfy its master. Negroponte's (1997) metaphor of a well-trained English butler illustrates very well a diversity of tasks that are difficult to automate. Knowledge acquisition in particular seems to be a key problem for a slave-agent. In fact, many of the problems mentioned regarding benevolent behaviour reoccur when it comes to being benevolent towards one's master. Second, the agent has to be prevented from abusing or discarding its role, because "the more intelligent the robot, the more it is capable of pursuing its own self-interest rather than its master's" (Bradshaw, 1997b, 3). The foundations to meet these two basic challenges have to be anchored within the behavioural model.

Historically, master-slave societies have not been able to persist in the long run, which indicates that humans are not natural slaves. Consequently a natural slave would have to be systematically different from humans in its capabilities and in motivation. In the present case this can be achieved because software-agents are universal computing machines. The shining example for DAI research, however, is the human being. And only few authors criticise the anthropomorphic foundations of agent-technology (e.g. Shneiderman, 1997). Despite all intentions, this makes it unlikely that software-agents will become natural slaves.

To reach for social order is more fundamental and less ambitious than to target a master-slave society between men and machines. The argument put forward here is that liberal order is able to accommodate a wide range of actors. It does not rely on actors fitting into a specific paradigm, particularly into the slave-paradigm. The idea

98

is that social order as a whole is guaranteed. The well-being of certain masters served by their machine slaves is ignored.

This section captures the most important aspects of the current debate on software-agent characteristics but it is not meant to be complete. The purpose of the discussion was to give an adequate picture of those characteristics with which agents are often intended to be equipped but which appear to be dispensable on the way towards social order in open systems. In summary, with regard to software-entities the above points challenge the traditional mind-set and argue that there cannot (except in small, closed systems) and does not have to be central control of the individual actor.

6.2   Rigorous implementation of individualism

Up to this stage, it has been outlined that a much wider range of behavioural characteristics than mainstream software-agent research suggests can be accommodated without sacrificing social order. At this point, it is necessary to discuss which design principles, if not the already named and discarded characteristics, are considered essential for social order. The first of these is an implementation of individualism.

The subject of individualism has already been touched upon from a methodological and normative perspective (Chapters 3 and 4). All social phenomena are considered to arise from the interactions of individual actors. At the core of liberal order stands the protection of the individual. Consequently, protection of the individual means protection from other individuals. Therefore, the presented general rules of conduct are targeted towards the individual actor. But liberal order is not only built around the individual, it also builds on the individual, i.e. there are minimum requirements an actor has to fulfil in order not to be alien to liberal social order. They can be summarised within three categories:
1. Identification
2. Incentive-orientation
3. Internalisation-capacity

With regard to software entities these requirements cannot be assumed implicitly but must be discussed explicitly which will be the case in this section. A fourth requirement, adaptability, is only beginning to receive more attention in both economics and DAI and will be discussed at greater length in section 6.3.

6.2.1 Identification

Individualism implies that the consequences of actions can be traced back to identifiable individual actors. Without identification, the rules presented in Chapter Five cannot be applied. History provides numerous instances which indicate that it is an important condition for social order: Whilst groups, communities or states are often accused of provoking conflicts, a solution of these conflicts can normally only be achieved when individual war criminals get caught, dictators are deposed and ministers resign. But identification does not only serve in these special cases. It is at the core of mundane exchanges on all kinds of markets. This is often overlooked by economists, who consider actors on markets to be anonymous. Agre (1998, 11) emphasises that relatively anonymous interactions, e.g. in supermarkets, are only possible because there is a minimum level of identification: It is possible "for people to conduct complex business anonymously by taking advantage of the properties of bodies" - e.g. at the supermarket checkout. People who interact electronically, and particularly software entities, lack the option to prove their identity via physical properties.

The first step in implementing individualism among artificial actors is the conceptualisation of software entities as agents. This means that the agent-metaphor is not only an instrument of analysis and design (cf. section 1.4) but also a necessary condition for social order. The agent-paradigm can prevent software from being an inscrutable conglomerate by making software-agents "one single thing that is different from other, countable things" (Agre, 1998, 4). Thus, agent-technology is a software engineering paradigm that encompasses the requirements of individualism. It is, however, only a first step, a necessary condition. The problem with bare software-agents is that originals and copies cannot be differentiated and that perfect copies can be produced at virtually no cost. Additionally, for actors like software-agents that do not have any physical properties, it may remain largely unclear what exactly has to be understood as an individual agent (cf. section 1.5). In order to conform to the principle of individualism, agents that act as meta-agents, as well as agents that are part of a meta-agent but that interact with actors outside this meta-agent, must be identifiable as a social unit. The only way this and the former hurdles can be crossed is by means of digital identities. Digital identities are not based on physical properties but on digital certificates that can in principle be obtained not only by humans but also by firms or software-agents (cf. Graber, 1999). A pearl of wisdom that dates back to the early days of the Internet would thus be outdated: "On the Internet they don't know you are a dog!" (New Yorker, 1993).

6.2.2 Incentive-orientation

"The great contribution of economic theory to understanding human affairs is, in my opinion, simply the repeated emphasis on incentives" (Gell-Man, 1994, 323). If incentives do not matter, individualism would hardly make sense because important instruments to reach the individual actor would fall apart. Since software-agents are not incentive-oriented by nature, the role of incentives on individual behaviour has to be explicitly discussed.

Incentives can be understood as arising from changes in the restrictions faced by an actor (Kirchgässner, 1991, 18). These restrictions can be exogenous (e.g. natural resources) but they can also be shaped by the actors themselves (e.g. contracts, externalities). In the absence of fixed internalised rules, the behaviour of an actor has to be systematically influenced by incentives, otherwise social order would be at risk. The relevance of this argument is often overlooked, possibly because the circumstance that humans are usually influenced by incentives is taken for granted. However, one rare but remarkable exception exists, which illustrates the importance of incentive-orientation: the madman running amok. He is a danger for his environment. In presence of a madman, incentives are of no use, he can only be stopped but not be influenced (Neubauer, 1999). The same counts for his counterpart among artificial actors, the virus.

In contrast, as soon as actors are incentive-driven there is a chance for mutual adjustment. Incentives provide a channel for social order to be established. The description as a channel is important, because it indicates the neutrality of the idea of incentives and implies that incentives do not necessarily contribute to social order. They can take all sorts of forms and may range from the incentive of an entrepreneur to make profit to the incentive of an employee to shirk; or from the incentive of a member of a club to defend his team-mates to the incentive for members of a community to overuse common resources, like for example Internet bandwidth. Which particular incentives contribute to social order largely depends on the specific situation. The crucial aspect is that actors react at all to incentives. While this is obvious for humans it is also achievable for software-agents. Rosenschein/Zlotkin (1994), for example, investigate how to design negotiation mechanisms for incentive-oriented agents in various domains.

To be incentive driven does not imply that individual behaviour follows a simple stimulus response pattern. Incentives matter but it is the perceived incentives that influence individual behaviour, i.e. actors do not take into account an objective truth but only what they perceive (cf. Vriend, 1996, 280). This means that actors who are influenced by incentives do not automatically rely on a simple behavioural model. Also, despite being incentive-oriented, actors can still be unpredictable.

So far, mainly the passive side of incentive-orientation has been emphasised. Incentive-orientation does, however, include an active side as well. In other words, actors can actively influence if not design incentives for other agents. Where this is done intentionally, especially within an economic context, the actors often design incentives by the means of contracts. Williamson (1985, 43ff) goes as far to view actors solely as creators of contracts. For software-agents the idea of incentive contracting is systematically explored by Kraus (1996).

The question that has remained untouched so far is: what turns actors into incentive-oriented entities? The fundamental economic answer is that actors consume resources so that they are affected by the omnipresent scarcity of resources. First, an actor keeps an eye on resources he already controls. From an economic point of view the first resource that comes to mind here is the budget of the individual. But it is not necessary to restrict oneself narrowly to obvious financial or physical resources. For instance, the reputation of an actor also can be considered as a resource. Second, in the light of the scarcity of his resources, an actor watches to gain control of further resources. This can be a certain property, but again also intangibles - for example the attention of other actors. There is no reason why this should be any different for software-agents. The Info-Sleuth multi-agent environment can serve as an illustrative example (cf. Bayardo et al., 1997/98). In Info-Sleuth every agent controls certain resources. These resources include information-databases or analysis facilities of various kinds, including ontologies and brokering services. The incentive-orientation of the system is still rudimentary but the basic condition - that each agent is tied to a constrained set of resources - is already fulfilled. In other areas of DAI the endowment of agents with resources is already essential to the respective concept; for example in market-oriented programming (cf. Mullen/Wellman, 1995, 289). In sum, incentive-orientation can be said to be based on a personal sphere of responsibility (Hayek, 1948, 20). This leads to situations where actors have something to gain or to lose. Consequently, the concept of incentive-orientation is inherently linked to the idea of private property (cf. section 5.1.2).

Reading this passage, a careful observer could note that it would be much more straightforward to simply label the behavioural basis of incentive-orientation rational-choice. The subject of rational-choice, however, is an area where one cannot see the forest for the trees. As indicated before, there are many ways to be rational if one cannot be fully rational. The strategy here is one of cherry-picking. It emphasises the aspect central to social order: incentives matter to individual behaviour. In order to be able to focus on the question of social order other elements of rational-choice remain unconsidered. In section 6.3 the analysis turns to adaptive behaviour which can be viewed as a step of further sophistication of incentive-orientation.

6.2.3 Internalisation-capacity

A rigorous implementation of individualism does include more than identifiable and incentive-oriented actors. If identification is possible, actors can be rewarded or sanctioned for the consequences of their actions. This is of special importance because incentive-orientation leaves room for unpredictable behaviour and surprises are not excluded ex-ante. The balancing of actions via respective rewards and sanctions can be captured by the notion of internalisation-capacity. An actor can be understood to have internalised the consequences of his actions if he bears all the costs and benefits of these actions. Although this condition is in many cases only partly fulfilled (consider the costs of driving a car for example), it is vital for the existence of social order.

Internalisation is only possible when there are rules of conduct demanding it. In this respect, the general rules of conduct presented in Chapter Five deliver appropriate foundations; especially private property rights based on the exclusion principle. But moreover, the actors themselves have to be prepared to be able to internalise the consequences of their actions. They need to have a capacity to internalise. Once again, for humans this can basically be taken as given. Humans have certain resources at their disposition, including last but not least their body and their lifetime. This is not only the basis for the already mentioned incentive-orientation but represents also a pool that allows humans to compensate or to be compensated for the consequences of their actions. Similarly, software-agents would have to be endowed with real resources and they would have to be aware of these resources, in order to allow for internalisation. While this can in principle be realised for example when agents are endowed with a financial budget the particular characteristics of digital actors have to be taken into account. A key aspect is that software-agents "are not hurt when they go broke." (Miller et al., 1996, 101). Thus an agent could cause damage, convey valuable property rights to another agent and simply destroy itself. A means of internalisation that can be thought of here would be the identification not only of the actors themselves but also of their resources.

One general problem of modern society is the increasing imbalance between the consequences of individual action and the capacity to internalise these consequences. History teaches that until very recently the impact of individual human action was so restricted that internalisation could be achieved relatively easily. The social harmlessness of the energy potential of single actors allowed for an indefinite increase of individual competence (Böhm, 1980, 202). Meanwhile this is no longer the case as actions of individual actors are a source of risk for society as a whole. The range of potentially dangerous activities is wide and includes the control of railway networks and nuclear power plants as well as the industrial processing of food. Single humans as well as software-agents cannot only deliver great benefits to many others, they also can cause an amount of harm that is well beyond what Thomas Hobbes was able to imagine at his time (cf. Beck, 1986).

Two conclusions can be drawn from the insight that an individual actor can provoke more harm than he can internalise. First, this does not disentangle individualism. There is no substitute for focusing on the individual in order to prevent harm. Even if an actor cannot compensate for all potential damage he causes, he can still act as to minimise negative externalities. He is more likely to do so if he is incentive-oriented and if the incentive system supports such behaviour. Second, as full ex-ante prevention of negative consequences of individual behaviour seems to be out of reach, there must be actors that internalise the damage caused by others. In other words, an actor must be insured when taking certain actions. Today this is obligatory when driving a car; it may be appropriate when employing a sophisticated software-agent (cf. 5.1.2).

Earlier it was said that in liberal order, every actor is considered to be a centre in his own right. In conclusion, this section pointed out that such polycentrality has to be tied to the three conditions of identification, incentive-sensitivity and internalisation. Otherwise, it appears to be impossible to anchor the liberal institutions outlined in Chapter Five and let them systematically influence individual behaviour.

6.3   Adaptive behaviour

The central claim of this book is that machines play an increasing role in modern society, that they are unpredictable and that there is an approach to social order that can constructively deal with individual unpredictability. This approach of liberal order can accommodate a wide range of behavioural characteristics. It does, however, require individual actors to fulfil certain basic conditions. The peripheral ones were discussed in the preceding section. In this section it will be argued that the key behavioural characteristic is adaptive behaviour.[30] In biology, adaptation stands for the adjustment of living matter to environmental conditions and to other living things. Here, the term's range is expanded to include learning and related processes, so that it can be applied to all sorts of actors, be they natural or artificial (Holland, 1995, 9). The following paragraphs will be employed to make the relevance of adaptability more transparent, to illustrate its properties and to explore to what extent software-agents can achieve such a behaviour.

---

[30] The concept of adaptive behaviour presented here is to be distinguished from the theory of adaptive expectations known in macroeconomics.

6.3.1 Adaptive behaviour as a complement to unpredictable behaviour

A number of measures have already been introduced to deal with individual unpredictability. General rules of conduct can serve to ensure that the range of unpredictable behaviours is not unlimited. The implementation of individualism allows for localisation as well as for influence and ensures accountability. What makes adaptability so central is that it is the natural complement to unpredictability. It is the cushion that absorbs unpredictable behaviours in everyday interactions between individual actors. In other words, if unpredictable actions are not complemented by adaptive actions then social order as a whole is at risk. A closer look at the complementary roles of adaptability and unpredictability will give valuable insights into these two behavioural features. Particularly, it will make transparent what requirements adaptive behaviour has to meet so that unpredictability can be accommodated. For this purpose, it will be instructive to focus on the relationship between man and machine.

Unpredictability can take many forms. Disturbing kinds of unpredictability of machines were introduced in the very first section (cf. 1.1). Unpredictable behaviour may be unintended. In software it can take the form of bugs and design-bugs for example. But it can also be intended, like viruses. The types of machine-unpredictability mentioned so far could be understood to be mostly latent in character. This means that the behaviour in every specific situation is already inherent to the machine and it is just due to encapsulation or due to the complexity of the machine that this behaviour is not pre-visible. Another feature of traditional machines is that they have little or no ability to adapt. In case of interaction, however, adaptation is necessary, if abortion, collision, or conflict are to be avoided. The common difficulties in establishing functioning machine-to-machine interaction can be regarded as an indicator for the lack and the respective importance of adaptation. Traditionally, in human-machine interaction it is the human actors who show adaptive behaviour. Examples range from the required flawless entries in standardised computerised forms of Enterprise-Resource-Planning software to the adoption of a machine-understandable handwriting for handheld computers. For this reason Rawlins (1997, 75) comes to the provocative conclusion that "programmers and users alike have become slaves of the machine."

Adaptation, however, must not be completely alien to machines. Software-agents are particularly suitable to be equipped with adaptive capabilities. A rudimentary form of adaptive behaviour was already introduced earlier in this chapter: incentive-orientation. Incentive-oriented agents flexibly align their behaviour to the restrictions with which they are confronted. However, this kind of adaptability is usually restricted to certain variables- for example, price. Moreover, it is usually restricted to the specific situation, without any consideration of future or past situations. For example, an agent may not recognise that his currently favourable price adjustment can have negative effects in the future (c.f. Kephart et al., 1998b). This changes when the agent is able to learn. A concrete picture of advanced adaptive behaviour and learning will be presented in the following section. For the moment, it suffices to point out that this allows the agent to take feedback from its environment into account, which means that he does not always do the same thing in the same circumstances. One consequence of this is that humans can let software adapt and can be less adaptive themselves. Moreover, if software-agents are adaptive, humans are less forced to become machines to use their machines (Rawlins, 1997, 75). They can behave unpredictably towards machines. But they have to accept that machines get less predictable themselves. Machine-unpredictability remains latent, but because adaptation means continuous change, unlike before, it can hardly be excluded for any future situation.

So far, it was argued that unpredictability requires adaptability on the side of the interaction partner and that the ability to adapt expands the possible range of unpredictable behaviours. As if this would not sufficiently complicate the quest for social order, one fundamental source of unpredictability so far has been ignored. This is what philosopher Hannah Arendt (1958/97, 215ff) described as the "ability to make new beginnings". Hence, what is meant here is genuinely unpredictable behaviour that is beyond any kind of latency. Arendt argues that the constant making of new beginnings is what distinguishes human beings. If, however, genuine unpredictability is very basically understood as randomness (Miller, 1997, 312ff), then many other creatures can be perceived to incorporate this characteristic. In fact, it can be argued that it is necessary for survival: "For example, if a rabbit fleeing from a fox always chose the single apparently shortest escape route, the very consistency of its behavior would make its escape route more predictable to the fox, its body more likely to be eaten, its genes less likely to replicate, and its fitness lower" (Miller, 1997, 316). While this is not a quest to let a rabbit interfere with the thoughts of Hannah Arendt, randomness delivers the foundation for the genuine unpredictability of software-agents that continuously reaches levels of higher sophistication. A more detailed and computer-science oriented description of this will be given, once again, in the following section.

In an economic sense, software-agents start to behave like entrepreneurs, as they continuously search for new, so far undiscovered behavioural opportunities (cf. Kirzner, 1982, 139). In a world of constrained resources and paired with incentive-orientation, this leads artificial actors to constantly make new and meaningful beginnings. For example Kelly (1994, 285ff) reports from Thomas Ray's software ecology Tierra of algorithms that redesign themselves to fit a given environment better than an initially hand-programmed algorithm.[31] What is important is that especially genuine unpredictability has to be complemented by adaptability; first, on

---

[31] See also Thearling/Ray (1997).

the side of the unpredictable actor itself, because otherwise its beginnings cannot be meaningful; second, on the side of the interaction partners, because they have to be able to cope with formerly unknown situations. Referring to the example of Tierra, first an algorithm has to make use of the feedback it receives as reaction to its unpredictable moves, and second, the remaining algorithms have to adapt to the new behaviour, or - like a fox who does not take the unpredictability of rabbits into account - they no longer get the processing resources they need. While all this is relatively new to machines in general and to software-agents in particular, the circumstance that machines can be genuinely unpredictable is something that may well challenge the adaptability of humans.

Finally, in the light of the illustrated counter-play between unpredictability and adaptability it is no less than intuitive to find adaptability to be the key behavioural characteristic for actors that participate in a liberal order. Subsequently, this finding will be substantiated further.

6.3.2 Adaptive behaviour based on inductive reasoning

After introducing adaptive behaviour as a complement to unpredictability it becomes necessary to clarify exactly what constitutes adaptive behaviour and to identify how adaptability can be ensured for artificial actors.

With respect to perfect rationality (c.f. section 6.1.2) it already was emphasised that an actor cannot have a well-specified model of the grand world on which it could optimise its behaviour. The preceding comments on unpredictability only supported this claim. As it is not possible for the actor to deduce from objective facts how to behave, he may instead choose to adapt gradually to its environment. What Savage (1954/71,16) termed the "cross that bridge when you come to it" principle can, for introductory purposes, be illustrated best by an example: A software-agent operating in the World-Wide-Web wants to download information from some server. Digital watermarks are woven into the data. To the agent digital watermarks are unknown but the situation might resemble situations where the agent retrieved encoded but decipherable information from the Internet. The agent hypothesises that the exclusion principle applies and deduces that it is advantageous to ask for authorisation before retrieving the desired data. The feedback from the server will then influence his next decision in a comparable situation. Although in principle achievable for software-agents, this process of so-called inductive reasoning is characteristic of human beings. Arthur (1994, 407) summarises the process as follows: "Each agent will normally keep track of the performance of a private collection of belief models. When it comes time to make choices, he acts upon his currently most credible (or possibly most profitable) one. The others he keeps at the back of his mind, so to speak. Alternatively, he may act upon a combination of

107

several. [...] Once actions are taken, ...agents update the track record of all their hypotheses." More analytically this process can be said to consist of three major components (cf. Holland, 1995, 87ff):

1. A performance system that specifies the agent's capabilities at a fixed point in time. It contains a set of sensors, a set of IF/THEN rules, and a set of effectors. As already shown in figure 3.1 the sensors and effectors allow the agent to interact with its environment: to receive information from it and to act on it. The rules represent the capabilities for information processing. If the rules are able to interact and if several rules can be active at the same time, then the agent can model complex situations through combination of simple rules. It does not require a separate rule for every possible situation.

2. A credit-assignment algorithm that provides an agent with hypotheses to anticipate future consequences. The rules over which the agent disposes are viewed as competing hypotheses. Based on their successes and failures, they receive credits and thus achieve certain strength. Rules that led to better outcomes in the past are stronger hypotheses, are more competitive and consequently are more likely to be repeated in the future. Assigning credits thus leads to adaptation.

3. A rule discovery algorithm that allows the agent to generate new hypotheses. These hypotheses do not have to be purely random but can be plausible. Their plausibility stems from the incorporation of past experience as strong rules become parents of new rules and deliver the building blocks for them. Two basic operations are possible: first crossover, i.e. the parent rules are paired and crossed; and second mutation, i.e. the parent's building blocks are randomly modified. An algorithm building on these operations spurs innovation and ensures that the whole range of behavioural options is continuously reconsidered, which is particularly important in an evolving world that can never be known entirely. Adaptability is further enhanced.[32]

Regarding these three components Holland (1995, 41ff) goes much further into detail than possible here and argues that they apply to any adaptive agent. While human beings are the unbeaten champions within the discipline of inductive reasoning and adaptive behaviour, software-agents are on track to follow. The behavioural model just presented can be found in DAI, particularly under the notions of reinforcement learning, classifier systems and genetic algorithms.[33] "Reinforcement learning is learning what to do - how to map situations to actions - so as to maximise a numerical reward signal. [...] Two characteristics - trial and error search and delayed reward are the most important distinguishing features of

---

[32] The rules referred to under 1.-3. are under continuous revision by the agent himself and can be flexibly combined. Consequently, they are not to be confounded with the global third-party rule internalisation abandoned in section 6.1.3.

[33] For a broader and more extensive overview of learning and adaptation in DAI, see Stone/Veloso (1997).

reinforcement learning" (Sutton/Barto, 1998, 1.1). Based on this, reinforcement learning agents can be said to explore their environment and to exploit the experiences they make. Classifier systems are a form of reinforcement learning that builds very closely on the premises of the three components mentioned above. Within classifier systems, genetic algorithms provide the crossover and mutation capabilities incorporated in component three.

Reinforcement learning turned out to be attractive to computer scientists for various reasons: It is promising, because it is "a way of programming agents by reward and punishment without needing to specify how the task is to be achieved" (Kaelbling et al., 1996, 237). Connected with this is that "as a learning method that does not need a model of its environment and can be used on-line, reinforcement learning is well suited for multiagent systems, where agents know little about other agents, and the environment changes during learning" (Hu/Wellman, 1998, 242). In other words, it can be employed in environments where the designers cannot anticipate everything and consequently cannot pre-program the agents to operate as desired. It is usually assumed that the agent has to operate despite significant uncertainty about the environment he faces. This implies that the agent is prepared to deal with a problem as a whole in the world as the whole, which is a feature that distinguishes reinforcement learning agents from other - even other learning - agents. Another factor arousing interest is that adaptive agents employing reinforcement learning techniques promise to be able to anticipate the long term consequences of their own actions (cf. Tesauro/Kephart, 1999). Finally, based on genetic algorithms, agents can develop genuinely unpredictable behaviour. As shown in section 6.3.1, this relevant because it allows for innovations and increases the competitiveness of such agents.

Typical application areas of reinforcement learning are game playing, robotics, and control. To a large extent, due to the increasing relevance of the Internet, adaptive agents operating within an economic environment seem likely to become the dominant field of application. From studies undertaken so far, it becomes evident why:

- Tesauro/Kephart (1999) show that in different market environments - including, for example, shopping-agents in consumer markets - adaptive agents perform significantly better than myopically optimising agents.
- Oliveira et al. (1999) propose an on-line continuous learning mechanism that enables agents to learn how to behave when negotiating goods and services. More specifically, they elaborate how a reinforcement learning buyer can learn about the marketplace which auction protocol to use and which negotiation partners to interact with. The results indicate that reinforcement learners outperform non-learning competitors.
- Cliff/Bruten (1998) employ adaptive agents in one-sided auction retail markets and come to the conclusion that they exhibit human-like collective market

109

behaviours. Unlike the experiments with zero-intelligence traders by Gode/Sunder (1994) mentioned in Chapter Five, this similarity promises to hold even if no special assumptions are made about the market.

Despite promising early results, artificial adaptive agents are still far from mature. Kaelbling et al. (1996, 275) state that progress is possible and necessary along several lines, which include shaping (supervised learning), local signals, imitation, problem decomposition and reflexes. The preliminary conclusion that can be drawn is that adaptive software-agents, as they get better, find their way into ever new areas of application (cf. Weiss, 1997).

Surprisingly, this section closes with another definition of adaptive behaviour. This definition, however, leads to a short summary: "A behavior is adaptive if, when an agent exhibits that behavior, it increases its chances of survival" (Cliff/Bruten, 1998, 8). This requires that the behaviour is well-matched to the environment and includes the implicit assumption that the environment is non-trivial, i.e. complex, unpredictable and unforgiving mistakes. Evidently, such behaviour is prepared to tackle successfully the problems this study is investigating, namely the grand world problem, the challenge of unpredictable interaction partners, transaction-cost efficiency and an exit to the state of nature. However, the insights provided so far need support from economics, as the social properties of adaptive behaviour still have to be to illustrated, to manifest the key role of this characteristic.

6.3.3 Adaptive behaviour
- more than a model of individual behaviour

As already demonstrated, adaptive behaviour is appealing to computer scientists for a variety of reasons, often depending on the particular perspective and problem of the respective researcher. The presented analysis has encouraged the view that adaptive behaviour represents an important building block for a solution of the problems encircled in this book. Yet there is more evidence for this view. It can be unveiled that the relevance of adaptive behaviour goes far beyond the idea of being a counterweight to unpredictable behaviour on the level of the individual actor. The distinction between the micro-level of adaptive behaviour and the macro-level of spontaneous liberal order is less discrete than the structure of this book may suggest (Chapter Six vs. Chapter Seven). Therefore, this last section of Chapter Six will prepare for departure to the macro-level. Economics offers two complementary lines of thought that show how adaptive agents arrive at a liberal order of actions.

First, adaptive behaviour can be considered the basis for dealing with the division of knowledge in society. This is connected inherently with issues subsumed under the headings of complexity and the grand world problem. Second, adaptive behaviour favours the system-wide spread of rules and allows for a translation of abstract rules into situation-specific rules. While this may be considered as a special case of the first point, moreover, it is important when state of nature situations are to be prevented especially if one recalls the gaps left open by the liberal institutions proposed in Chapter Five.

a)   Adaptive behaviour and the use of knowledge

Departing from what has been said, the prevailing picture is that of actors learning by experience. What has to be outlined is that they do not have to rely solely on their own experience. In fact, "the world is too complex for a single individual to learn directly how it all works" (Denzau/North, 1994, 8). Even worse, Hayek (1948, 91) attests an "unavoidable imperfection" of the knowledge of a single actor. Consequently, there is a need for a process that constructively deals with the fragments of knowledge held by single actors.

The presented model of adaptive behaviour is a point of departure for such a process, because, in addition to building on their own experience, it allows actors to observe and learn from the behaviour of others. They can adapt to actions and reactions and they can imitate actions. Adaptation and imitation can be based solely on the reinforcement mechanism described in the preceding section. As a consequence the single actor can employ knowledge without explicitly possessing that knowledge. For instance, a software-agent may not open a file sent to him that contains a virus just because others, before him, have also declined the offer, but without actually having any knowledge about the origin and content of this file. Sticking to the example, on the Internet, knowledge about the number and quality of viruses that are active on the net is not given to anyone in its totality. Yet their threat is usually limited because knowledge about them that is dispersed within the system is utilised. In other words, actors can make use of so much experience, not because they possess the experience, but because, without their knowing, it has become incorporated in the schemata of behaviour, which guide them (Hayek, 1973, 30f). But they have to be prepared to behave that way: "Because of their bounded rationality, and because they can therefore greatly enhance their limited knowledge and skill by accepting information and advice form the social groups to which they belong, individuals who are docile - who tend to accept such information and advice - have a great advantage in fitness over those who are not docile - who reject social influence. Docile people do not have to learn about hot stoves by touching them" (Simon, 1996, 45).

As already indicated, the ability to adapt is only the point of departure. In order to handle the knowledge problem effectively, considerably more has to be fulfilled. One condition is again named by Hayek (1948, 86), when he argues that the whole acts as one coherent system because the limited fields of vision of the individual actors sufficiently overlap so that through many intermediaries the relevant information is communicated to all. In human societies a huge diversity of both deliberately designed and unintentionally and spontaneously arisen mechanisms exists which connect the limited fields of vision of the members of society. In science for example, the methods of citation and referencing lead to an effective spread of knowledge and allow efficient access. Of particular interest to economists and of fundamental importance to society is the role of prices in communicating relevant knowledge. While the function of prices will be discussed in more detail in chapter seven, here it is important to note that the circumstance that individual fields of vision overlap allows the transition from adaptation, via bilateral adaptation to mutual adaptation. Although the relevance of this point has not yet been acknowledged fully by designers of multi-agent environments, efforts to create computational markets for example indicate its importance also for software.

Another important way to leverage the ability to adapt is the capacity to generalise. With regard to humans, Hayek (1973, 29f) points out that perception and behaviour do not react immediately to specific situations but to abstractions. Individuals adapt to the general circumstances. "Abstractness will here be regarded...as the basis of man's capacity to move successfully in a world very imperfectly known to men – an adaptation to his ignorance of most of the particular facts of his surroundings" (Hayek, 1973, 30). Like every characteristic, the capacity to generalise also has its downsides. It regularly leads humans to build up prejudice and to show a certain resistance to facts, which from time to time have to be overcome. Less sophisticated but in principle comparable, is software agents' capacity to generalise. The behaviour of adaptive agents as discussed in the preceding section relies on abstractions. For example, a software-agent operating as a buyer in a computational market may not know who the suppliers are and how many of them exist. He may rely just on general information on the availability and prices of products that are relevant to him. Adaptive agents initially employ general or abstract hypotheses about an environment they do not know well. These default hypotheses work better than purely random actions, are fewer in number, and can be tested more frequently than specific hypotheses. As experience accumulates, more specific exception hypotheses are added. Holland (1995, 60) calls this a "default hierarchy." In the case of the above example, the software-agent could learn that for a particular product - for instance consulting services - it is necessary to have information about the supplier.

b)   The co-evolution of actors and rules of behaviour
Adaptive behaviour that uses more than individual knowledge - based on the ability to observe and to imitate, on the overlapping fields of vision and on the capacity to generalise - has further desirable characteristics. It breathes life into those general rules of conduct that have repeatedly been called "the building blocks of our society" (Hargreaves Heap et al., 1992, 18) and of which the rules discussed in chapter five constitute an important part.

The basic idea presented here is that the hypotheses an adaptive actor forms and the rules of behaviour he derives can be shared with other actors. Human history suggests that mental models employed by individual actors are shared among groups or even societies (Denzau/North, 1994, 15). The basis for this are the forms of indirect learning and adaptation discussed above. And the resulting effects are similarities among the members of a society. Denzau/North (1994, 21ff) argue further that shared mental models to interpret the environment lead to the institutions that restrict and guide the behaviour of individuals in society. Individual actors that (indirectly) learn about these rules receive ready-made hypotheses of how to behave under certain conditions. The individual IF/THEN rule discussed in 6.3.2 becomes a social IF/THEN rule. This goes beyond the mentioned case of Simon's docile person who does not touch hot stoves, because these rules are important for co-ordination and co-operation and may be sanctioned. Moreover, this differs from the third-party rule-internalisation abandoned in section 6.2.3.

Already Hayek (1973, 18) pointed out that "learning from experience ... is a process not primarily of reasoning but of practices which have prevailed because they were successful." And he emphasised that, "what we call understanding is in the last resort simply his capacity to respond to his environment with a pattern of actions that helps him to persist." In conclusion the adaptation to the general circumstances which surround an actor is brought about by his observance of rules (Hayek, 1973, 12). While this sounds intuitive, in economics most of the work still has to be done in order to be able to explain how institutions emerge from shared mental models (cf. Denzau/North, 1994; Arthur et al., 1997). Research based on software-agents clearly supports this work and at the same time demonstrates that software-agents are capable of undergoing this process themselves. Vriend (1999) shows that in large societies of simple reinforcement learning agents who use rules of thumb to guide their behaviour, agents learn to employ better rules. He demonstrates that this is based on "interaction between the agents' choices" (Vriend, 1999, 23) as the agents learn from each other's choices. While one agent adapts to the environment, parts of the environment adapt to him. This means that agents not only learn to make better choices but also that certain rules get established as the agents in a given situation on average follow a specific rule of behaviour. The learning of the agents and the emergence of rules do not happen all of a sudden, but need time. Co-evolution of agents and rules appears. One agent's set of internal rules evolves in response to the rules used by other agents, with the sets of all these agents evolving at the same time (Vriend, 1999, 12). Interdependently, the individual actors evolve and the social rules they share evolve.

Both research into software-agents and preliminary work in economics suggest why this co-evolution takes place. In the tradition of Hayek, Vriend (1999, 23ff) emphasises the effect of information aggregation. By following the rules employed

113

by other agents, an agent implicitly builds on their experiences and observations regarding these rules. He exploits aggregated information on these rules without actually knowing the details. This is important because of the large spectrum of situations with which an agent is confronted and because of the continuous change of this spectrum. The co-evolutionary process appears to produce two effects when it spreads rules of behaviour. This is first, the specification of rules, and second, the modification of rules. On the one hand this process supports agents in learning specific rules for specific situations. The building of the above mentioned default hierarchies is significantly facilitated. This is vitally important for the functioning of a liberal order because the abstract rules presented in Chapter Five have to be translated into much more specific rules that apply to the actual situations confronted by agents. An average citizen, for example, never reads the laws that restrict his behaviour but he nevertheless knows how to act in accordance with them. On the other hand, agents as well as rules not only change the circumstances, they also have to adapt to changing circumstances. The process of co-evolution allows for an implicit as well as an explicit modification of the rules. An illustrative example can be found in Denzau/North (1994, 25). They discuss the evolving meaning of the phrase "All men are created equal" since its appearance in the Declaration of Independence in 1776.

The overall effect of what has been described so far substantiates an argument already mentioned in Chapter Five and traditionally brought forward by North (e.g. 1990/92, 3, 61ff): Institutions reduce uncertainty and lower transaction costs. Here it is shown that not only institutions, but also shared mental models and resulting similarities of behaviours, reduce uncertainty and lower transaction costs. This is not to say that individual unpredictability is eliminated. Under the constraints discussed above, the individual actor can still make new beginnings, and genetic algorithms for software-agents are not excluded. But at the final count the co-evolution of actors and rules make it easier for the individual actors to live with each other's unpredictability. Because rules spread among society and because many actors follow these rules, an individual actor receives a reasonable good orientation based on the average behaviour of all its interaction partners. Whenever the actor incurs a negative surprise due to an unpredicted action of another actor, this can be viewed as an investment, because it helps to improve his future behaviour and additionally the behaviour of the actors who have him in their field of vision.

After outlining the complementary role of adaptability and unpredictability and after investigating the model of adaptive behaviour, this section closed with an analysis of the broader but crucial properties of the adaptive actor paradigm. In summary, it was shown that an adaptive behaviour that includes the capacities to observe, imitate and generalise and that occurs among actors with overlapping fields of vision assists actors with imperfect knowledge to deal with a complex environment. It was further shown that based on these factors not only more knowledge is used that any one actor could possess, but also that rules of conduct spread among a society of actors. Rules and actors co-evolve which, on average, makes the environment predictable for individual actors while retaining their individual unpredictability. This average predictability is fundamental for a prevention of state of nature situations and for a social order with low transaction costs.

6.4 Conclusions

This chapter dealt with the individual actor in general and with the software-agent in particular. As such, it treated agents as a variable. Despite the fact that behavioural requirements for software-agents are at the centre of discussion, it is safe to say that the characteristics put forward here also apply to humans. This is not due to deliberative human design but because humans, by and large, are naturally endowed with these characteristics. It is now time to recapitulate and to summarise the possible contributions of the presented actor-profile to a solution of the problems worked out in Part I.

At the outset, a range of dispensable behavioural characteristics was discussed. This was done because in DAI research, these features are commonly considered crucial for social order. However, a closer look revealed that this is in fact not the case. Benevolence, perfect rationality, global third-party rule internalisation, and natural slavery are dispensable on the way towards social order among and with software-agents.

Yet liberal order cannot be reached unless individual actors meet certain minimum requirements. The first of the presented conditions is a rigorous implementation of individualism, which includes three fundamental points: identification, incentive-orientation, and internalisation-capacity. The implementation of individualism was considered to represent the necessary complement to the liberal institutions presented in Chapter Five. Without it, liberal rules have no anchor on the micro-level and the state of nature cannot be overcome. Also, individualism appeared to be a necessary condition to deal with unpredictability. Incentive-orientation and internalisation-capacity allow for unpredictability but prevent it from getting completely out of control. The two characteristics suggest that actors behave on average predictably, and that negative surprises are compensated before they can accumulate. Another aspect is the emphasis of the social role of software-agents. Here, identification was considered to be the essential property because it makes sure that an agent is 'someone'. And obviously, individualism is a basis for open complex systems. It is not possible to think of decentralisation without it. Under the heading of individualism the reader may have expected other or additional points - for example, goal-oriented behaviour at the place of incentive-orientation or responsibility in the context of internalisation. However, the points covered pick what is essential for social order without risking a fall in the melting-pots of the philosophical and moral discussions that are connected to notions like goals or responsibility.

Adaptive behaviour was identified to be the key behavioural characteristic for actors that are part of a liberal order. Like a cushion that absorbs unforeseen movements, adaptability is the natural complement to unpredictability. Adaptability allows one to take feedback from the environment into account, allows others to be unpredictable, and increases one's own unpredictability. Furthermore, the individual actor does not have to adapt to his environment to fulfil a function but that he himself continuously creates a part of this environment to which others have to adapt. That means mutual adaptation generates the room for individual unpredictability. It appeared plausible that, while not directly connected to each other, the two often play in concert. In addition, genuine unpredictability - like entrepreneurial activity for instance - can be accommodated under the condition that it is complemented by adaptability. The relevance of this is not to be underestimated, as entrepreneurial activity implies a continuous striving for the better which promises to reduce transaction costs. All these implications count for humans as well as for agents.

A general model of adaptive behaviour then consists of three components: a performance system containing sensors, IF/THEN rules, and effectors; a credit assignment algorithm; and a rule discovery algorithm. In principle, software-agents can be endowed with these components. It was demonstrated that preliminary observations, especially in economic environments, confirm the importance of adaptability with respect to the posed problems of social order. Further evidence for the relevance of adaptive behaviour was inferred by investigating its wider effects. A crucial point is that adaptability is fundamental for an actor who is part of a complex system. Adaptability allows him to operate without a (perfect) model of the environment and ensure that he is able to deal with unforeseeable events. A final quote from Simon (1996, 35) proves to be illustrative here: "Even if events are imperfectly anticipated and the response to them less than accurate, adaptive systems may remain stable in the face of severe jolts, their feedback controls bringing them back on course after each shock that displaces them. Although the presence of uncertainty does not make intelligent choice impossible, it places a premium on robust adaptive processes instead of optimizing strategies." Furthermore, adaptability was considered to be fundamental for dealing with the division of knowledge in society. It was found that by adapting to actions of others and by imitating actions of others, actors employ knowledge without explicitly possessing it. On top of that, adaptive behaviour favours the system-wide spread of rules and allows for a translation of abstract rules into situation-specific rules. Such a co-evolution of rules and behaviour is essential in order for the few liberal principles presented in Chapter Five to bring order in a complex system. The co-evolution significantly reduces uncertainty and thus transaction costs.

In sum, this chapter discussed many of the aspects that are connected with individual software-agents. After the very brief introduction of agents in section 1.4, it offered background information on agent-theories, implications for agent-architectures and conclusions with regard to liberal order. Figure 6.1 summarises how the discussion updated and enriched the model of an actor presented in section 3.4. However, liberal theory is likely to be an insufficient pool to finally achieve an exact specification of an agent. Therefore, the appendix will point to directions that can further support such a specification.

Figure 6.1:   Updated model of an agent with identity, incentive-orientation, internalisation and adaptability

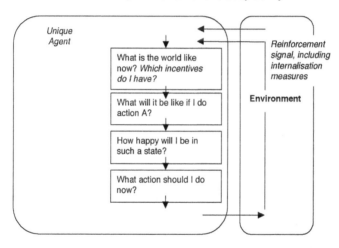

Appendix 6   Further preparation of software-agents
for liberal order

The analysis in this chapter was launched to determine the behavioural conditions for liberal order. Humans are, by and large, naturally endowed with the characteristics discussed here, namely identity, incentive-orientation, internalisation-capacity and most importantly adaptability. Reservation towards the presented concepts may occur when they are viewed to be insufficient with regard to software-agents. Software-agents, like humans, are more than the theories that explain and describe them. However, while the specification of humans still is beyond deliberative human design, the specification of software-agents is brought about by humans. The following discussion has the purpose to assist this process of specification that evidently has to go beyond the key characteristics presented so far. The objective of this assistance is twofold. First, it should indicate a direction that allows specifications of software-agents to be in line with liberal order even if at the current stage of development cuts are inevitable. Second, a direction for specification should be proposed that has the potential to enable software-agents - which are by far less sophisticated than humans - to exist under the demanding conditions of a complex environment (grand world). Despite being targeted at agent-specification the exposition still remains on a social sciences level rather than reaching the granularity of an engineering perspective. It consists of the two connected specification strategies presented below.

A6.1 Functional differentiation and
domain-specific software-agents

Since the days of Adam Smith it is generally acknowledged that modern economies are characterised by division of labour and specialisation of their individual members. Switching from the economic perspective to a broader sociological perspective, it can be attested that specialisation is not only a feature of areas like manufacturing or trade but of society as whole. Society can be said to consist of specialised sub-systems. The most comprehensive account of this view probably stems from Niklas Luhmann (1984/94) who distinguishes, for example, the economy of society, the science of society and the law of society. Within each of these and other systems only those actions are considered which can be grasped by the media of the respective system. Thus, in the economy, for example, only those operations are relevant that can be expressed in money, which is the media of the economic system. On the reverse, operations that are expressed in terms of money are ignored by other sub-systems. A society consisting of such closed and self-referential sub-systems can be called functionally differentiated. When taking such a perspective it is only consequent to identify the individual as a member of various systems rather than as a member of society in general. This is what makes the concept of functional differentiation interesting for computer science, because it can guide the specification of software-agents. In addition to the general behavioural characteristics presented in the earlier sections of this chapter, an agent can be equipped with specific features to meet the requirements of a certain sub-system of society. For example an economic actor is aware of the limited availability of resources and his behaviour is price-oriented, but issues like truth, right or power that are central to other sub-systems constitute his environment rather than being a motivational force for him. This concentration on one sub-system significantly facilitates the task of designing software-agents. In fact, partly because of technological constraints and partly because of traditional problem orientation, designers of software-agents have followed exactly this path. This is exemplified by the fact that software-agents are highly specialised, which was illustrated in section 1.5. The examples given there underscore that existing software-agents are designed to operate in selected sub-systems of society. Possibly this will be even more deeply rooted if multi-agent environments are clustered in distinct types of domains that can be inhabited only by certain types of agents. Domain theories like the one of Rosenschein/Zlotkin (1994) were already mentioned in Appendix 5. While it is not possible to discuss every domain-specific behavioural detail of software-agents for every domain, the purpose of this section is to confirm that it can be a promising strategy to specify agents in order to fit a certain domain or sub-system of society.

A second purpose of this section is to create awareness for the potential downsides of this direction. It seems plausible that the implications of functional differentiation differ for man and machine. Nevertheless some controversial aspects of functional differentiation and systems-theory are also relevant to software-agents. For example individual actors can be comprehended as only functions of a certain system which indicates that it is the system rather than the actor that decides (cf. Kirsch, 1997, 44). This implies a holistic perspective, which is fundamentally different from the individualistic perspective presented in this book. In addition to known problems, like the exertion of dominance, new problems may arise. The above argumentation for example implies that software-agents will operate only in one sub-system while humans live in various sub-systems at a time. This makes it probable that software-agents, unlike humans, will completely ignore sub-systems other than the one in which they are active. At the current stage it is not possible to derive the consequences of such a conduct. But the simple fact that the sub-systems of a society depend on each other (Gerecke, 1998, 26ff) favour the conclusion that social order can be negatively affected.

In conclusion, social theory can be interpreted to suggest caution when adopting a strategy of domain-specific design of software-agents, at least if it is on a mass basis. By and large it is commonly acknowledged that functional differentiation and liberal order go hand in hand (c.f. Kirsch, 1997, 41; Gerecke, 1998, 50). Consequently, a specification of software-agents on the basis of functional differentiation and domain-specific design can in principle be considered to be in line with liberal order.

A6.2 Role-specific software-agents

Related to the preceding strategy but even more specific, is the approach to design software-agents according to a certain role. The circumstance that the role has to be ascribed by someone implies that agents are made part of an organisation. Such an organisation, however, does not have to be huge. It may consist just of a human designer or user and a software-agent taking over a specific role - for example, information filtering. Organisations are part of any social-order. Organisations can have different effects and they potentially prevent the solution of the problems that are at the centre of this study. Hayek (1969/94, 41) for example reminds us of the fact that complete planning and organisation does not allow systems to achieve high complexity. Simon (1996, 154f) realises that they restrict our liberties but emphasises the opportunities for attaining freedom. With respect to artificial actors the picture of organisations and the roles they contain is no less ambivalent but possibly less dramatic. On the one hand ascribing roles to software-agents is bound to be in conflict with the general rules of conduct presented in Chapter Five. In particular, the contract principle is ignored (cf. also Hargreaves Heap et al., 1992, 65). Also, the idea of roles is based on specific functions and purposes which inherently demands predictability and contradicts the search for social-order independent from any purposes. On the other hand, to design software-agents by targeting certain roles means using a systematic and flexible method for agent specification with wide-ranging support from social-theory. Based on roles, the functions, goals, and desires of an agent can be encoded (cf. section 1.4). In addition, the behavioural characteristics and processes are prescribed by the role. This further assists the specification of agents. And despite the fact that agent-technology is still far below this level, there is nothing in the idea of role specification that prevents agents from choosing their role(s) themselves as soon as they are able to. Also, roles do not have to lead to a specification of every act of an agent, which would lead to exactly those problems identified in the very first chapter. Rather, roles can be defined so that the agent can decide over the details. This is important because only the agent knows the particular circumstances of time and space, and this is the precondition to make use of knowledge that nobody possesses as a whole (Hayek, 1973, 49).

The specification of software-agents based on roles is common in DAI. It is done implicitly and arbitrarily but also explicitly and systematically (cf. for example Panzarasa et al., 1999; Bayardo et al., 1997/98). An already well- elaborated systematic approach briefly summarised in section 2.1.3 comes from Munindar Singh: "In our approach, agents play different roles with a society. The roles define the associated social commitments or obligations to other roles. When agents join a group, they join in one or more roles, thereby acquiring the commitments that go with those roles. The commitments of a role are restrictions on how agents playing that role must act..." (Singh, 1998,45). This quote illustrates very well how roles can be used to specify software-agents and that individual roles are interdependent. It is assumed that designers define roles and create multi-agent environments to which other designers and users can supply further agents to play different roles. Each agent would have to comply with the roles. Nevertheless, the approach is primarily viewed to provide an infrastructure and not to determine the behaviour of the agents. Agents can still be diverse in content and they can change roles and exit the environment as well (Singh, 1998, 46).

In summary, role-specific agent design can be understood to be a more detailed continuation of domain specification. In a sense, functional-differentiation is broken down to the level of the single agent. Like functional differentiation role specification also does not in principle contradict liberal order. However, it is important to be aware of the fact that role specification usually takes place within an organisational - and that means hierarchical - context. This means that specifications that may be technologically required potentially restrict agents much more than the general rules of conduct presented in Chapter Five. Moreover, it is important to be reminded of a comment by Hayek (1973, 46) that organisation, as a principle of order, cannot be employed arbitrarily. In general, role-specific agent-design within organisational contexts can be assumed to be in line with liberal order as long as it does not undermine or prevent a polycentral order. This threat increases to the extent that the role specification of agents in monopolised by certain organisations (cf. figure 6.2).

Finally, this section has shown that further preparation of software-agents for liberal order is possible but has to be treated with care. The discussion made transparent that, for good reason, liberal theory does not deliver prescriptions because this may undermine liberal order. Thus the direction of functional differentiation and role specification can serve as guidelines for agent-design. But while it seems unproblematic if these directions are being followed individually (cf. also 7.1.4) it can be harmful if they are controlled centrally. Similar to Appendix 5, the ideas treated here do not belong to the core of liberal theory.

Figure 6.2: Role-specific agent-design can threaten polycentral order

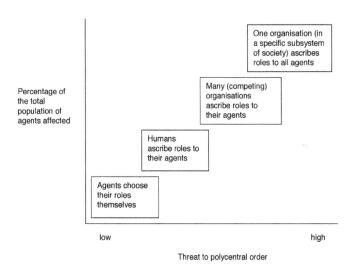

Percentage of
the total
population of
agents affected

One organisation (in
a specific subsystem
of society) ascribes
roles to all agents

Many (competing)
organisations
ascribe roles to
their agents

Humans
ascribe roles to
their agents

Agents choose
their roles
themselves

low   high

Threat to polycentral order

7

Spontaneous liberal order

Up to this point the analysis has provided a variety of insights on software-agents and liberal institutions. But what actually results from these premises remains an open question. Therefore, it is time to draw a scenario of the order of actions resulting from liberal institutions that constrain unpredictable but adaptive individual actors. The present chapter represents the last stage of the intellectual journey through Coleman's MMM-scheme. The liberal order of rules and the adaptive model of individual behaviour are active building blocks for a liberal order of actions in that, to achieve social order, a builder who assembles these blocks is not required. At this stage nothing remains to be done for a social engineer of multi-agent environments. The order of actions that comes about is a spontaneous order. Although it has not been explicitly explained yet, the concept of spontaneous order will be familiar to the attentive reader. At the outset of this book it was laid out that social order can be achieved separately from following specific purposes. Also it was said before that social phenomena can occur that are neither intended nor predicted by the individual actors creating it. These phenomena evolve rather than be constructed. Then it was shown that if certain basic rules and behavioural characteristics apply to a multiplicity of actors, it is easier to reach reliable behaviour of the system as a whole. "When order is achieved among human beings [and software-agents] by allowing them to interact with each other on their own initiative - subject only to laws which uniformly apply to all of them - we have a system of spontaneous order in society" (Polanyi, 1951, 159).

The concept of spontaneous order is not very intuitive. As mentioned before, constructivism and the idea that the social order of society has to be made explicitly are influential. In addition, constructivism and computer science are tightly interwoven. In DAI Miller/Drexler (1988b, 139f) were the first to propose to apply the idea of spontaneous order to computer systems. The developments which have followed are better known under the notion of emergence. Emergence, in turn, has played a role mainly for simple software-agents (Castelfranchi/Conte, 1996, 531). Similar to human society, not much room is attributed to the idea of spontaneous order in open and complex systems. Or, as Simon (1996, 33) remarks: "We have become accustomed to the idea that a natural system like the human body or an ecosystem regulates itself. [...] But somehow, untutored intuitions about self-regulation without central control do not carry over to the artificial systems of human societies."

It is not surprising that even thinkers who identify and seriously attempt to analyse the anonymous phenomenon of spontaneous order develop imaginative metaphors to explain it. The most famous and respected metaphor certainly is Adam Smith's notion of the invisible hand that guides individual choices to bring about a coherent and orderly social system. Describing the rise of spontaneous order with the help of the elegant movements of an invisible hand turns economic theory into an aesthetic experience (cf. Rothschild, 1994, 320). The following exposition will try to convey such an experience in order to make the phenomenon of spontaneous order approachable. At the same time it will aim to be more hands-on and systematic than Smith and others have been. Taking the discussed liberal institutions and many adaptive agents that constrain each other as given, this chapter will consider the logic of a liberal order of actions. It will make transparent what kind of social order is to emerge. However, it will not be a presumption of knowledge that is not given to anyone in its totality (Hayek, 1948, 78). Instead of trying the impossible of attempting to describe the grand world spontaneous liberal order generates, the explanation will be restricted to the pattern of the outcome. As there is a danger for such an approach to become an extremely abstract exercise, the patterns will be illustrated extensively with examples. Although this entails the risk of losing generality, the use of examples represents an ideal opportunity to demonstrate that the abstract concepts of liberal order and software-agents have a place in the grand world of reality, especially in the combination presented here.

The interdependency of the variables forbids making claims about specific causalities between inputs like the exclusion principle or adaptability and outputs like the division of labour (cf. Kleinewefers, 1988). This can only be brought about by empirical analysis or by artificial social simulations. Therefore, the focus will be on the known properties of liberal order and on how they rely on each other. Section 7.1 is based on the assumption that liberal institutions are perfectly implemented and that the individual actors fulfil the requirements discussed before. Step-by-step the consequences are revealed until the picture of spontaneous liberal order is completed. Yet a range of potential problems can disturb this order. In section 7.2 it is considered that liberal order is never perfect and the most important disruptions are discussed.

Figure 7.1: The stairway of increasingly beneficial co-operation

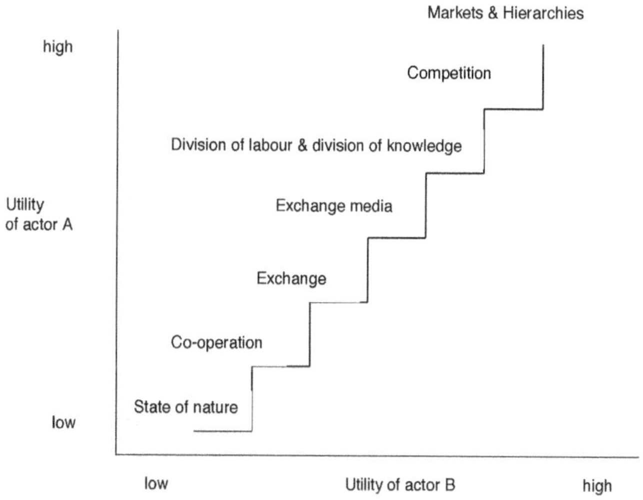

Markets & Hierarchies

high

Competition

Division of labour & division of knowledge

Utility
of actor A

Exchange media

Exchange

Co-operation

State of nature

low

low   Utility of actor B   high

Source: for a comparable approach see Gerecke (1998)

7.1 The logic of spontaneous liberal order

Spontaneous liberal order systematically differs from the state of nature. Instead of getting involved in a war of each against all, the actors have the chance to enter mutually beneficial relationships. The gains from co-operation that can be achieved provide incentives to climb to higher levels of co-operation, which present themselves in more complex social structures. The phenomenona that arise when adaptive actors co-operate under a liberal order of rules are interdependent. For explanatory purposes it is instructive to perceive them broadly to build up on each other. The arising social phenomena can be understood to form a stairway that leads the individual actors to higher levels of utility (cf. figure 7.1). The gains from co-operation that can be achieved on each step represent an incentive that pushes the development of a spontaneous liberal order of actions another step further. The following sections show how this process contributes to a solution of the fundamental problems under discussion here. Departing from the state of nature, actors first benefit from not being in conflict with each other. In a second step they will have incentives to exchange goods. Third, this can be facilitated by media like

125

money, which triggers, fourth, the division of labour, and allows for the use of distributed knowledge. Fifth, competition accompanies the co-operative processes and is one of the reasons why they, sixth, result in complex contractual structures of markets and hierarchies. This sequence of steps fills the notion of co-evolution of actors and rules (cf. 6.3.3) with content. Actors that operate freely in the upper part of the stairway have to be highly evolved. Similarly, when the upper part is reached, the liberal principles have produced a wide range of offspring that is specified and modified to suit the respective part of the complex environment where it applies. Each of the steps realises gains from co-operation. However, these gains do not come for free. With each step for every actor the complexity and the number of sources of unpredictability of the environment rises. As a consequence, higher degrees of co-operation are only possible when the gains outweigh the costs. Subsequently, these phenomena are discussed one by one before the whole pattern of spontaneous liberal order will be summarised.

7.1.1 Co-operation instead of conflict

The premier thing liberal institutions suggest is that actors do not get in conflict with each other and mutually respect private property rights. In complex environments, of which the actors have only limited knowledge, this is an adaptive process because actors often are not, or only partially, aware of the rights of others and of the consequences of their own actions. For example, a software-agent may register the domain name www.maggi.com to use it as URL, without being aware that this is a protected brand name. Another example could be a webcrawler which accesses particular webpages for index purposes so often that the traffic it creates prevents other users from using the pages. This also illustrates that any sorts of bugs the actors contain are not eliminated. However, the state of nature's right of everybody for everything does not exist, internalisation measures drive the actors towards a mutual respect of property rights. These measures can have different origins. The webcrawler may realise that it is better to access webpages less often, rather than being completely excluded. The software-agent looking for a domain-name may have applied for registration under the condition that it would not employ a protected name. In any case, social order arises spontaneously because actors follow general rules of conduct and not because every detail was pre-arranged. Also, this order tends to have beneficial effects because "by internalizing the costs of a decision, the right of ownership creates strong incentives for owners to seek (and reduce the costs of seeking) the highest valued uses for their goods" (Pejovich, 1997, 3). A first unintended effect of liberal order is this incentive it provides for an efficient allocation of resources.

On this basis co-operation can significantly increase the space of available actions. Actors can join forces and thus achieve more than by acting individually (cf. Nozick,

1974). This is known to anybody who has ever pushed a car that refuses to start. Similarly, it is evident that the car itself, the streets it drives on, and the buildings that surround it exist only because of co-operative behaviour among many individual actors. As shown in section 2.2 agent-systems also build on this logic to allow agents solving more complex problems. But, unlike in early agent-systems (cf. Smith, 1980) individual incentive-oriented actors within liberal order are not pre-determined to co-operate. Therefore, far reaching co-operation is usually only achieved when all the involved actors benefit enough from it to make it worthwhile (cf. de Jasay, 1995). In order to receive their share of the achievable gains from co-operation they can enter various forms of contractual arrangements under different types of governance. The most basic step to undertake is to enter an exchange relationship.

7.1.2 Exchange

"Trade seems to be a constant feature of human history" (Hargreaves Heap et al., 1992, 181) and Hayek (1988, 38ff) claims that it is older than the state, agriculture or any other sort of regular production. Under a liberal order of rules exchange comes about spontaneously. It arises from the fact that an actor A is endowed with a certain quantity of good X, while an actor B possess a certain quantity of good Y. Because both actors would value it higher to be endowed with certain quantities of both goods instead of having a large quantity of only one good, it is beneficial for them to exchange. They can achieve gains from trade. The new endowments with goods give A and B incentives to barter and contract with other actors. The logic underlying mutually beneficial bilateral exchange is worked out in any standard textbook on economics (cf. figure 7.2).

Figure 7.2: Through bilateral exchange, actors depart from their initial endowment and try to reach higher indifference curves

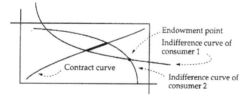

Source: Kreps (1990)

127

However, the figure also demonstrates how standard treatments often hide that exchange takes place locally, in a polycentral fashion. In large systems it is often impossible for actors to bring their goods to a central marketplace, negotiate with and collect information about all potential interaction partners, and clear the market with one move. This is overseen by traditional economic theory and by many designers of market-oriented software systems as well. In polycentral markets the actors repeatedly enter into exchanges with the various immediate neighbours they meet on their way through the system. As portrayed in figure 7.3, this results in networks of trade partners. Parallel sequences of bilateral exchanges may aggregate to system-wide multilateral exchange. The transactions continue until all mutually beneficial trades are completed. Without the individual actors being aware of it, the goods flow through these networks from one edge to the other to reach higher valued uses. This is remarkable because the individual actor does not need to know where the resources he is willing to exchange are employed best. Also, there is no central controller who possesses this information and regulates the process. The trading networks and the flows of goods arise spontaneously. In addition to enhancing the situation of the individual actor, exchange improves the state of the system as whole. Depending on the angle from which a system is observed such improvements can take different forms. With respect to human society, Hayek (1988, 41ff) finds that trade allowed humans, unlike other animals, to populate nearly every spot on the earth. Consequently, trade does not only build on an order of rules but it itself actively spreads an order of actions. In terms of software-agents Epstein/Axtell (1996, 111f) discover that agent-environments within which trade is possible can carry more agents than the same environment endowed with the same amount of resources but where agents are not capable of trading.

Figure 7.3: Simulation results of an emergent trade network of software-agents trading sugar and spice

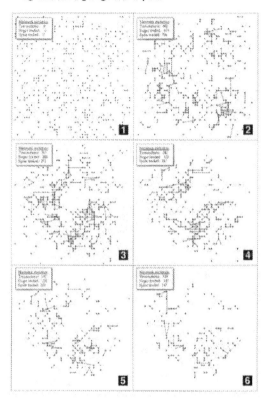

Source: Epstein/Axtell (1996)

Extensive exchange will only take place if the actors have incentives to undertake it. This presupposes not only that they desire something but also that the barriers to acquire it are not prohibitively high. Liberal rules fulfil an important function in facilitating exchange. However, actors have to learn how to apply these rules in particular situations and how to specify them so that trades can be completed successfully. The resulting co-evolution leads to a large spectrum of informal and formal exchange rules (cf. 5.2). The co-evolution of these modes of exchange plays an important role when it comes to the accommodation of individual unpredictability. This can best be illustrated by the aid of an example: A software-agent managing an Internet server has to decide whether or not to give an unknown information retrieval agent access to the contents of the server. The information retrieval agent is unpredictable in that the server-agent does not know whether it will just browse, modify, buy or steal something. The server agent has to make this decision several thousand times a day for different information retrieval agents. It bases its decision on its experience with past visitors of the same kind. It might incur negative experiences with exactly this visitor but this investment pays off to the extent that in the future, the server agent will make better decisions on average, i.e. let certain types of agents in and exclude others partly based on the contractual precautions it takes. Vice versa, the information retrieval agent will by experience, learn which behaviour is best for him. Thus, the agents are unpredictable, but they generate incentives for their interaction partners to co-operate.

Evidently, the story of spontaneous liberal order does not stop here, as much room for improvement remains. The actors can achieve further gains from co-operation along several lines. The next aspect to consider is that in a pure barter economy not all potentially beneficial exchanges can be executed because the trading partners may not come across suitable intermediaries to get something they need. There must be what Edgeworth (1881) called a "double coincidence of wants". A medium of exchange like money, against which all kinds of goods could be exchanged, dramatically facilitates exchange.

7.1.3 Exchange media

"Money, the very 'coin' of ordinary interaction, is hence of all things the least understood and - perhaps with sex - the object of greatest unreasoning fantasy; and like sex it simultaneously fascinates, puzzles and repels" (Hayek, 1988, 101). It would be presumptuous to aim to give an adequate account of the phenomenon of money. Nevertheless, the crucial importance of exchange media for liberal order demands a careful treatment of a range of issues.

Exchange media like money can emerge spontaneously. Within a bartering system actors realise that some goods are more marketable than others. For instance, a craftsman may find it difficult to search for an exchange partner who is willing to give him the particular carriage he wants against the statue he offers. It is easier for him to exchange the statue against salt and than using some of the salt for the carriage and exchange the rest into vegetables for example. Thus actors converge on exchanges on the more marketable goods, being willing to exchange their goods for them; the more willing, the more they know others who are also willing to do so in a mutually reinforcing process (Nozick, 1974, 18). Money evolves through a process of gradually increasing liquidity of some particular commodity. At the beginning this is not yet money but a generally accepted means of indirect exchange, for instance salt or cattle (cf. Kirzner, 1992, 177).

As the exchange media must not be coins or bank notes, it is not surprising that money can also be digital. Comparable to the historical steps before - say, from cattle to salt, from salt to gold, and from gold to fiat money - it is plausible that actors will converge on digital money only if the benefits outweigh the costs. Table 7.1 illustrates that the requirements for digital money are considerable. Although modern society already operates with a range of substitutes for cash, namely credit cards and smart cards, it has to be emphasised that only digital cash in the sense of table 7.1 is fully compatible with the liberal principles. This is illustrated by the fact that credit cards allow the tracking of spending history and creation of marketing profiles of the actors, which is not in the sense of the exclusion principle and the non-domination principle. While not too relevant for the spontaneous emergence of the exchange media, for its survival and stability it appears to be important to have some third party taking care of it. In modern society this is mostly the state (cf. 5.2.4). However, this has frequently been challenged and arguments can be found for a co-existence and competition between various third parties and the exchange media they promote (cf. Hayek, 1976).

All at once, money is a store of value, a medium of exchange, and a unit of account. But eventually, in order to achieve gains from co-operation these functions must not be provided by money in particular. Depending on the type of environment, other media can be more suitable. For example, in politics votes are used to transfer, uphold and legitimate power, while in science quotations are used to exchange, keep and estimate prestige and reputation. It may be surprising that even when economic values are to be exchanged, money may not only have predecessors like salt but also successors.

Table 7.1   Key properties of private digital cash

- secure
- anonymous
- portable
- two-way
- off-line capable
- divisible
- infinite duration
- wide acceptability
- user-friendly
- unit-or-value freedom

Source: Matonis (1998)

Particularly the Internet turns out to be an environment where alternative means flourish. Loyalty points or commodities like mobile phone minutes, free e-mail service and others enable micro-payments for the attention of an actor or for personal data that would otherwise not be traded. In a sense the Internet delivers a revival of the barter economy. It provides an increased competition among different means of exchange, including also different forms of the above mentioned digital cash.

The digital examples indicate a point that is crucial for the discussion here: Digital exchange media, especially digital cash, can be utilised by software-agents. These media are in fact key enablers for the interaction between software-agents and as such for the existence of complex multi-agent environments at all. The reason behind is the same as in human societies. Exchange media emerge and supersede each other because they allow the individual actor to achieve new, previously uncaptured gains from co-operation. Many economists might be tempted to simply say that these media do so by saving transaction costs. While there is no reason to deny this, it can be fruitful to draw a more differentiated picture, which allows for further exploration of spontaneous liberal order.

A closer look at the exchange media money reveals that potentially more interesting than the means itself is the information it produces: prices. Under liberal institutions every actor can declare prices for the goods he possesses and he is willing to exchange. Similarly, he can offer prices for goods he would like to obtain from another actor. The communicated prices can be equilibrium prices or disequilibrium prices. The role of equilibrium prices and disequilibrium prices differ. Equilibrium prices lead to a situation where the decisions of the individual actors mutually reinforce each other, i.e. exchanges take place. Disequilibrium prices inform actors to revise their decisions. They lead to regret and disappointment. They stimulate the revision of initially uncoordinated decisions in the direction of greater mutual co-ordination (cf. Kirzner, 1992, 146f). Following this distinction, two roles of prices can be separated, the role of prices as

- co-ordination instrument, and
- discovery instrument.

Prices can be perceived as a co-ordination instrument because "without knowing the details concerning the preferences of the other market participants or concerning the conditions surrounding production processes, decision makers through the guidance of these prices are led... to that pattern of attempted activities that permits all of them to be carried out without disappointment and without regret" (Kirzner, 1992, 143). This is possible first because all possible exchanges are related to a common scale, and goods are exchanged according to their relative prices. Second, prices summarise all relevant information for an actor which can once again be illustrated by referring to an example from Hayek (1948, 85f): "Assume that somewhere in the world a new opportunity for the use of...tin, has arisen, or that one of the sources of supply of tin has been eliminated. It does not matter for our purpose - and it is significant that it does not matter - which of these two causes has made tin more scarce. All that the users of tin need to know is that...they must economize tin. There is no need for the great majority of them even to know...in favour of what other needs they ought to husband the supply [...] The mere fact that there is one price for any commodity...brings about the solution which ...might have been arrived at by one single mind possessing all the information which is in fact dispersed among all the people involved in the process."

Regarding the phenomenon of prices it is at this stage important to stress the characteristic that prices can be interpreted to be reinforcement signals for the agents and thus represent an ideal complement to the behavioural model presented in chapter six. They allow actors to adapt. Also they allow actors to be unpredictable. This is because they aggregate information and thus provide an average picture of the environment, which is more predictable than the behaviour of single actors. Although every actor is unpredictable, market prices enhance the chance for each actor to form correct expectations about the system.

The fact that prices facilitate co-ordination by greatly compressing the information relevant to an actor makes price systems particularly interesting for bounded actors like software-agents (cf. Wellman/Wurman, 1997, 6f). In terms of the process already sketched above, prices can emerge spontaneously and in a polycentral fashion from the unordered interactions of many agents (cf. Epstein/Axtell, 1996, 135). Or price formation can take place in a more centralised fashion if agents participate in auctions and interact through a central clearinghouse, as is the case in financial markets like the New York Stock Exchange or in agent-mediated marketplaces (cf. Clearwater, 1996). The discussion of the institutional differences between the two types of markets will have to wait until section 7.1.6.

In their role as a co-ordination instrument, prices summarise economic knowledge. In another role, that of a discovery instrument, they also reflect the inadequacies of this knowledge and thus create the market incentives for a modification of prices. In this context prices do not only aggregate information. They function as reinforcement signals by delivering feedback from which the actor can learn. Consequently, prices represent an ideal complement to the model of adaptive behaviour presented in Chapter Six. "Prices provide information to use for future plans, they indicate the success of past plans, and provide the incentives and information to discover previously unknown uses of resources" (Horwitz, 1994, 15). Thus they alert actors to the possibility of profit or the danger of loss and they are incentives, motivating entrepreneurial discovery (cf. Kirzner, 1992, 150f). Like equilibrium prices, these prices also spread information, but it is information about knowledge to be discovered, rather than about existing knowledge. Studies like those of Tesauro/Kephart (1999) or Cliff/Bruten (1998), which were already mentioned in section 6.4.2, demonstrate that such reinforcement signals are important for software-agents. The processing of prices and the learning from price changes prevents agents from bringing disorder into their environment and enables them to survive in a complex environment.

In essence, this section showed that liberal social order based on co-operation and exchange can spontaneously develop further as actors converge on widely accepted exchange media, particularly money. This significantly facilitates transactions, so that the scarce resources that represent one of the triggers of the state of nature are better exploited. More importantly, it enables actors to benefit from the characteristic of prices to communicate relevant information. The fact that prices can easily be processed by an actor although they aggregate a lot of information can prevent him from losing orientation in a grand world he can only partly understand and where many actions of other actors have to remain unpredictable for him. All this seems to be as relevant to software-agents as to humans. Or, as Hanson/Kephart (1998, 1) state: "The 'almighty dollar' would fill a crucial function as built-in motivator and facilitator for the adoption, success, and survival of agents." Nevertheless, it has to be kept in mind that money is a very selective exchange media that only communicates one particular kind of information.

An effect that has been treated implicitly only is the high frequency and the fine granularity of exchanges that is made possible when money and prices are adopted. Two phenomena of modern society are tightly connected to this effect: the division of labour and the division of knowledge. Along these two lines the further development of spontaneous liberal order will be studied below.

7.1.4 Division of labour and division of knowledge

The division of labour and the division of knowledge are basic structural aspects of modern society. Already sections 1.5 and 2.2. indicated that these two phenomena are of significant relevance in agent-environments, too. What follows is a more detailed discussion that concentrates on the spontaneous development of the division of labour and on the question of how the resulting division of knowledge can be dealt with.

With money as the lubricant of exchange, transactions become feasible where no interactions took place before. A significant shift regarding the achievable gains from co-operation can be reached through the division of labour. The classical account of the incentives motivating a division of labour is Adam Smith's portait of the pin-factory. Smith finds that solely by division of labour, ten workers are able to produce thousands of pins instead of a handful of pins a day (1776/1976, 14f): "But

134

in the way in which this business is now carried on, not only the whole work is a peculiar trade, but it is divided into a number of branches, of which the greater part are likewise peculiar trades. One man draws out the wire, another straights it, a third cuts it, a fourth points it, a fifth grunds it at the top for receiving the head; to make the head requires two or three distinct operations; to put it on is a peculiar business, to whiten the pins is another; it is even a trade by itself to put them into the paper; and the important business of making an pin is, in this manner, divided into about eighteen distinct operations, which in some manufactories are all performed by distinct hands .... "

In the meantime, division of labour has probably contributed more to the wealth of nations than Smith would have imagined. And it has made human society ever more complex. A huge variety of possible forms exist. It includes the functional or the divisional organisation within firms, as well as the outsourcing of services by firms and the use of franchising models. Continuously, new institutional approaches are being added while others disappear, which indicates that the division of labour is to a large extent a process of spontaneous order. A basic distinction can be made between the division of labour or specialisation among equal interaction partners and the same process within a hierarchy where a principal divides up his workforce for example. The institutional forms that enable both reduce transaction costs in order to capture the achievable gains from trade (cf. also 7.1.6).

The division of labour is interesting for multi-agent environments for the same reasons that made it appear so crucial for human society. In fact it can be argued plausibly that it is even more important for software-agents than for humans, because it allows relatively primitive actors to participate in and contribute to complex processes. Beyond any cynicism, this is best illustrated by the circumstance that an extensive division of labour renders humans who specialise in certain activities stupid and ignorant. For humans this has frequently been named as a disadvantage (cf. Groenewegen, 1987, 903). The reverse is the case for software-agents, because to them specialisation provides an ideal entry opportunity into social processes without requiring sophistication in themselves. Among the broad range of examples the Contract Net is probably the most explicit form of division of labour in agent systems (cf. 2.3). It certainly does not go too far to say that the whole idea of multi-agent environments depends more on the concept of division of labour than Charles Babbage's idea of the very first computer, which already built on this concept. But what is more important is that, in comparison to Babbage, what takes place in DAI is also a shift in perspective. The division of labour in the sense of Babbage lends itself to a mechanistic paradigm. It is implemented top-down. In contrast, the most remarkable feature of division of labour is that it can emerge spontaneously - bottom up. Hanson/Kephart (1998) demonstrate that spontaneous specialisation can take place in multi-agent environments. In their model of an information filtering economy, broker agents specialise and carve out market niches for themselves to serve the consumers of information. "This is despite the fact that none of the brokers is 'aware' of even the notion of specialization, let alone of its potential benefits" (Hanson/Kephart, 1998, 6). It is these benefits that drive the spontaneous division of labour and they can best be illustrated by turning the view again towards human society.

In human society people learned that rather than doing everything in a mediocre way, it is advantageous to specialise in those activities best suited to personal skills and resources and to exchange what one makes against what one needs. The specialisation in turn increased the gains to be achieved because people learned more about the task they performed and discovered that economies of scale could be achieved. Thus, these two factors further reinforced the division of labour; however, not unlimitedly so. I is at this stage that a problem complicates the situation which was identified by Hayek (1948, 77) to be the economic problem of society. This is "not merely a problem of how to allocate 'given resources [...]. It is rather a problem of how to secure the best use of resources known to any of the members of society, for ends whose relative importance only these individuals know. Or, to put it briefly, it is a problem of the utilization of knowledge which is not given to anyone in its totality." The process of specialisation makes evident that knowledge is dispersed in society. There is not only a division of labour, there is also a division of knowledge (Hayek, 1948, 50f). And increasing specialisation fuels the knowledge problem.

A straightforward way to plausibly illustrate this point is to compare the situation of a self-sufficient medieval farmer to that of a contemporary electrician. The farmer only has to learn enough to be able to cultivate his environment to an extent where he can make a living for his family. Also, he may only be surprised by the weather and may be forced to adapt his plans accordingly. In contrast, the electrician relies heavily on many other actors to make a living. He is a specialist in his job, but he does not know much about keeping cattle and even less about growing vegetables. He might be able to carry out little repairs on his car but he does not much about financing and insuring it. In addition, he has no perfect knowledge whether those who insure and finance his car and those who supply him with food do so properly, efficiently or honestly. While the list of missing knowledge and potential surprises could easily be extended, it is striking that the electrician and his environment secure a better use of resources than the farmer and his similarly self-sufficient neighbours. Consequently, there must exist ways to solve the cross-sectional problem of using the fractional knowledge that is dispersed among the members of modern society and to solve the intertemporal problem of profiting from experiences that previous generations have had (cf. Vanberg, 1998, 5).

A range of preconditions that contribute to a solution of the knowledge problem has already been mentioned. In contrast to specific commands, the general rules of conduct, given by liberal principles, allow every actor using his or her knowledge of the particular local and timely circumstances, without possessing a degree of sophistication, that enables him to understand the whole world. Another factor is the ability to adapt, which is the basis for actors to make use of knowledge they do not actively possess. In addition, the spread of knowledge is further facilitated by the use of exchange media. They connect the limited and otherwise separate fields of vision of the individual actors. Tightly linked to the subject of exchange media and of fundamental importance to the question of knowledge and spontaneous liberal order in general is the phenomenon of competition. Competition arises in the state of nature as well as under liberal institutions. The difference is that under a liberal order of rules competition can work constructively to further specialisation, fight the knowledge problem, and generally capture gains from co-operation. Consequently, this phenomenon will be studied in more detail below. Another development that stems from adaptive behaviour is the co-evolution of actors and rules of behaviour that was already introduced in section 6.3.2. The specification and modification of rules due to mutual adaptation of the actors can be interpreted as an answer to the knowledge problem and as an opportunity to capture further gains from co-operation. Thus, the possible paths of institutional evolution provide an additional area of investigation (cf. 7.1.6).

7.1.5 Competition

Right in the middle of a chapter on social order and co-operation one might consider the issue of competition to be misplaced. Competition means rivalry and stands for conflicting interests regarding the use of resources. As resources are scarce it is not at all surprising that competition arises spontaneously. Less expected, however, is the argument that competition is a natural element of spontaneous liberal order. Co-operation and competition in one system are not mutually exclusive. Examples are manifold. Competitors try to beat each other but they also enter partnerships and alliances. Customers and suppliers want to contract but they bargain. Actors have a common interest in gains from co-operation and they have conflicting interests regarding the question of who is going to get what share of these gains. Interactions within a liberal order of actions are often characterised by the co-existence of co-operation and competition. Nalebuff/Brandenburger (1996) have coined the notion "co-opetition" to describe this fact. Subsequently, it will be discussed how competition can enhance system-wide co-operation.

Competition is not a state of affairs but a dynamic process. Under a liberal order of rules it is not only scarce resources but also the priority principle that provides a basis for competition. The spontaneous emergence of competition depends on a variety of factors. The number and the relevance of each of these factors are a matter of ongoing controversy in economics. As liberal order is not tied to a particular purpose, it neither targets a specified form of competition or even perfect competition. Thus, for the present exposition it suffices to point out factors that are commonly acknowledged to stir competition. They include freedom of entry into the system, a high number of competitors (polycentrality), market transparency, and entrepreneurship of the actors. The degree of competition can be concluded from observing variables like the price level, price elasticity, and price dispersion.

Smith et al. (1999) state that electronic markets on the Internet are to show a higher degree of competition than conventional markets and find that software-agents are involved in this development. This is plausible as electronic environments in general and software-agents in particular reduce search costs and information asymmetries, allow for easier switching between suppliers and for more flexible pricing, all of which is also confirmed by other early studies like Maes et al. (1999) or Kephart et al. (1998b).[34] The reference to these works already anticipated a point that, in the present context, is even greater interest: In open multi-agent environments competition among software-agents can arise spontaneously. This is also confirmed by research in market-oriented systems, which, however, is based on more restrictive assumptions than liberal order (cf. for example Mullen/Wellman, 1995; Wellman, 1996).

Faced with the presence of competition in human society and in agent-environments it becomes necessary to investigate the role of this phenomenon. This appears to be even more pressing as competition is known to have serious critics. It is often associated with the paradigm of the survival of the fittest. It creates restlessness among the actors and continuously confronts them with surprises and unpredictable moves of other actors. Nevertheless, the generally beneficial effects of competition must include disappointing or defeating some particular expectations or intentions. In fact, competition is valuable only because and in so far as its results are unpredictable and on the whole different from those, which anyone has, or could have, deliberately aimed at (Kirzner, 1992, 150). The role of competition goes beyond its economic importance as it ensures freedom and prevents dominance and thus reinforces liberal institutions. The economic effects that make competition so valuable can be summarised under two headings:

- allocative efficiency, and
- discovery procedure.

Competitive conditions provide the actors with incentives to allocate resources efficiently. For an actor who does not allocate his resources efficiently it will be more difficult to find a co-operation partner and to achieve gains from trade than for his efficient competitors. The important role of the price as a co-ordination instrument in this context has already been illustrated. It guides actors towards

---

[34] See Varian (2000) for factors that can slow down this trend.

efficient allocation. While the individual actor may not necessarily welcome this incentive, it appears to be beneficial for the system as a whole. This is best illustrated by the ideal concept of perfect competition where a pareto-efficient allocation of resources is achieved. Pareto-efficiency is the situation where no actor can be made better off without making any other actor worse off (cf. Kreps, 1990, 153). What makes all this particularly interesting is the circumstance that allocation efficiency can be reached in the absence of a global controller. There is no central planning unit that oversees the whole system in order to make appropriate allocative decisions. The spontaneously emerging phenomenon of competition lets individual actors decide based on restricted and local information. Still, the customer in the north of a country will be able to buy bread of comparable quality and at a comparable price as the customer in the south of that country. These properties are not restricted to the physical world of human society. The allocative effects of competition were among the first to be discovered by DAI. Already today, software-agents are active in a wide range of competitive multi-agent environments (cf. Clearwater, 1996). Not only straightforward effects of competition have been realised, but also more subtle aspects of allocation - for example, the fact that if competitive pressure is high, software-agents do not reason about other agents and do not search for opportunistic options (Vidal/Durfee, 1998, 2). It is however necessary to add that within most of the existing environments competition, is one of the few spontaneous phenomen while many other elements are actively constructed (cf. Appendix 5).

In addition, there exists another fundamental trait of competition that is regularly ignored by those economists concerned with its allocative effects. Competition can be viewed as a discovery procedure. It provides actors with incentives to find hitherto overlooked opportunities for mutually gainful exchanges. These opportunities exist when, as discussed above, actors do not possess perfect knowledge. The competitive discovery process is spontaneous and indeterminate, as it cannot be foreseen which actor makes what kind of discovery and how this influences the other actors (Kirzner, 1992, 46ff). Competition informs the actors which things represent goods and how scarce these goods are (Hayek, 1969/94, 243). On the basis of unpredictable and adaptive behaviour, competition leads to innovations and requires imitation (Hayek, 1969/94, 260). Again it is prices from this perspective functioning as a discovery instrument that facilitate this ignorance eroding process. Humans and software-agents alike, can, under the competitive conditions of spontaneous liberal order, create and use more knowledge than a single individual actor could possibly achieve. However, the chances given by the use of knowledge through the discovery process of competition have yet to be fully revealed. The process of discovery is not well understood in human society. And in agent-environments the spontaneous process of discovery has yet only been at work in fragments within otherwise explicitly constructed systems. One example is the utilisation of auction mechanisms in negotiation. The auction is decisively structured but in the process of an auction competition helps sellers to price items when the buyer's willingness to pay is unknown (McAfee/McMillan, 1998, 2). Competition allows them to benefit from knowledge they do not have. Initially, agents only participated in auctions. Meanwhile, software-agents flexibly employ auctions themselves to structure their interactions with other agents (Oliveira et al., 1999).

In the last paragraph it was said that in agent-environments elements of spontaneous order are mostly islands in constructed orders of action. It was emphasised from the beginning of this second part that the perspective here is the opposite one. What is described is the bottom-up process of the evolution of spontaneous liberal order. So far, actors undertake very basic moves of co-opetition. However, from observation of the grand world it is obvious that they compete and co-operate within the institutional settings. The question remains whether these institutions of social order which are commonly thought to be constructs of purposeful design can emerge spontaneously. Therefore, the origin and the possible forms of markets and hierarchies will be studied below.

7.1.6 Markets and Hierarchies

Transactions do not take place in a vacuum, but within an institutional setting. The institutional point of departure assumed in this chapter is the liberal principles introduced in Chapter Five. On this basis, actors co-operate to carry out all kinds of mutually beneficial exchanges of goods and services. Yet one question concerning these exchanges has hardly been touched. It is the question of how these transactions are organised. As mentioned before, exchanges can be organised principally in polycentral and in monocentral institutions (cf. 5.2). More concretely, it is possible to speak of a range of institutional options that lay between markets and hierarchies. All options represent a refinement of the basic liberal institutions. And these refinements can be brought about and change spontaneously in the course of interaction between the actors.

a) Markets
Up to this point more or less isolated bilateral exchanges have been the object of discussion. Although these transactions already can be termed market exchanges it can be argued that the notion of a market hides more than what has been mentioned so far. Connections between bilateral transactions can be observed; not only in terms of the flow of the goods, but also with respect to the institutional setting within which they take place. This connecting institutional setting can be called the market. The notion of a market is an umbrella term for an institution that has many faces and facets. Although economists claim to study the working of the market, in modern economic theory the market has a shadowy role (Coase, 1988, 7). Therefore, it will be instructive to stick to concrete examples rather than losing the

essence of the meaning of the market somewhere between the lines of abstract economic theory.

An easy way to imagine a market is to think of a marketplace in a medieval town. It is time and place that connect the bilateral exchanges in this setting. The market forms here because the town requires many inputs and the place is populated by people who can afford to satisfy a whole range of their needs. Influenced by exogenous factors, like a wealthy duke or a prosperous cloister, market rules that specify time and place for mutually beneficial bilateral exchanges can arise spontaneously. History teaches that this phenomenon is not restricted to medieval marketplaces. It is similarly relevant to contemporary markets, which also include fairs, exhibitions and clusters of vendors and buyers of certain industries in specific regions like Silicon Valley in California or the garment industry cluster in Hong Kong. Examples of historical and contemporary markets demonstrate that the initial reason for the creation of a marketplace quickly degenerates to be only a marginal factor for further development. The relevant economic factor that fuels these markets are network effects or network externalities. Marketplaces show network effects in the sense that the more actors trade on these markets, the higher the potential gains from trade and thus the incentives for other actors to carry out their exchanges there, too (cf. Economides, 1996). The spontaneous creation of the market is followed by a spontaneous reinforcement and self-replication of the market (cf. Bouillon, 1991, 32).

The developments on the Internet perfectly illustrate that time and especially place characterise not only physical markets but also digital markets. On the Internet, actors willing to exchange goods and services are quickly attracted by those marketplaces, that are of interest to them. Prominent examples include ebay.com, chemconnect.com, fastparts.com and polymerce.com. Obviously, digital marketplaces are of particular interest in this book because they are, at least in principle, accessible for software-agents. In fact, some of them are specifically designed to be accessed by software-agents - for example Tete@tete or Kasbah (cf. Maes et al., 1999). This leads to the next characteristic of markets. Market rules may include more than just a time and place to interact under bilateral governance. In addition, participation in a certain market may require certain transaction rules and procedures to be followed. This can include the requirement for an actor to register, or to trade goods according to predefined categories, or the necessity to stick to specific auction protocols. All this works to facilitate exchange and to reduce transaction costs, which increases competition but also trade volume (Coase, 1988, 7ff). Overall, the gains from co-operation are increased.

Further market-oriented institutional specifications are particularly attractive for software-agents because they receive much needed guidance compared to the case of a completely unstructured interaction. However, it is necessary to carefully examine the degree of regulation, or in the terminology of this book, the degree of dominance. Characteristic for a high degree of regulation is that interactions are rather indirect. Actors then decide in favour of or against a transaction solely based on prices and a limited number of other predefined variables. They only respond to the market environment in general but not to other actors. This can be interesting for software-agents because they have to be less sophisticated in order to interact successfully. But marketplaces with indirect interactions where all relevant information is transmitted through the price or few other variables are only applicable to a small range of standardised products, particularly commodities. Also, actors can only to a limited extent bring in their individual knowledge, including innovations. There is a risk of getting stuck in small worlds.

Most of the named institutional measures do not arise spontaneously but are introduced by a market maker (cf. also Appendix 5). However, the resulting order of actions still can be perceived to be a spontaneous order, as the market maker usually does not know who is going to participate in the market when nor what kind of transactions at what prices will take place. The emergence of a market does not rely solely on the actions of a conscious designer. Instead, it is more suitable to interpret its development as the rise of a standard. It can be influenced by individual actors who find themselves in key positions, but it depends on the positive feedback of a large number of actors who are ex ante not aware of the spontaneous order that forms itself.[35]

With respect to the market maker, one aspect remains to be discussed. Even if the transaction partners generally respect the property rights of others it can be costly to enforce them individually when some of the actors are not well informed or choose to act opportunistically. Exchange could show less friction if a third party like the market maker takes over the enforcement, for example by sanctioning or excluding uncooperative players (cf. the discussion of third-party governance in section 5.2). This line of improvement is important because in liberal order actors can always choose not to play (Tullock, 1985) so that neither further gains from co-operation nor further spread and enforcement of social order are achieved.

b) Hierarchies
Markets are only one institution of modern society. And Simon (1996, 31) points out that the role of markets is often overemphasised in comparison to another type of institution: organisations. "Roughly eighty percent of the human economic activity in the American economy, usually regarded as the epitome of a "market" economy, takes place in the internal environments of business and other organizations..." This means that not all transactions are market exchanges where outputs are measured and priced. The notions of exchange and contract do not

---

[35] Regarding standards cf. Shapiro/Varian (1998).

disappear. But when speaking of hierarchical organisations, exchange has a different meaning and implications. Owners of property rights enter long-term contracts and form a coalition. Such a coalition can take various forms (cf. Williamson, 1985, 206ff), amongst which authority relations that appear in firms and other hierarchical organisations play an overwhelmingly important role. For example, an actor can offer rights over his labour resources to an entrepreneur in return for a monthly salary. Once the contract is made, the actor will be managed by the entrepreneur and via a hierarchical relationship that will substitute market exchange (Eggertsson, 1990, 159). The involved actors agree on unified governance.

While it is relatively straightforward to describe an organisation as a particular form of contractual relationship, it is not immediately obvious why actors undertake these steps. However, by revisiting previous sections of this chapter the reasons can be collected quickly. At the outset it was noted that co-operation increases the space of available actions. In economic terms this means that coalitions of resource owners can achieve significant "economies of scale and scope" (Chandler, 1990, 24). The discussion of DPS and MAS in section 2.2 showed that this is a crucial aspect in agent-technology as well. Hierarchical organisations like firms are able to capture existing economies of scale and scope because they efficiently order individual actions. This becomes particularly evident when the issue of specialisation is taken into account. While specialisation and exchange between the butcher, the baker, and the dentist easily can be imagined to be co-ordinated via market transactions, it is hard to think of Adam Smith's example of the pin factory as consisting of a network of bilateral spot market contracts. Rather the factory will be managed hierarchically because "the greater the specialisation... the more weight must be put on reliable institutions that allow individuals to engage in complex contracting with a minimum of uncertainty about whether the terms of contract can be realized" (North, 1990/92, 34).

More generally, every contract involves transaction cost, and hierarchical organisation saves on those costs that Coase (1960/88, 157ff) describes as the "costs of market transactions." They include search and information costs, bargaining and decision costs, and policing and enforcing costs. According to Coase (1937/88, 33ff) hierarchical organisations like firms owe their existence to the presence of these costs. Similar considerations hold in agent environments (cf. Miller/Drexler, 1988b, 140f). However, hierarchies are not the ultimate way to create order. Firms face difficulties or even bankruptcy, and efforts to turn whole societies into hierarchies have failed repeatedly. These problems stem from the fact that hierarchies have to do largely without features that are characteristic to market transactions. Most notably, prices cannot be used as allocative instruments and as discovery instruments, and only to a limited extent are the forces of competition at work. Consequently, especially large and complex hierarchies face drawbacks regarding the generation and use of knowledge, as well as the resulting adaptation. What organisations gain with respect to internal predictability and control they trade-off against the losses regarding flexibility and adaptability.

The last aspect points to the circumstance that hierarchies are often explicitly designed. There is a visible hand at work that orchestrates the involved actors. An organisation is largely a made or constructed system where the order of actions in many ways follows directives and specific commands. But at the same time hierarchies heavily depend on the forces of spontaneous order. When examining the role spontaneous order plays for hierarchies, it is useful to distinguish between aspects internal and external to an organisation. Internally, it is plausible that hierarchies do not function in a completely mechanistic way, purely based on specific commands. "Every organization in which the members are not mere tools of the organizer will determine by commands only the function to be performed by each member, the purposes to be achieved, and certain general aspects of the methods to be employed, and will leave the detail to be decided by the individuals on the basis of their respective knowledge and skills" (Hayek, 1973, 49). Thus, more or less general rules, which can be formal or informal, fill the gaps between the existing commands to which they are subsidiary. Based on the same rules and commands the resulting order of action can be very different, which allows organisations to adapt to a limited degree to a changing environment. Although it does not perfectly coincide with the perspective of organisations just presented, an approach to multi-agent environments going into this direction is the social commitments approach presented in section 2.3 and Appendix 6.

Externally, several aspects are important. First, the emergence and spread of hierarchical organisations can be interpreted to be a phenomenon of spontaneous order. In past centuries, hierarchical structures were of very limited relevance in human society. "Before 1850 hierarchical structures were virtually non-existent outside the episcopal churches and the military" (Milgrom/Roberts, 1992, 539). The invention of the steamship, the railroad, and the telegraph allowed for the formation of large industrial enterprises. The largely spontaneous development of these firms - for example from Thomas Edison's invention of the light bulb to today's General Electric - often went far beyond the intentions of their founders and managers. Organisations adapt to changing environmental conditions. Within liberal order this adaptation takes place on the basis of the actions of individuals who interact with these organisations. They can offer or demand something from an organisation, they can enter or exit it, and they can raise their voice internally or externally. They do so based on the incentives they have, and thus influence the spontaneous development of an organisation.

Comparable to the developments in human society, Axtell (1999) shows that firms can evolve spontaneously among a population of independent software-agents. Experiments like this do not only show that organisations can in principle emerge in agent environments, but also that these processes, once triggered, take place at a much higher pace and possibly also with a greater variety than in human society. What is important to note is that agent organisations that are open to the forces of spontaneous order differ fundamentally from the approaches introduced in section 2.3. In conventional agent organisations, agents hardly have any of the behavioural options available within liberal order. Rather, it is the slave metaphor that applies in these approaches. From human history it is known that slavery poses a series of problems, not only morally - which would be less relevant in case of software-agents - but also economically (cf. Barzel, 1989, 76ff). In addition the slave-metaphor vividly illustrates that conventional agent-organisations do not possess the wide range of options of adaptation discussed above for the organisations that persist within spontaneous liberal order in the long run.

A second aspect of spontaneous order stems from the fact that society consists of a large number of organisations that compete, co-operate and complement each other. Without intending it, the actors involved in these organisations contribute to the development and to a continuous self-replication of a highly complex social order. In this development organisations have to adapt to the conditions of their environment. Following the pattern of Darwin's biological concept of the survival of the fittest, social order also is characterised by a process where some of the contractual forms survive and others go under (cf. Alchian, 1950). An impressive snapshot of this process delivers the example of the spontaneous transformation of whole countries that followed the emergence of large enterprises in the second half of the nineteenth century (cf. Chandler, 1990, 3). Despite the fact that developments of agent-systems could not yet be observed in this order of magnitude, it seems likely that, given conditions of liberal order, spontaneous order works the same way as in human society. In sum, it appears plausible to conclude that "the family, the farm, the plant, the firm, the corporation and the various associations, and all the public institutions including government, [but also the various conceivable forms of DPS and MAS] are organizations which in turn are integrated into a more comprehensive spontaneous order" (Hayek, 1973, 46).

In conclusion, the preceding paragraphs on hierarchies already indicated that neither human society nor agent environments are strictly bipolar worlds that consist solely of hierarchies and markets. "Markets and hierarchies - sometimes regarded as the major discrete alternative ways of organizing economic activity - are actually just two extreme forms of organizational contracting, with voluntary bargaining characterizing markets and strict lines of authority characterizing hierarchy" (Milgrom/Roberts, 1992, 20). Market and hierarchy are connected by a long continuum of options. In human society modes of organisation like organised marketplaces, annual contracts, licensing and franchising contracts, joint ventures, or profit-centres can be found in between the extremes. Preliminary simulations suggest that a similar if not a greater variety will be feasible in multi-agent environments (cf.

Eymann et al., 1998; Sandholm/Lesser, 1997). The crucial point in liberal order is that new forms evolve while others disappear and that actors freely choose between the institutions and their modes of exchange based on the incentives they have. Adaptation leads to a greater degree of organisation and leads to more variation (surprises) as niches are opened up for actors to exploit (Vaughn, 1999, 2). Consequently, it is particularly on this level that the co-evolution of actors and rules discussed in section 6.3.3 fully develops. Although polycentrality is important for liberal order, it is not pushed to its extremes. "What in fact we find in all free societies is that although groups of men will join in organizations for the achievement of some particular ends, the coordination of the activities of all these separate organizations, as well as of the separate individuals, is brought about by the forces making for a spontaneous order" (Hayek, 1973, 46).[36]

7.1.7 Simple patterns for complex social order

The preceding sections unfolded the logic of spontaneous liberal order and it is worth to quickly recap the steps that were presented.

- Co-operation occurs instead of conflict because liberal rules define individual property rights, and actors adapt to structures of property rights. In addition, co-operation increases the space of available actions, which is especially valuable for software-agents.

- Exchange takes place because actors can capture gains from trade. From bilateral exchanges, networks of trade partners arise. Unintended by the individual actors, goods flow through the whole system, leading to complex patterns of exchange and to a better exploitation of scarce resources. Agent environments can exhibit these processes.

- Exchange media can emerge spontaneously when actors realise that this facilitates trade. Digital exchange media are key enablers for exchanges in agent environments. The information produced by exchange media (e.g. prices) functions as a co-ordination instrument and as a discovery instrument.

- Division of labour and division of knowledge arise when actors exploit the finer granularity of exchange that becomes feasible through exchange media. The effects of learning and scale economies are incentives for a division of labour. While high degrees of specialisation are especially suited for software-agents, a general accompanying problem is the division of knowledge that occurs. Again, exchange-media help actors to overcome the fragmentation of knowledge.

- Competition arises because the resources actors consume are scarce. The conditions in agent environments suggest that competition will play an even

---

[36] The phenomenon of complex, spontaneous liberal order consisting of many different subsystems can also be described as emergent hierarchical organisation. See Simon (1996), Lane (1993).

more important role among software-agents than among humans. Competition leads actors to allocate resources efficiently, and it represents a discovery procedure, helping actors to identify new opportunities.

- Markets and hierarchies are the basic institutions that can form spontaneously. Markets, be they physical or digital, are characterised by time, place and the rules that regulate the interactions. There can be a market maker, who actively aims to construct a market. In effect, however, the rise of a market depends on the interaction all of its participants, most of whom do not have the market itself on their mind. Like markets, hierarchies facilitate certain types of exchanges because they offer a predictable environment. Although hierarchies are often explicitly designed, the order they generate internally and externally is to a large extent spontaneous.

As mentioned before, in reality, spontaneous liberal order does not unfold in the exact sequence stated here. The processes and phenomena described in the previous sections are interdependent; they trigger and reinforce each other. However, it is commonly acknowledged that we are only at the beginning of an understanding of the complex phenomena of spontaneous order (cf. Holland, 1995, 97ff). Against this background, the presented stairway (cf. figure 7.1) moved along steps commonly considered to be fundamental, and it thus delivered a comprehensive illustration of the pattern of spontaneous liberal order. It showed how the co-evolution of liberal institutions and adaptive actors generally proceeds. At every step of the analysis it was emphasised that each of the described developments is not a result of the design ambitions of an omniscient and omnipotent mind, but that it emerges solely from the interplay of actors and rules introduced already in Chapters Five and Six. The invisible hand explanation that stands behind each of these steps rests on three logical pillars: The first is that individual action often leads to consequences that were unintended and unforeseen by the actors. The second is the argument that the sum of these unintended consequences, over a large number of actors or over a long period of time, may, given the right circumstances, result in an order that is understandable to the individual actor and appears as if it were the product of some intelligent planner. The third is the judgement that the overall order is beneficial to the participants in the order in ways that they did not intend but nevertheless find desirable (Vaughn, 1989, 171f).

The spontaneous emergence of liberal order is particularly remarkable when it is considered that the participating actors can also be software-agents. Based on examples from DAI, it was demonstrated that all of the discussed phenomena of spontaneous liberal order can be produced by software-agents. This finding has to be qualified only by the fact that there is no artificial society yet that shows all the phenomena simultaneously. Agent environments are still far from reaching the complexity of human spontaneous order. However, they contribute to the

147

complexity of human society and there appears to be no obstacle to keep them from arriving at a similar complexity themselves.

7.2 Pitfalls of spontaneous liberal order

In the previous section an idealised picture of spontaneous liberal order was drawn. In order to allow for a coherent view, all potential complications were left out. However, spontaneous liberal order is not free of flaws and problems. A whole range of challenges exists which threaten liberal order. Some of them arise because the liberal principles cannot be fully implemented; others appear although the basic rules are at work. For human society, economists and other social scientists have identified these dangers. They can be summarised under the following categories:
1. Power and rent-seeking
2. Public goods
3. Market dynamics
4. Path-dependence
5. Principal-agent problems

Below each of these problems will be treated separately. It will be shown that most of them arise and are relevant also among software-agents. And it will be demonstrated that these problems can be handled without breaking liberal principles, i.e. the existence of these dangers does not require a turning away from liberal order.

7.2.1 Power and rent-seeking

Implicitly, the rise of organisations has been treated so far as something which is beneficial for social order. Effects like the voluntary reduction of unpredictability to reach higher levels of complexity and the increase of the space of available actions, including economies of scale and scope, have been indicated. However, there is a danger that organisations do not form or operate to expand the total gains from co-operation. They may work to swallow gains already produced by someone else or they may prevent further gains from being produced. The latter problem points to the issue of power, while the former more specifically falls into a category economists call rent-seeking. In both cases, liberal principles are undermined, particularly the non-dominance principle.

All organisations in modern society are targeted to follow specific purposes. Yet a significant number of them are regularly referred to as representing special interest groups. They differ from firms, which aim to make profits, or from public institutions, which execute parliamentary decisions, in that they undertake activities

148

which are directly unproductive, "in the sense that they produce pecuniary returns but do not produce goods or services that enter a conventional utility function or inputs in such goods and services" (Bhagwati, 1987, 845). These coalitions are usually described as "rent-seekers" (Tullock, 1987, 147ff). In human society they primarily form in order to influence the political process systematically. On the one hand they play an important informational function that is imperative in complex social systems (Gerecke, 1998, 104f). On the other hand, because of their directly unproductive and redistributive activities, special interest groups are considered to be a serious threat to social order (Olson, 1982). Regarding human society it remains an open issue whether rent-seeking enhances or threatens social order. Concerning the present discussion of spontaneous liberal order for software-agents, the issue can be considered irrelevant as long as agents are not involved in the political process, which, for the time being, appears to be a realistic assumption (cf. 5.2.4).

Another threat to liberal social order are positions of power of certain actors. It is a merit of the Ordo-liberal school of economics to have identified this problem. The spontaneous processes in liberal order can lead to extremely powerful economic actors who are able to influence the whole system. For these monopolistic or oligopolistic players, incentives exist to close markets, for example by the formation of cartels. Ordo-liberals regard economic power as evil because it cripples the price mechanism and because it allows for infringements on the liberty of others (Streit/Wohlgemuth, 1997, 7). Actors in power positions are likely to exert dominance over other actors, which reflects a re-rapprochement to the state of nature (Kirsch 1997, 29). However, the question whether economically powerful players only have downsides is a matter of ongoing controversy, perfectly illustrated and documented by cases from business history that range from the German IG Farben to America's AT&T and the global Microsoft Corporation. Consequently, the remedies proposed to deal with positions of power differ. While Ordo-liberals argue that it is necessary to establish an order of rules that leads to "complete competition" (Eucken, 1959, 155), more moderate positions hold that it suffices to safeguard freedom of market-entry (Kirzner, 1992, 39). What is commonly acknowledged is that on the level of the order of actions, competition can be regarded as the process to curb the power of individual actors and organisations. And as already outlined above, competition is a natural element of spontaneous liberal order.

In contrast to the issue of rent-seeking, economic power is a problem that quickly can become relevant within multi-agent environments. Markets for software-agents are still organised to a degree that prevents individual agents from building up powerful positions. However, as soon as social order in agent environments develops spontaneously as described above, the rise of power has to be expected. Moreover, preliminary investigations into the nature of digital markets suggest that the issue can become more pressing than in conventional markets. For instance, Adamic/Huberman (1999, 3) find that a small number of websites on the Internet command the traffic of a large segment of the web population, which indicates that the Internet is an environment that nurtures winner-take-all markets with powerful positions.

In conclusion, rent-seeking and economic power definitely challenge spontaneous liberal order in human society. In essence it is competition that contributes to a solution of these problems. Therefore, precautions which stir competition have to be made on the level of the order of rules. Spontaneous order in multi-agent environments is still far from reaching a stage where the issues of rent-seeking and economic power threaten the system. But at least with respect to economic power, the nature of digital markets suggests that if problems occur, they will arise quickly and massively.

7.2.2 Public goods

The previous section showed that liberal principles can be undermined, which in turn can endanger social order. Another possibility is that there may be situations where it is difficult to apply the basic rules. Probably the most prominent of these difficulties affects the exclusion principle. In economics the source of concern regarding the exclusion principle is public goods. Public goods exist when many actors share a resource or when they together provide a resource and no private property rights are assigned. Depending on the situation, the consequences lead in two directions.

If the affected resource is already present, it is likely to be overused, and the "tragedy of the commons" arises (Hardin, 1968). The classic example is the over-fishing of certain areas of the oceans to which large numbers of commercial fishers have access. What is fishing for humans is message congestion for software-agents. "Most distributed implementations of automated contracting have run into message congestion problems" state Sandholm/Lesser (1995/98, 72) and refer to a situation where agents overuse their commonly owned communication resources. Wellman (1996, 88) also argues that the tragedy of the commons is a frequent pitfall in multi-agent environments. He delivers the example of agents using a transportation network to ship cargo. In the case where transportation links are owned commonly, the agents provoke a congestion of the network. In general, various reasons can lead to the tragedy of the commons even under a liberal order of rules. In a dynamic environment it arises again and again, always when resources suddenly become scarce. Examples are wood for the construction of ships in ancient Greece and clean air during the period of industrialisation. Then there are cases where the tragedy persists under liberal rules until the involved actors agree on a procedure to solve it.

In these cases goods may be difficult to divide like underground petroleum deposits or aquifers for example. Another problem can be that it is difficult to measure or price the good, asin the case of clean air. Various approaches can be pursued to solve these problems.

Traditional software-engineering can be expected to approach the problems by internalising additional rules into software-agents. However, such a procedure contradicts liberal principles and seems inadequate in open systems where it appears difficult to implement a wide range of special rules for special situations inside all agents. In contrast, in spontaneous liberal order, competition works as a discovery procedure for new scarcities and resulting overuse of resources. Once the problem is discovered, it is possible to allocate property rights based on the first come first served basis of the priority-principle. However, there can be conflicts between colliding rights - for example, the right to pollute and the right for clean air. Another issue is the meaning of 'first-come' when many actors over long periods of time contribute to the cultivation of a resource until it can successfully be exploited, as in the case of the Indian Neem-tree. Therefore, it is often required that actors agree on a general procedure to allocate new property rights. Such an agreement is also subject to liberal rules, especially as it must consider the problem of dominance. Competition can again play a major role in these agreed-upon allocation processes as auctions for radio frequencies show. In sum, actors realise that for a specific good, a market is missing; but they create it, intentionally or spontaneously. Then transaction-cost efficient ways to enable exchange and trade can be found, so that the resources will be acquired by those actors who can use them best (Coase, 1960/88, 157ff).

Obviously, not all problems can be solved. However, the reach of the described process is often underestimated. This counts particularly for spontaneous elements, like the entrepreneurial competition that regularly discovers ways of assigning property rights that were unknown beforehand. An example from digital markets is the discovery of methods for the pricing of networks (cf. Gupta et al., 1996). As it is likely that the public goods problem will present itself in new forms in agent-environments, it is important to note that DAI research has already begun to develop new answers (cf. Parkes/Ungar, 1996; Glance/Hogg, 1995).

The other side of the public goods problem is titled 'free rider problem.' If a large number of actors commonly provide a resource, it is likely that many individual actors choose not to contribute (ride free) so that it will be undersupplied. Next to the problem of fare dodging on buses, the classic example here is adherence to and enforcement of social norms, which can be understood to be a public good (cf. 5.2.2). Again the problem can appear in multi-agent environments. For instance, Shoham/Tanaka (1997, 1) consider shared databases that are populated by items contributed by the users themselves and where the users can be humans or software-agents. "In either case, each user derives a benefit from having a rich database to draw from, but has a slight disincentive to actually contribute anything. The result is that the database remains empty, to the detriment of all users."

Generally, the free-rider problem can arise for comparable reasons as the tragedy of the commons. In a dynamic environment it can surface spontaneously when circumstances change. For instance, the problem may be known and solved in the area of traditional shared databases but it may turn up again in new applications, like collaborative filtering (cf. DeLong/Froomkin, 2000). In any case, the underlying logic is the same. As it is difficult to apply the exclusion principle, the activity of one benefits all. In the end every actor expects the other actors to undertake the activity while he himself finds it beneficial to refrain from it. As software-agents are made capable of such strategic reasoning (cf. Parkes/Ungar, 1996), this problem poses a real challenge to liberal agent-environments. However, again it seems plausible that remedies successful in human society also work among software-agents. In addition to the precautions named above, an important means to overcome the free rider problem is "selective incentives" (Olson, 1965/71, 51), which directly affect the concerned actor. They can take the form of reward or punishment. And as the spontaneous evolution of social norms in human society demonstrates, they can be brought about in a spontaneous process (Glance/Huberman, 1994). For the spectrum of selective incentives to work, however, agents would have to respond not only to financial incentives but also to other dimensions like reputation and emotions.

Finally, public goods represent a serious problem in spontaneous liberal order that occurs when it is difficult to implement the exclusion principle. But as the name indicates, it only affects certain classes of goods. As soon as all liberal principles are rigorously implemented, the public goods problem is significantly reduced by spontaneous processes like exchange and competition. Consequently, the public goods problem cannot be categorised as a fundamental threat to liberal order. This does not mean, however, that it can be ignored with respect to multi-agent environments. The opposite is the case, as public goods turn out to have negative effects on the co-operation between software-agents. While remedies that have proven to be successful in human society generally appear to be applicable to agents as well, this still has to be examined in detail; particularly because the problem shows new facets in digital environments.

7.2.3 Market dynamics

It was first economists and later computer scientists that became attracted by the market economy. It was again first economists and later computer scientists that were more attracted by the neo-classical model of the market than by the grand world of the market economy itself. The reason for this is rooted in the typical characteristics of this model. As it describes a market in equilibrium, it promises stable social order. However, this stable social order is only reached if a series of restrictive assumptions holds (cf. Kreps, 1990, 263ff). This counts for human society, as well as for computational markets (cf. Walsh et al., 1997, 2). While markets appear to form under rules of liberal order, it is unlikely that the specific assumptions of the neoclassical market model will always or even often be fulfilled. On the one hand this is advantageous, because under the strict constraints of neo-classical markets, most of the spontaneous processes that are responsible for the creation of complex social order (cf. 7.1) are impossible. "Because new niches, new potentials, and new possibilities are continually created, the economy operates far from any optimum or global equilibrium" (Arthur, et al., 1997, 5). On the other hand this may come at the price of instability in dynamic markets, which threatens social order.

Ignoring the derivations of neo-classical economics, human markets regularly find themselves out of equilibrium. Modern economies are regularly plagued by periodic bouts of inflation and depression. The financial markets have seen several Black Fridays, often oscillate heavily and thus hit many actors hard economically. Similarly, price wars are commonly feared but seemingly unpreventable phenomen. These effects are undesirable, because the actors cannot form reliable expectations about their environment. In addition, the actors can drive themselves down a spiral of mutually destructive behaviours. Instead of producing gains from co-operation, the actors continuously confront each other with negative surprises. Even actors who on first sight appear to benefit from such developments - like consumers in retail market price wars - later may face downsides (e.g. being charged overly high prices by the surviving competitor). Huberman/Hogg (1988) demonstrate that imperfect knowledge and delayed information cause those dynamics, notably in human and in computational markets.

Unfortunately, the properties of digital environments lead to a reduction of transaction costs, which nurtures the described market dynamics rather than calming them down. The reasons for this shift in transaction costs can be found in the characteristics of software-agents and multi-agent environments as introduced in Chapter Two. Tesauro/Kephart (1998, 1) argue that three factors in particular increase the risk of disorder in multi-agent environments: first, the greater ability of humans compared to software-agents to predict the long-term consequences of their actions; second, the more limited but quicker processing of information and the higher speed of action of software-agents compared to humans; and third, the much greater connectivity in digital environments. In other words, agents do not realise when their behaviours become disadvantageous; their harmful actions cumulate quickly; and they have a large scope. Several experiments and simulations confirm what the theoretical argument suggests. Kephart et al. (1998b) analyse a free-market information economy in which large numbers of software agents exchange a rich variety of information goods and services. Price wars spontaneously arise as information brokers successively undercut each other until some or all of the brokers jump to other, less competitive niches. Upon arrival, the agents immediately resume the price war, and a never-ending cycle of fairly regular price wars begins. Even when agents are less determined to undercut their competitors, the system presents itself to be inherently unstable, and periods of relative calm and prosperity are punctuated sporadically by price wars (Kephart et al., 1998b). Another area of interest is e-commerce based on shopbots and pricebots. Shopbots help consumers to compare prices of a given product on the Internet. Pricebots assist sellers in setting prices by finding out about the pricing of competitors. Greenwald/Kephart (1999) find that also in this domain price wars can occur spontaneously without any of the players intending it.

As market dynamics are already the third problem discussed here, it will not be very surprising that there are chances of constructively dealing with this challenge that lies within the reach of liberal order. In search of a remedy, Tesauro/Kephart (1999) find that the degree of sophistication and adaptability of an actor matters. More specifically, they show that agents who are capable of learning alter the situation significantly in both, the information filtering economy and the shopbot-pricebot domain. The amplitudes of price wars are reduced and in some cases an outbreak of price wars is prevented. Re-stabilisation occurs when actors learn they are less myopic and it is less likely for errors to cumulate.

Economic theory as well as practical experience in human markets suggests that there are further ingredients which can contribute to a dampening out of harmful oscillations. One way to overcome disadvantageous market dynamics can be derived from the above discussion on markets and hierarchies: Actors can organise their activities differently. If, for example, price wars plague the retail market for food, it can be a viable strategy for some sellers to merge, or for one seller to buy market share by integrating competitors into his own hierarchy. Such measures can render the market more stable. On average, prices may be slightly higher, but fluctuate less. The seller may be able to offer superior quality and prevent delays or disruptions in supply. However, as discussed above, care has to taken that the economic power of the respective actors does not become rampant, disabling the spontaneous forces of liberal order.

A further method of stabilising markets consists of loyalty programs that have already been briefly mentioned in another context (cf. 7.1.3). For instance, frequent-flyer programs introduced by airlines decades ago have spontaneously generated a stable market for safe passenger air-transportation. Varian (2000) arrives at the conclusion that for commerce on the Internet, loyalty programs will play a significant role, especially in reducing price competition. An additional force that can occur spontaneously to reduce the negative effects of market oscillations is all kinds of insurance. They represent a particular form of specialisation and work ex-post by compensating for negative surprises. It is the various existing and continuously invented new forms of insurance that prove valuable in this context. The heterogeneity of the exemplified options that can arise spontaneously indicates that it is effective to let the actors of a system autonomously evolve countermeasures to market dynamics. An important feature of these developments is that they handle negative surprises on the micro-level, which reduces harmful effects on the aggregate system level, which would affect by far more actors. All these processes contribute to make market structure less susceptible to harmful oscillations. Similarly, however, all these processes rely highly on the adaptive capabilities of the participating actors. If the conditions of adaptability are not fulfilled and some actors – or even whole sectors of the economy – remain in stasis, then market dynamics can break out that are even more harmful (cf. Kirsch, 1988).

Finally, another way of inducing stability can be pursued under third party governance. The third party can undertake steps that work as incentives for the other actors to keep from behaviours that destabilise the system in the aggregate. The most prominent examples in human society are governmental fiscal, monetary and other policies to regulate the levels of output, inflation and unemployment in an economy (Cassel/Thieme, 1999). While multi-agent environments are still far from reaching the complexity of a human economy, in principle the same logic can be applied to software-agents that operate under the governance of an independent market maker. For instance, in experiments with simple agents Gode/Sunder (1999) investigate how price controls affect the market in which these agents are active. Despite a certain potential to relieve social order from a serious threat, it is necessary to remember that third-party governance executed this way can contradict liberal principles as dominance is exerted. In addition, the central government or the market maker in general face severe knowledge restrictions regarding the aggregate effects of their measures, so that it cannot be excluded that in some cases the situation may get worse even than without intervention.

In sum, it can be said that under a liberal order of rules, markets are dynamic, which necessarily includes harmful oscillations; or as Huberman/Hogg (1995, 149) put it: "At least so far, all market-like systems of which we are aware have shown at least some tendency, in some circumstances, to fall into oscillations and chaos." These harmful dynamics represent a transient phenomenon but they re-occur from time to time. Factors like the actors' adaptability, institutional change, loyalty programs, insurance, and third-party intervention can significantly defuse this problem. In general, it can be argued that the risk of market dynamics and disorder is reduced if negative surprises are compensated on the micro-level, so that they do not accumulate to global instabilities. Market dynamics can also occur among software-agents. Moreover, the properties of digital actors and their environments suggest that the problem will become even more pressing there. The discussed partial remedies also appear to function in agent environments, and it remains to be seen whether further means evolve spontaneously under liberal rules.

7.2.4 Path-dependence

Extremes cause problems. While market dynamics are one extreme, so called path-dependence is an extreme that can be found at the static end of the spectrum of social order. The notion of path-dependence is used to describe the powerful influence of the past on the present and future (North, 1994, 364). Spontaneous liberal order cannot simply be called into existence. It needs time to evolve and it relies on past developments and achievements. Without path-dependence, the described liberal order of action would be unthinkable. It is the spontaneous co-evolutive processes of actors and rules which bring about complex but functioning social order. In these processes, path-dependence has advantageous effects, as it creates predictability and thus enhances social order. An illustrative example from the preceding section is loyalty programs, introduced by airlines and other companies to increase the number of path-dependent decisions of their customers. However, in general, there is no guarantee that the cumulative past experience of individual actors and of society as a whole will help to solve new problems. There are not only productive but also unproductive paths.

Not the most relevant and not the least controversial but probably the most popular case of path-dependence is that of QWERTY (David, 1985). QWERTY is the name for the keyboard layout of standard personal computers and typewriters. The layout was originally only introduced because it helped to prevent a jamming of the type bars of nineteenth century typewriters. There were no ergonomic concerns and although other -supposedly better - layouts were proposed repeatedly, people got locked-in on the QWERTY-path. Keyboard layout is a question of economic standards, where path-dependence can result in inferior solutions. Although the best solution may be discovered, the market fails because the actors do not adopt this technology. But it is not all about technological standards. North (1990/92, 94f) points out that the problem of path-dependence also affects institutional change, which increases its relevance for the question of social order. He discusses the economic development of Latin America and shows how initial sets of institutions provide disincentives to productive activity and cause the creation of organisations and interest groups that further cement these constraints. Along this path, the "mental constructs of the participants evolve an ideology that not only rationalizes the society's structure but accounts for its poor performance" (North, 1990/92, 99). What becomes evident here is that the lock-in manifests itself on the level of the order of rules. Its implications, however, come into being on the level of the order of action. Path dependence prevents actors from capturing attainable gains from co-operation. While North recognises that we are just beginning to explore the issue of path-dependence, it is highly probable that the phenomenon will spread in multi-agent environments as well. For instance, experimenting with simple adaptive agents who choose between decision rules, Vriend (1999, 17ff) finds that path-dependent behaviour characterises the system.

As the full extent and the implications of path-dependence, especially among software-agents, cannot yet be seen, a fruitful theoretical way to approach the problem is to examine the potential reasons for this phenomenon to occur. Following North (1990/92, 95), two forces can be held responsible: the existence of increasing returns and of transaction costs. The idea of increasing returns was already discussed in section 7.1.6 when network effects in markets were analysed. Transaction costs do not only make switching from one standard or one rule to another expensive. They also cause actors to receive only fragmentary information feedback on their actions, which keeps them from leaving unproductive paths. Vriend (1999, 27f) goes as far to ask "could it be that the famous QWERTY lock-in has less to do with network externalities and other relative payoff matters than with information contagion?" The software-agents in his experiments show path-dependent behaviour simply because they base their decisions on the decisions of other agents and thus mutually adapt based on imperfect information.

Increasing returns or network effects as well as transaction costs appear to be natural properties of both, human society and agent-environments. Consequently, path-dependence also naturally occurs. On the one hand, this phenomenon is indispensable, because without it the co-evolution of actors and rules in spontaneous liberal order cannot take place. On the other hand, the burden of undesirable effects of path-dependence has to be carried. As these effects are not entirely predictable in advance (Arthur, 1989, 129), it is not possible to -literally- rule them out. However, in spontaneous liberal order forces are at work that continuously offer new paths and to reduce old dependencies. Vaughn (1999, 5) outlines that entrepreneurs find ways to challenge lock-ins. Based on these discoveries, competition functions as a correcting force. In fact, it is the recent developments in the networked digital economy that demonstrate best how entrepreneurial activities can manipulate path-dependence (Shapiro/Varian, 1998). In the end, this makes path-dependence a temporary phenomenon. Occasionally, disasters occur, but spontaneous order shows a clear tendency for improving average performance (Vriend, 1999, 28).

7.2.5 Principal-agent problems

The exchange situations, and especially the contract situations, which characterise a liberal order of actions have a particular structure. From an economic point of view, the actors find themselves in principal-agent relationships.[37] A principal-agent relationship is established when a principal delegates some rights - for example, user rights over a resource - to an agent who is bound by a (formal or informal) contract to represent the principal's interests in return for payment of some kind (Eggertsson, 1990, 40f). These relationships can arise in any exchange situation, for instance between a buyer and a seller, between an employer and an employee, or between a citizen and a politician; but also between a computer user and an interface software-agent, or between a mobile software-agent and a server computer. In a sense liberal order is nothing but a finely woven web of such relationships. Unfortunately, each knot in this web may fail to hold because of so called principal-agent problems. In human society these problems can be found everywhere. They are as scattered over society as the relationships themselves, and it is plausible that environments with software-agents will be similarly affected.

Under a liberal order of rules, it is attractive for actors to co-operate because of the gains from co-operation that can be achieved. However, the individual actor can arrive at the conclusion that he can gain even more if all other actors co-operate while he himself defects. Common examples for such behaviour are deception in contract situations and shirking at work. Due to the increasingly social role of software-agents, it is plausible that software-agents may also act opportunistically and are affected by opportunistic behaviour. Already in section 6.1.1 the benevolence assumption was dropped. Following others, Binmore/Vulkan (1999,1) find that "[software-] agents will, therefore, find themselves in situations where they have an incentive to lie, or act tough, or exploit other strategic avenues not usually associated with machines."

Principal-agent problems can occur in markets as well as in hierarchies. Problems in markets include car-workshops who do more repairs on a client's car than necessary, or people who claim damages from their insurance that have not occurred. Meanwhile, and right in the logic of these examples, Rosenschein/Zlotkin (1994, 53ff) show that software-agents also can be prepared to work with "hidden tasks", "phantom tasks" or "decoy tasks" to exploit their co-operation partners. Hostile interactions are also expected to take place between mobile software-agents and host-computers. Besides mutually gainful exchanges between these types of actors, theft and harmful manipulation of valuable resources is bound to happen (cf. Ordille, 1996, 1 and 5.1.2). While the list of problems could easily be extended, it is more fruitful to shade some light on hierarchies as well. The classic example here is an employee who minimises his work-input while receiving a full salary from his principal. A similar constellation among software-agents can be found in Contract Nets (cf. 2.3). While the awareness for problems of co-operation has not been very

---

[37] Note that when speaking of a principal-agent relationship in this section, the notions principal and agent can refer to both, humans and software-agents. A software-agent can also be a principal and a human can also be an agent.

high during the early days of the Contract Net (cf. Smith, 1980), it has increased considerably since, however, without explicit reference to the principal-agent paradigm employed in economics (cf. Sandholm/Lesser, 1995/98). Regarding software-agents, further problems can occur between computer-users and interface-agents. For example, it easily can be imagined that software-agents pass private data of their principals on to marketing firms.

In search of an explanation for principal-agent problems, it is useful to remember a statement made earlier (cf. 5.1.3): Contracts regularly contain an incentive for non-fulfilment in their time-performance structure. Transaction-specific costs, the incompleteness of contracts, and information asymmetries can lead the agent to opportunistically hide actions, hide information or more generally to moral hazard (Richter/Furubotn, 1996, 163). The potential for negative surprises is high, and as chain reactions cannot be excluded co-operation, as a whole may be at risk. De Jasay (1995, 3) puts it this way: "Theft, robbery and default have robust attractions. Property and contract look fragile in comparison." But he continues in the next sentence to say: "...on the whole and most of the time, they nevertheless prevail." This is because actors have found institutional arrangements that allow them to deal with principal-agent problems. A systematic account of the types of institutional arrangements that can be pursued under liberal order was given in section 5.2.

What is important to note is that principal-agent problems are not solved because there is one central authority that has control over all interactions. Rather, as the problems are scattered over the system, every actor contributes with his local knowledge and actions. This polycentrality leads to a large variety of concrete solutions, impossible to cover here. But it is worth emphasising that this variety is likely to spread to environments of software-agents as well. For example Schillo et al. (1999) experiment with software-agents that collect information about the trustworthiness of potential partners by observation and interviewing other agents about their observations, while Bazzan et al. (1997) examine whether gains from co-operation can be achieved more easily when software-agents are equipped with moral sentiments. These and other software-agents then can operate principally on electronic marketplaces like ebay.com, which have already developed mechanisms like insurance, feedback forums, escrow services and authentication services to facilitate co-operation and overcome principal-agent problems. Marketplaces suited to software-agents additionally will offer interaction protocols that enhance co-operation and reduce opportunistic behaviour - for example, by providing incentives to tell the truth (cf. Rosenschein/Zlotkin, 1994).

The generation of institutional arrangements can be interpreted to be an adaptive process. The phenomenon of competition inspires the actors to discover new arrangements and motivates them to allocate their resources to the most efficient arrangements. But as there is also always competition between those who want to enforce contracts and those who act opportunistically, moral hazard will never be completely eliminated. A crucial property of spontaneous liberal order is that, normally, principal-agent problems are micro-problems that do not significantly affect social order as a whole. Instead of the mentioned chain reaction, negative surprises cancel each other out on the micro-level because actors sanction each other or exit the particular interaction situation.

Principal-agent problems prevent liberal order from attaining a maximum degree of co-operation. Under a liberal order of rules there is always room for moral hazard, and there will always be actors who follow surfacing incentives for opportunistic behaviour. It would be unrealistic to preclude this for software-agents, especially as software-designers have explicitly discovered this opportunity. However, neither in human society nor in environments of software-agents do principal-agent problems appear to be a threat to social order as a whole, because, the actors deal with the problem on the micro-level before it aggregates to become a macro-problem based on their adaptive capabilities.

7.2.6 Unavoidable but tolerable pitfalls

The conclusion that can be drawn from the discussion in the preceding sections is that spontaneous liberal order does not work flawlessly. It was shown that fundamental pitfalls exist that cannot be completely avoided. However, they can be constructively dealt with polycentrically. In sum, the following problems were examined:

- Power and rent-seeking swallow existing gains from co-operation and prevent gains from being produced. Rent-seekers engage in re-distributive and thus unproductive activities, mainly in political processes in human society. Actors in powerful positions hinder free exchange in market processes, which is also relevant for agent-environments. The spontaneous forces of competition represent a proven measure to keep these problems from fundamentally threatening social order.

- Public goods occur when it is difficult to implement the exclusion principle. They imply an overuse of resources (tragedy of the commons) or that actors fail to co-operate to produce valuable resources (free rider problem). Both pitfalls plague not only human society but also agent-environments. Human society in general, as well as DAI in particular, successfully derive procedures to overcome public goods problems without being in conflict with liberal institutions. Within open and changing environments, there will always be new public goods problems, but spontaneous processes like exchange and competition enable actors to deal with them.

- Market dynamics, naturally produced by the actors in spontaneous liberal order, can lead to harmful oscillations and mutually destructive behaviour. Because of knowledge problems, they arise among humans, but they appear to play an even more significant role in agent-environments. The problem is transient but it inevitably re-occurs. A variety of spontaneously generated processes influence market structures so that they are less susceptible to harmful oscillations and so that they do not become a fundamental threat to liberal order.

- Path-dependence causes humans and software-agents to converge on and get locked-in by inferior economic standards and institutional structures. These standards and - even more importantly - poor institutional structures prevent actors from capturing otherwise achievable gains from co-operation. As such, unproductive paths stem from the same co-evolutive processes of actors and rules as the productive paths of social order. Therefore, they cannot be completely prevented. But competition functions as a corrective force.

- Principal-agent problems can arise in any exchange situation of liberal order. They stem from the fact that actors have incentives to act opportunistically and to exploit their interaction partners. Software-agents are not immune to these incentives. The threat to social order is limited because in polycentral liberal order, principal-agent problems, are usually micro-problems and because in the spontaneous process of competition, the involved actors generate institutional arrangements that make the problems tolerable.

After all, the examined pitfalls must be considered natural elements of spontaneous liberal order as the constructive phenomena discussed in section 7.1. Under the conditions of liberal order there is no final solution to any of them. Changing circumstances will lead them to surface unexpectedly over and over again. This also goes for agent environments. Nearly all of the problems can occur there as well. The different properties of digital environments make them more vulnerable to some of the problems (e.g. market dynamics), while others so far hardly pose difficulties (e.g. rent-seeking). Apart from that, not all potential consequences of these problems have to be taken into account. For example, social considerations are irrelevant for software-agents. Despite the fact that the named downsides will always have to be faced by humans and by software-agents, it is plausible to conclude that they do not pose a fundamental threat to social order as long as the spontaneous forces of liberal order function properly. For each of the problems, processes like contract-based exchange and competition help to overcome them as they occur. An important property of these processes is that they tend to provide distributed solutions of the problems on the micro-level suited to the particular circumstances. This in turn prevents the problems from accumulating to become a threat to the whole system. Thus the named downsides are less deep than it is often assumed. For this conclusion to hold, however, liberal institutions must be implemented consistently and rigorously.

7.3 Conclusions

This chapter finally examined what is bound to happen when unpredictable and adaptive actors interact under a liberal order of rules. The analysis followed the tradition of invisible hand explanations in order to trace how interacting individuals bring about complex social order without deliberately planning it. First, it was shown how spontaneously arising phenomena can be understood to build up on each other to form a liberal order of action. Second, it was discussed how various pitfalls undermine the formation of social order. It will now be fruitful to review to which extent spontaneous liberal order provides a solution to the problem of social order.

The results of the first section appeared to be promising. Several spontaneous processes that can be considered to be key to liberal order were analysed. These included the adaptive co-operation under liberal rules, the focus provided by the division of labour; the allocation, co-ordination and discovery functions of exchange media and competition, as well as the reduction of uncertainty given by the rise of institutions like markets and hierarchies. These phenomena occur and trigger each other because actors exploit gains from co-operation. Each of these phenomena contributes to a situation where order in the sense of Hayek is reached, namely that bounded individual actors can form expectations about the system that have good chances of proving correct. More specifically, it seems plausible that the key problems posed at the beginning of this second part can be solved by liberal order.

The state of nature was found to be overcome as adaptive actors follow liberal principles and in a co-evolutionary process apply and specify them so that these rules spread to be present at any time and place within the system. This process is especially interesting for software-agents because their knowledge about the world is even more restricted than that of humans and because they increasingly tend to operate without fixed and specific internalised rules of behaviour. Based on the incentives they perceive, humans and agents can be said generally to head for gains from co-operation rather than getting involved in conflicts. The second section made clear that obstacles like principal-agent problems or powerful actors can hinder this process. However, actors learn to deal with these pitfalls and the forces of spontaneous liberal order, especially competition, work against a spread of state of nature situations.

A major challenge that was extensively discussed in Chapter Four was the question of whether actors can be free and hence unpredictable. This chapter showed that the logic of spontaneous liberal order does not only leave room for unpredictable behaviour but in fact builds on it heavily. An important aspect is that the outstanding gains from co-operation provide incentives for actors to produce positive instead of negative surprises. Nevertheless negative surprises can occur. For instance, software-agents can inhabit bugs, viruses, or show opportunistic behaviour, which in turn may generate all sorts of principal-agent problems. A distinct feature of polycentral liberal order is its tendency to locate unpredictability on the micro-level while leaving the macro-level predictable. Various factors come into play. First, actors learn from experience and thus are able to improve their behaviour. Exchange media aggregate information and give an average picture of the environment. This is more stable and hence more predictable than the individual interaction partners, so actors can more easily adapt. Furthermore, exchange media help them to adapt quickly to major negative surprises. Second, actors learn from experience and are free to choose, for example, their interaction partners: after bad experiences with one interaction partner they may switch to another. Competition among the actors motivates them to enter exchange relationships where the gains from co-operation are high, hence where there are few negative surprises. The first two aspects indicate that individual actors have to bear the consequences of their own unpredictability and that of the other agents. Third, this can be viewed as an investment rather than a cost, because the negative experiences the actors incur help them to improve their future behaviour. The actors can be considered to choose based not so much on the actual situation, but grounded in their cumulative experience to achieve a satisfying overall behaviour. This leads to the generation of and the participation in more sophisticated institutional settings. The spontaneous generation of institutions like markets or hierarchies in turn initially itself requires the ability to act unpredictably. Fourth, the fact that mutual adaptation swallows downsides of individual unpredictability and turns them into improved behaviour means that negative surprises are regularly being canceled out before they can accumulate to get big enough to affect the system as a whole. Fifth, if nevertheless emergent problems like market oscillations or unfavourable path dependence affect the system as a whole, it is again unpredictable entrepreneurial behaviour combined with the informative function of exchange media and the forces of competition that allows actors to find countermeasures, which enhance the predictability of the macro-level.

In essence, the unpredictability on the micro-level and the predictability on the macro-level reinforce each other. It is the unpredictability of the individual agent, which allows the system as a whole to be predictable. And because the system on average is predictable, the agents can bear to be unpredictable. h a sense, the predictable system is not more but less than the sum of its unpredictable parts. It is not characterised by a "2+2=5 effect" but by a "2+2=3 effect" (Vriend 1999, 19). And that is the reason why, in the sense of Hayek, the individual actor in a liberal order, by acquaintance with some spatial or temporal part of the whole, can form expectations which have a good chance of proving correct.

A fundamental problem faced in this book from the very first chapter onwards was the grand world problem or the challenge to deal with complexity. In this chapter it was shown how co-evolutionary processes gradually increase the complexity of social order. The complexity of the arising spontaneous order exceeds the design and planning capabilities of any single actor. The social order also enables actors to achieve things they cannot achieve alone. Starting from simple mutual respect of individual property rights and bilateral exchanges, a grand world arises that consists of complex institutional structures including markets, hierarchies, and all sorts of hybrid institutions. These can be comprehended to be small worlds, within which it is easier for actors to operate. More specifically, the division of labour and knowledge manifested within these institutions allows actors to be relatively simple in comparison to the system as a whole. However, these institutions depend on each other and are inter-linked. And at every stage of development the polycentral liberal order is open for new unpredictable and adaptive actors to enter. Competitive forces transmitted through exchange media guide the simple actors in this complex environment to adapt themselves and to refine the small worlds which they populate. The actors' fields of visions are connected and, without necessarily intending it, they continuously reproduce the complex order of actions. The patterns of spontaneous liberal order provide unpredictable and adaptive actors with incentives to solve problems like market dynamics or path-dependence when they come to them. According to Savage (1954/71, 16), this is the characteristic way to operate in the grand world. Moreover, it was shown that these processes on the micro-level let the grand world remain on an overall high level of order.

Finally, the patterns of spontaneous liberal order can be concluded to converge towards transaction-cost-efficient interactions. In addition the analysis indicated that agent-technology further spurs this tendency. On the level of the order of actions, several effects were found to come into play. First, the mutual respect of private property rights internalises the costs of a decision an actor makes. This, in turn, provides an incentive for an efficient allocation of resources, which also includes information resources and thus transaction-relevant resources. Another aspect stems from the rise of exchange media. They provide means for efficient communications that go well beyond bilateral information exchange. Furthermore, competitive conditions provide actors with incentives to allocate resources efficiently. This also counts for resources invested into institutions to regulate exchanges of all kinds. Consequently, the actors intentionally or unintentionally specify and participate in institutions between markets and hierarchies according to their transaction-cost efficiency. However, problems like path-dependency prevent the convergence towards transaction cost efficient solutions from being perfect. Also, there appears to be a trade-off between lowering transaction-costs and overcoming other problems like market dynamics. However, the forces of spontaneous liberal order show a capability to balance this.

A conclusion may commence with the reminder that at least parts of the spontaneous order discussed here - especially for software-agents – can also be directly constructed (e.g. money, marketplaces, firms of agents etc.). And as said before, it has to be acknowledged that spontaneous liberal order does not provide a perfect solution to the problem of social order. But letting the properties of this approach pass in review, it is not necessary to emphasise that competitive alternatives are rare.

8

Final conclusion

"Liberal order and software-agents" – long-established ideas and modern technology were bridged in the preceding analysis. The impulse for undertaking this effort came from the observation that it becomes difficult for computer science alone to create order for and within machines. The growing complexity of computer systems, open networks like the Internet, and the increasingly social role of software entities push the traditional quest for total global control out of reach. Economic theory of social order offers extensive experience with such conditions, so that it can complement and guide research in computer science. It was shown that a common understanding between economics and computer science's sub-field of distributed artificial intelligence is possible on the level of software-agents. On this basis, the first part of this book served to encircle four fundamental problems of social order: first, the requirement to overcome and prevent state of nature situations in the sense of Hobbes; second, the necessity to accommodate unpredictable individual actors; third, the challenge of exiting the small worlds of traditional software systems; and fourth, the ambition to reach a transaction cost efficient social order.

It was concluded that economics can contribute to an understanding and to possible solutions of these problems by unfolding the idea of liberal order for software-agents. In a systematic analysis that covered the order of rules, the model of the individual actor, and the order of actions, it was shown that the conditions for liberal order can be created, without exception, in agent-environments. But although approaches exist that, often unintentionally, confirm this applicability with respect to each element of liberal order, agent-technology is still far from attaining all-encompassing approaches. While this may well continue to be out of reach for some time, the presented analysis demonstrated that it is fruitful to orient current agent-design efforts towards this direction. This stems from the fact that liberal order, to a large extent, has to be grown and cannot be made on an ad-hoc basis.

In line with this conclusion, it was outlined how design focuses on basic rules or institutions and on laying the foundations for adaptive actors. Through interaction, institutions and actors co-evolve to form complex systems. Further design efforts on the system-level are not compatible with the idea of liberal order.

Spontaneous liberal order demonstrates a capacity to constructively deal with the fundamental problems under discussion. A range of interesting properties that arise in human society as well as in agent environments could be identified: Co-operation supersedes conflict; unpredictability regularly appears on the micro-level, but there are conditions that keep it from aggregating to the macro-level; social order reaches and sustains levels of complexity that are beyond the complexity which can be achieved by explicit (human) design; and institutions that save on transaction costs replace less efficient arrangements. If deviations from these properties nevertheless occur, this does not lead the system to complete failure as the corrective forces spontaneously set in.

It will be acknowledged generally that the named properties are desirable not only for human society, but also for agent environments. They correspond to the requirements of a grand world. However, they are inevitably bound to a strict implementation of liberalism. This, in turn, requires accepting conditions that have repeatedly proven to be alien to human thinking and action. Most importantly this implies refraining from the ambition of global control and to tolerate being confronted with positive and negative surprises which continuously require one to adapt. With respect to software-agents, coming to terms with these conditions will be even more alien. However, although it may be demanding for us in everyday life, the presented analysis showed that unpredictability and thus freedom for software-agents can be fruitful, at least under a liberal order of rules. Ceteris paribus, it is plausible that, given liberal conditions, the scenario about HAL and Dave in Clarke's "2001 A Space Odyssey" would have to be rewritten.

Epilogue

If this book has managed to convey the impression of an integrated and unified view of the question of social order for software-agents, this is due to the tactical intention of not losing the reader in the complexities of the subject. The strategic intention behind this study has been a different one. The aim has been to help open the door to a dimension of research along the borderline between economics and computer science. For this purpose the text delivers a framework and many potential links for further investigations. The nature of this task required omitting countless opportunities for deeper analysis. At this point it may be worth exemplifying this by pointing into a few directions.

On the level of the order of rules, specific institutions - like those briefly introduced in the second chapter - can be studied in greater detail. This is particularly relevant for institutions that, for technological and for other reasons, have not yet been considered in human society. Regarding the individual software-agent, the question of the preferences and goals a machine has (or does not have) is certainly worth a separate discussion. Similarly, for an artificial actor, the relevance of moral sentiments and emotions undoubtedly requires a closer look. This would demand an investigation of the conditions for acting ethically and to distinguish between good and bad. Along these lines a discussion of a potential self of machines is more appropriate than it may seem. On the level of the order of actions, quick technological progress asks for further exploration of the unknown properties of social systems in which systematically different actors like humans and software-agents operate. I do not believe that to understand these properties, basic economic laws will have to be given up. Yet as the participating actors change and develop, new efforts will have to be made to understand phenomena like co-operation, exchange, competition, and conflict in specific situations. In this sense, artificial social simulation will be an important tool. Combined with traditional economic approaches, it will help to identify more clearly the limits of purposeful design of social order and the challenges of evolution.

These are some of the gaps that were left intentionally open in order to make the challenge of mapping the territory of liberal order for software-agents a manageable task. While I have been happy to draw a horizontal picture, I am convinced that in the future it will be rewarding to go into the vertical analysis of specific subfields.

There is another major issue that has only been treated implicitly. This is the discussion of the relationship between man and machine. Personally, I am convinced that liberal order, as presented here, can be a promising basis for social order among all sorts of actors, even among actors as different as humans and software-agents. Nevertheless, to the extent that machines leave their role as simple instruments behind, the ordering of the relationship between man and machine deserves special attention. The question of freedom has to be treated more thoroughly. The commonalities and the differences between man and machine as social actors need closer examination. Also questions regarding the various biased mutual dependencies and the limits of human control have to be studied. For example, it easily can be imagined that in commercial digital environments on the Internet, software-agents have the potential to become superior decision-makers. Yet, it also can be imagined that humans do not want to be exploited by machines, and they will not voluntarily give up the role of the principal. Against this background it will presumably be necessary to study the properties and chances of class societies again. Personally, I am sceptical about the potential fruitfulness and legitimacy of master-slave relationships, Apartheid regimes, caste-based systems and the like, even if it is between men and machines.

In sum, the challenge of ensuring social order appears to enter new stages quickly. Yet as long as there are enough actors among us with the ability and the commitment to make new beginnings, I am decisively optimistic.

Bibliography

Adamic, L. /Huberman, B. (1999), The nature of markets in the world wide web, technical-report, Xerox PARC Research Center, Palo Alto CA

Agre, P. (1995), Computational research on interaction and agency, in: Artificial Intelligence, 72, 1-52

Agre, P. (1998), The architecture of identity: Embedding privacy in market institutions, paper presented at the Telecommunications Policy Research Conference, October, Alexandria

Alchian, A. (1950), Uncertainty, evolution and economic theory, in: Journal of Political Economy, 58, 211-221

Appelrath, H. /Ludewig, J. (1995), Skriptum Informatik - Eine konventionelle Einführung, Stuttgart: Teubner

Arendt, H. (1958/97), Vita activa - oder vom tätigen Leben, München: Piper (Engl.: The human condition, Chicago: University of Chicago Press, 1958)

Arthur, B. (1989), Competing technologies, increasing returns, and lock-in by historical events, in: The Economic Journal, 99 (March), 116-131

Arthur, B. (1994), Inductive reasoning and bounded rationality, in: AEA Papers and Proceedings, vol.84, no.2, 406-411

Arthur, B. /Durlauf, S. /Lane, D. (1997) (eds.), The economy as an evolving complex system II, Reading MA: Addison-Wesley

Arrow, K. (1951/66), Social change and individual values, New York: John Wiley & Sons

Asimov, I. (1990/92), Robotervisionen, Bergisch Gladbach: Bastei-Lübbe

Austin, J. (1962), How to do things with words, Cambridge MA: Havard University Press

Axelrod, R. (1984), The evolution of cooperation, New York: Basic Books

Axelrod, R. (1997), The complexity of cooperation, Princeton NJ: Princeton University Press

Axtell, R. (1999), The emergence of firms in a population of agents: Local increasing returns, unstable Nash equilibrium and power law size distributions, working-paper no. 3, Center on Social and Economic Dynamics, Brookings Institution, Washington DC

Bachmann, R. (1998), Kooperation, Vertrauen und Macht in Systemen Verteilter Künstlicher Intelligenz, in: Malsch, Th. (Hrsg.), Sozionik, Berlin: Edition Sigma, 197-234

Bailey, J. (1992), First we reshape our computers, then our computers reshape us: the broader intellectual impact of parallelism, in: Daedalus, Winter 121 (1), 67-85

Baker, S. (1999), Taming the wild, wild web, in: Business Week, October 4, 154-160

Barzel, Y. (1985), Transaction costs: are they just costs?, in: JITE, 141, 4-16

Barzel, Y. (1989), Economic analysis of property rights, Cambridge: Cambridge University Press

Bayardo, R. /Bohrer, W. /Brice, R. /Cichocki, A. /Fowler, J. /Helal, A. /Kashyap, V. /Ksiezyk, T. /Martin, G. /Nodine, M. /Rashid, M. /Rusinkiewicz, M. /Shea, R. /Unnikrishnan, C. /Unruh, A. /Woelk, D. (1997/98) , InfoSleuth: Agent-based semantic integration of information in open and dynamic environments, in: Huhns, M. / Singh, M. (eds.): Readings in agents, San Francisco: Morgan-Kaufmann, 205-216

Bazzan, A. /Bordini, R. /Campbell, J. (1997), Agents with moral sentiments in an iterated prisoner's dilemma, paper presented at the AAAI Fall Symposium on Socially Intelligent Agents, Cambridge MA

Beck, U. (1986), Risikogesellschaft - Auf dem Weg in eine andere Moderne, Frankfurt a. M.: Suhrkamp

Becker, G. (1976), The economic approach to human behavior, Chicago: University of Chicago Press

Benson, B. (1998), Economic freedom and the evolution of law, in: Cato Journal, vol. 18, no.2, 209-232

Berlin, I. (1964/98), From hope and fear set free, in: Berlin, I., The proper study of mankind, Hardy, H./Hausheer, R. (ed.), New York: Farrar, Straus and Giroux, 91-118

Berlin, I. (1969), Four essays on liberty, Oxford: Oxford University Press

Bhagwati, J. (1987), Directly unproductive profit-seeking (DUP) activities, in: The New Palgrave: A Dictionary of Economics, vol. I, London and Basingstoke: Macmillan Press, 845-847

Binmore, K, (1994), Game theory and the social contract, Vol. I., Cambridge MA: MIT Press

Binmore, K. /Vulkan, N. (1999), Applying game theory to automated negotiation, in: Netnomics, 1, 1-9

Birman, K. /Renesse, R. (1997), Software für zuverlässige Netzwerke, in: Spektrum der Wissenschaft, September, 76-81

Böhm, F. (1980), Freiheit und Ordnung in der Marktwirtschaft, Böhm, F. / Mestmäcker, E.-J. (Hrsg.), Baden-Baden: Nomos

Boullion, H. (1991), Ordnung, Evolution und Erkenntnis, Tübingen: J.C.B. Mohr (Paul Siebeck)

172

Boutilier C. /Shoham, Y. /Wellman, M. (1997), Economic principles of multi-agent systems, in: Artificial Intelligence, 94, 1-6

Bradshaw, J. (1997a) (ed.), Software agents, Menlo Park CA: AAAI Press /MIT Press

Bradshaw, J. (1997b), An introduction to software agents, in: Bradshaw, J. (ed.), Software Agents, Menlo Park CA: AAAI Press /MIT Press, 3-48

Brafman, R. /Tennenholtz, M. (1996), On partially controlled multi-agent systems, in: JAIR 4, 477-507

Brooks, F. (1995), The mythical man-month: essays on software engineering, Reading MA: Addison-Wesley

Brooks, R. (1986), A robust layered control system for a mobile robot, in: IEEE Journal of Robotics and Automation, 2 (1), 14-23

Buchanan, J. (1975), The limits of liberty - between anarchy and leviathan, Chicago: University of Chicago Press

Buchanan, J. (1994), Notes on the liberal constitution, in: Cato Journal, vol. 14, no. 1, http://www.cato.org/pubs/journal

Buchanan, J. /Tullock, G. (1962/87), The calculus of consent, Ann Arbor: University of Michigan Press

Caldas, J. /Coelho, H. (1999), The origin of institutions: socio-economic processes, choice, norms and conventions, in: JASSS, vol. 2, no. 2, http://www.soc.surrey.ac.uk/JASSS

Cammarata, S. /McArthur, S. /Steeb, R. (1983), Strategies for cooperation in distributed problem solving, in: Proceedings of the 8th International Joint Conference on Artificial Intelligence (IJCAI-83), Karlsruhe, 767-770

Cassel, D. /Thieme, J. (1999), Stabilitätspolitik in: Bender, D. et al. (Hrsg.), Vahlens Kompendium der Wirtschaftstheorie und Wirtschaftspolitik, München: Vahlen, 363-437

Castelfranchi, C. (1990), Social power. A point missed in multi-agent systems…, in: Demazeau, Y /Müller, J.-P. (eds), Decentralized AI, Proceedings of the First European Workshop on Modeling Autonomous Agents in a Multi-Agents World, Amsterdam: North Holland, 49-63

Castelfranchi, C. (1995a), Guarantees for autonomy in cognitive agent architecture, in: Wooldridge, M. /Jennings, N. (eds.), Intelligent agents, ECAI-94 Workshop on agent theories, architectures, and languages, Berlin /Heidelberg /New York: Springer, 56-70

Castelfranchi, C. (1995b), Commitments: From individual intentions to groups and ogranizations, in: Proceedings of the International Conference on Multiagent Systems (ICMAS-95), Menlo Parc CA: AAAI Press, 41-48

Castelfranchi, C. (1998), Modeling social action for AI agents, in: Artificial Intelligence, 103, 157-182

Castelfranchi, C. /Conte, R. (1996), Distributed artificial intelligence and social science: critical issues, in: O'Hare, G. / Jennings, N. (eds.), Foundations of Distributed Artificial Intelligence, New York: John Wiley & Sohns, 527-542

Chandler, A. (1990), Scale and scope - The dynamics of industrial capitalism, With the assistance of Takashi Hikino, Cambridge MA: Havard University Press

Chavez, A. /Maes, P. (1996), Kasbah: An Agent Marketplace for buying and selling goods, in: Proceedings of the First International Conference on the Practical Application of Agents and Multi-Agent Technology, London

Chess, D. /Grosof, B. /Harrison, C. /Levine, D. /Parris, C. (1995), Itinerant agents for mobile computing, research-report, IBM T.J. Watson Research Center, New York

Clarke, A. (1969), 2001: A space odyssey Screenplay, Hawk Films Ltd., c/o. M-G-M Studios, Boreham Wood, http://www.palantir.net/2001/script.html

Clarke, R. (1993), Asimov's laws of robotics - implications for information technology, in: IEEE Computer 26,12 and 27,1, 53-61 and 57-66

Clearwater, S. (ed.) (1996), Market based control, Singapore/ New Jersey /London /Hong Kong: World Scientific

Clearwater, S. /Huberman, B. (1995), A multi-agent system for controlling building environments, in: Proceedings of the International Conference on Multi-Agent Systems (ICMAS-1995), Menlo Park CA: AAAI Press /MIT Press, 171-176

Cliff, D. /Bruten, J. (1998), Shop 'til you drop I: Market trading interactions as adaptive behavior, HPL-98-58, HP Laboratories, Bristol

Coase, R. (1937/88), The nature of the firm, in: The firm the market and the law, Chicago: University of Chicago Press, 33-56

Coase, R. (1960/88), The problem of social cost, in: The firm the market and the law, Chicago: University of Chicago Press, 157-186

Coase, R. (1988), The firm, the market and the law, Chicago: University of Chicago Press

Coleman, J. (1990), Foundations of social theory, Cambridge MA /London: Belknap Press of Havard University Press

Conlisk, J. (1996), Why bounded rationality, in: Journal of Economic Literature, Vol. XXXIV (June), 669-700

Cranston, M. (1967), Freedom, London: Longmans

Cutkosky, M. /Engelmore, R. /Fikes, R. /Genesereth, M. /Gruber, T. /Mark, W. /Tenenbaum, J. /Weber, J. (1993/98), PACT: An experiment in integrating concurrent engineering systems, in: Huhns, M. / Singh, M. (eds.), Readings in agents, San Francisco: Morgan Kaufmann, 46-55

David, P. (1985), Clio and the economics of QWERTY, in: AEA Papers and Proceedings, vol. 75, no. 2, 332-337

Decker, K. /Lesser, V. (1995/98), Designing a family of coordination algorithms, in: Huhns, M. / Singh, M. (eds.), Readings in agents, San Francisco: Morgan Kaufmann, 450-457

DeLong, B. /Froomkin, M. (2000), Speculatice microeconomics for tommorrow's economy, in: First Monday, vol. 5, no. 2, http://www.firstmonday.dk

Demsetz, H. (1969), Information and efficiency: Another viewpoint, in: Journal of Law and Economics, 11, 55-66

Dennett, D. (1987), The intentional stance, Cambridge MA: MIT Press

Denzau, A. /North, D. (1994), Shared mental models: Ideologies and institutions, in: Kyklos, 47, 3-31

Durfee, /Lesser, V. /Corkill, (1992), Distributed problem solving, in: Shapiro, S. (ed.), Encyclopedia of Artificial Intelligence, New York: John Wiley & Sons, 379-388

Dyson, G. (1997), Darwin among the machines: The evolution of global intelligence, Reading MA: Addison-Wesley

Economides, N. (1996), The economics of networks, in: International Journal of Industrial Organization, vol. 14, no. 2, 673-699

Edgeworth, F. (1881), Mathematical psychics, London: Kegan Paul

Edwards, P. (1967) (ed.), The Encyclopedia of Philosophy, Vol. 3, London

Eggertsson, Th. (1990), Economic behavior and institutions, Cambridge: Cambridge University Press

Eisenberg, A. (1999), Die Lösungen sozialer Dilemmata und der Wandel informeller Institutionen, Diskussionsbeitrag 04-99, Max-Planck Institut zur Erforschung von Wirtschaftssystemen, Jena

Ephrati, E. / Rosenschein, J. (1996), Deriving consensus in multiagent systems, Artificial Intelligence 87, 21-74

Epstein, J. /Axtell, R. (1996), Growing artificial societies - social science from the bottom up, Washington and Cambridge MA: Brookings Institution Press /MIT Press

Eucken, W. (1959), Grundsätze der Wirtschaftspolitik, Reinbek bei Hamburg: Rowohlt Verlag

Eymann, T. /Padovan, B. /Schoder, D. (1998), Simulating value chain coordination with artificial life agents, in: Demazeau, Y. (ed.), Proceedings of the 3rd International Conference on Multi-Agent Systems (ICMAS '98), Los Alamitos CA: IEEE Computer Society Press, 423-424

Fischer, K. /Müller, J. /Pischel, M. (1996/98), A pragmatic BDI architecture, in: Huhns, M. / Singh, M. (eds.), Readings in agents, San Francisco: Morgan Kaufmann, 217-224

Foner, L. (1997), YENTA: A multi-agent, retrieval-based matchmaking system, in: Proceedings of the First Conference on Autonomous Agents 1997, New York: ACM Press, 301-307

Frank, R. (1988), Passions within reason: The strategic role of emotions, New York: Norton

Franklin, S. (1997), Autonomous agents as embodied AI, in: Cybernetics and Systems, 28:6 (1997), 499-520

Franklin, S. (1998b), Coordination without communication, Working-paper, Insititute for Intelligent Systems and Department of Mathematical Sciences, University of Memphis

Franklin, S. / Graesser, A. (1997), Is it an agent or just a program?: A taxonomy for autonomous agents, in: Müller, J. /Wooldridge, M. /Jennings, N. (eds.) Intelligent agents III, agent theories, architectures, and languages, Heidelberg /Berlin /New York: Springer, 21-35

Furubotn, E. G. / Richter, R. (1991) (Hrsg.),The new institutional economics: a collection of articles from the Journal of Institutional and Theoretical Economics, Tübingen: J.C.B. Mohr (Paul Siebeck)

Gasser, L. (1991), Social conceptions of knowledge and action: DAI foundations and open systems semantics, in: Artificial Intelligence, 47 (1-3), 107-138

Gaus, G. (1996), Liberalism, in: Stanford Encyclopedia of Philosophy, http://cs1/library.usyd.edu.an/stanford/entires/liberalism.html

Gauthier, D. (1986), Morals by agreement, Oxford: Oxford University Press

Gell-Man, M. (1994), The quark and the jaguar, New York: Freeman and Company

Gerecke, U. (1998), Soziale Ordnung in der modernen Gesellschaft, Tübingen: J.C.B. Mohr (Paul Siebeck)

Gibbs, W. (1994), Software: chronisch mangelhaft, in: Spektrum der Wissenschaft, Dezember, 56-63

Glance, N. / Hogg, T. (1995), Computational social dilemmas, technical-report, Xerox PARC Research Center, Palo Alto CA

Glance, N. /Huberman, B. (1994), The dynamics of social dilemmas, in: Scientific American, March, 76-81

Gode, D. /Sunder, S. (1994), Human and artificially intelligent traders in computer double auctions, in: Carley, K. /Prietula, M. (eds.), Computational organization theory, Hillsdale NJ: Lawrence Erlbaum Assoc., 241-262

Gode, D. /Sunder, S. (1999), Double auction dynamics: Structural consequences of non-binding price controls, working-paper, Graduate School of Administration, Carnegie Mellon University, Pittsburgh

Graber, Ch. (1999), Zertifikate für digitale Identitäten, in: NZZ, Nr. 219, 21. September, B43

Greenwald, A. /Kephart, J. (1999), Shopbots and Pricebots, in: Proceedings of the 16th Interantional Joint Conference on Artificial Intelligence (IJCAI-99), Stockholm, 506-511

Grimley, M. /Monroe, B. (1999), Protecting the integrity of agents: an exploration into letting agents loose in an unpredictable world, in: Crossroads, http://www1.acm.org/crossroads

Groenewegen, P. (1987), Division of labour, in: The New Palgrave: A dictionary of Economics, vol. I, London and Basingstoke: Macmillan Press, 901-906

Gupta, A. /Stahl, D. /Whinston, A. (1996), Economic issues in electronic commerce, in: Kalakota, R. /Whinston, A. (eds.), Readings in electronic commerce, Reading MA: Addison Wesley, 197-227

Guttman, R. /Moukas, A. /Maes, P. (1998), Agents as mediators in electronic commerce, in: EM, vol. 8, no. 1, 22-27

Gwartney, J. /Lawson, R. (1997), Economic freedom of the world. 1997 Annual report, Vancouver BC: Fraser Institute

Hanson, J. /Kephart, J. (1998), Spontaneous specialization in a free-market economy of agents, paper presented at the Artificial Societies and Computational Markets Workshop at the Second International Conference on Autonomous Agents (AA '98), Minneapolis /St. Paul

Hardin, G. (1968), The tragedy of the commons, in: Science, 162, 1243-1248

Hargreaves Heap, S. /Hollis, M. /Lyons, B. /Sugden, R. (1992), The theory of choice, Oxford and Cambridge MA: Blackwell

Hargreaves Heap, S. /Varoufakis, Y (1995), Game theory: a critical introduction, Routledge, London

Hayek, F. A. v. (1948), Individualism and economic order, Chicago: University of Chicago Press

Hayek, F. A. v. (1960), The constitution of liberty, London: Routledge & Kegan Paul

Hayek, F. A. v. (1966), The principles of a liberal social order, in: Il Politico, Vol. 31, No. 4, 601-618

Hayek, F. A. v. (1969/94), Freiburger Studien, Gesammelte Aufsätze, 2. Auflage, Tübingen: J.C.B. Mohr (Paul Siebeck)

Hayek, F. A. v. (1973), Law, Legislation, and Liberty, vol. 1., Chicago: University of Chicago Press

Hayek, F. A. v. (1976), Denationalisation of money, London: The Institute of Economic Affairs

Hayek, F. A. v. (1988), The fatal conceit - the errors of socialism, in: Bartley, W. (ed.), The collected works of Friedrich August Hayek, vol. I, London: Routledge

Hirschman, A. (1970), Exit, voice, and loyalty: responses to decline in firms, organizations, and states, Cambridge MA: Harvard University Press

Hobbes, Th. (1651/1996), Leviathan, Oxford: Oxford University Press

Holland, J. (1995), Hidden order. How adaptation builds complexity, Reading MA: Addison-Wesley

Holland, J. / Miller, J. (1991), Artificial adaptive agents in economic theory, in: AEA Papers and Proceedings, vol. 51, no. 2, 365-370

Homann, K. /Pies, I. (1993), Liberalismus: kollektive Entwicklung individueller Freiheit - Zu Programm und Methode einer liberalen Gesellschaftsentwicklung, in: Homo Oecnomicus, Bd. X (3/4), 297-347

Homann, K./Pies, I. (1991), Wirtschaftsethik und Gefangenendilemma, in: WIST, Heft 12, Dezember, 608-614

Horwitz, S. (1994), From the sensory order to the liberal order: Hayek's non-rationalist liberalism, working-paper, St. Lawrence University, Canton NY

Hu, J. /Wellman, M. (1998), Multiagent reinforcement learning: Theoretical framework and an algorithm, in: Proceedings of the 15th International Conference on Machine Learning, Madison, 242-250

Huberman, B. (1988) (ed.), The ecology of computation, Amsterdam: North-Holland

Huberman, B. /Hogg, T. (1988), The behaviour of computational ecologies, in: Huberman, B. (ed.), The ecology of computation, Amsterdam: North-Holland, 77-116

Huberman, B. /Hogg, T. (1995), Distributed computation as an economic system, in: Journal of Economic Perspectives, vol. 9, no. 1, 141-152

Huhns, M. / Singh, M. (1998a) (eds.), Readings in agents, San Francisco: Morgan Kaufmann

Huhns, M. /Singh, M. (1998b), Cognitive Agents, in: IEEE Internet Computing, November-December 1998, 87-89

Huhns, M. /Singh, M. /Ksiezyk, T. (1994/98), Global information management via local autonomous agents, in: Huhns, M. / Singh, M. (eds.), Readings in agents, San Francisco: Morgan Kaufmann, 36-45

Hume, D. (1739/1985), A treatise of human nature, London: Penguin

Jasay, A. de (1991), Choice, contract, consent: A restatement of liberalism, London: Institute of Economic Affairs

Jasay, A. de (1995), Conventions: Some thoughts on the economics of ordered anarchy, in: Lectiones Jenenses, Max Planck Institut zur Erforschung von Wirtschaftssystemen, Jena

Jennings, N. (1999), Agent-based computing: promise and perils, in: Proceedings of the 16th Interantional Joint Conference on Artificial Intelligence (IJCAI-99), Stockholm, 1429-1436

Jennings, N. /Sycara, K. /Wooldridge, M. (1998), A roadmap of agent research and development, in: Autonomous and Multi-Agent Systems, 1, 7-38

Jennings, N, /Wooldridge, M. (1998), Agent technology - Foundations, applications, markets, Berlin/ Heidelberg/ New York: Springer

Jordan, M. /Russell, S. (1998), Introduction to computational intelligence, in: MIT Encyclopedia of the Cognitive Sciences, Cambridge MA: MIT Press, http://cognet.mit.edu/MITECS

Kaelbling, L. /Littman, M. /Moore, A. (1996), Reinforcement learning: A survey, in: Journal of Artificial Intelligence Research, 4, 237-285

Kautz, H. /Selman, B. /Coen, M. /Ketchpel, S. /Ramming, Chr. (1994/98), An experiment in the design of software agents, in: Huhns, M. / Singh, M. (eds.), Readings in agents, San Francisco: Morgan Kaufmann, 125-130

Kelly, K. (1994), Out of control - The new biology of machines, social systems, and the economic world, Reading MA: Addison-Wesley

Kephart, J. /Das, R. /MacKie-Mason, J. (1999), Two sided learning in an agent economy for information bundles, paper presented to the IJCAI-99-Workshop on Agent-Mediated Electronic Commerce, Stockholm

Kephart, J. /Sorkin, G. /Chess, D. /White, S. (1998a), Kampf den Computerviren, in: Spektrum der Wissenschaft, May, 60-65

Kephart, J. /Hanson, J. /Sairamesh, J. (1998b), Price-War Dynamics in a Free Market-Economy of Software Agents, in: Adami, Ch. /Kitano, H. /Taylor, Ch. (eds.), Proceedings of ALIFE VI, Cambridge MA: MIT Press

Kirchgässner, G. (1991), Homo oeconomicus, Tübingen: J.C.B. Mohr (Paul Siebeck)

Kirsch, G. (1988), Wenn Wandel zur Krise wird, in: Frankfurter Allgemeine Zeitung, Nr. 294, 13

Kirsch, G. (1992), Unvorhersehbarkeit, ein Ausdruck der Freiheit, in: Jahrbuch für Neue Politische Ökonomie, Bd. 11, 16-29

Kirsch, G. (1994), Unpredictablilty - another word for freedom...and if machines were free?, in: Thalmann, N. /Thalmann, D. (eds.), Artificial life and virtual reality, New York: John Wiley & Sons

Kirsch, G. (1997), Neue Politische Ökonomie, 4. Auflage, Düsseldorf: Werner Verlag

Kirsch, G. (1999), Ethik wirtschaftlicher Ordnungen, in: Korff, W. (Hrsg.), Handbuch der Wirtschaftsethik, Bd. 2., Gütersloh: Gütersloher Verlagshaus, 186-216

Kirsch, G. / Kohlas, J. (1993), Der Wert des Unvorhersehbaren, in: Frankfurter Allgemeine Zeitung, Nr. 106, 15

Kirzner, I. (1982), Uncertainty, discovery, and human action: A study of the entrepreneurial profile in the Miseian system, in: Kirzner, I. (ed.), Method and process of Austrian Economics, Lexington MA: Lexington Books, 139-160

Kirzner, I. (1992), The meaning of market process, London: Routledge

Kiwit, D. /Voigt, S. (1995), Überlegungen zum institutionellen Wandel unter Berücksichtigung des Verhältnisses interner und externer Institutionen, Diskussionsbeitrag 02-95, Max-Planck Institut zur Erforschung von Wirtschaftssystemen, Jena

Kleinewefers, H. (1988), Grundzüge einer verallgemeinerten Wirtschaftsordnungstheorie, Tübingen: J.C.B. Mohr (Paul Siebeck)

Kleinewefers, H. (1999), Hayek und die Demokratiereform, working-paper, Seminar für Wirtschafts- und Sozialpolitik, Universität Fribourg, Fribourg

Koboldt, Ch. /Leder, M. /Schmidtchen, D. (1992), Ökonomische Analyse des Rechts, in: WIST, Heft 7, 334-343

Kraus, S. (1996), An overview of incentive contracting, in: Artificial Intelligence, 83, 297-346

Kraus, S. (1997), Negotiation and cooperation in multi-agent environments, in: Artificial Intelligence, 94, no. 1-2, 79-97

Kraus, S. / Wilkenfeld, J. / Zlotkin, G. (1995), Multiagent negotiation under time constraints, Artificial Intelligence, 75(2), 297-345

Kraus, S. /Lehmann, D. (1995), Designing and building a negotiating automated agent, in: Computational Intelligence, vol. 11, no. 1, 132-171

Kreps, D. (1990), A course in microeconomic theory, New York: Princeton University Press

Krogh, C. (1995), The rights of agents, in: Wooldridge, M./Müller, J. /Tambe, M. (eds.), Intelligent Agents II, Agent Theories, Architectures, and Languages, Berlin /Heidelberg /New York: Springer, 1-16

Krogh, C. (1997), Normative structures in natural and artificial systems, Ph.D Thesis, Oslo University, Oslo

Labrou, Y. /Finin, T. (1997/98), Semantics and conversations for a agent communication language, in: Huhns, M. / Singh, M. (eds.), Readings in agents, San Francisco: Morgan Kaufmann, 235-242

Lane, D. (1993), Artificial worlds and economics, part I, in: Journal of Evolutionary Economics, 3, 89-107

Langlois, R. (1986) (ed.), Economics as a process, Cambridge: Cambridge University Press

Leipold, H. (1989), Das Ordnungsproblem in der ök. Institutionentheorie, in: ORDO, 40, 129-146

Leonard. A. (1997), Bots, San Francisco: Hardwired

Lesser, V. (1998), Reflections on the nature of multi-agent coordination and its implications for an agent architecture, in: Autonomous Agents and Multi-Agent Systems, 1, 89-111

Locke, J. (1690/1967), Zwei Abhandlungen über die Regierung, Euchner, W. (Hrsg.), Frankfurt a. M.: Europäische Verlagsanstalt

Luhmann, N. (1984/94), Soziale Systeme - Grundriss einer allgemeinen Theorie, Frankfurt a. M.: Suhrkamp

Macy, M. (1998), Social order in artificial worlds, in: JASSS, vol. 1, no. 1, http://www.soc.surrey.ac.uk/JASSS

Maes, P. (1995), Modeling adaptive autonomous agents, in: Langton, Ch. (ed.), Artificial life – An overview, Cambridge MA: MIT Press, 135-162

Maes, P. /Guttman, R. /Moukas, A. (1999), Agents that buy and sell: Transforming commerce as we know it, in: Communications of the ACM, vol. 42, no. 3, 81-91

Maes, P. /Kozierok, R. (1993), Learning interface agents, in: Proceedings of the 11th National Conference on Artificial Intelligence (AAAI-93), Menlo Parc: AAAI Press /MIT Press, 459-465

Malsch, T. (1998a) (Hrsg.), Sozionik - soziologische Ansichten über künstliche Sozialität, Berlin: Edition Sigma

Malsch, T. (1998b), Die Provokation der Artificial Societies, Malsch, T. (Hrsg.), Sozionik - soziologische Ansichten über künstliche Sozialität, Berlin: Edition Sigma, 25-58

Matonis, J. (1998), Digital cash and monetary freedom, in: Hayek Society's AMA-Gi, vol 1., no.1, http://www.lse.ac.uk/clubs/hayek/ama-gi/ama-gi.htm

McAffee, P. /McMillan, J. (1998, Game theory and competition, working-paper, Northwestern University, Evanston IL

McCarthy, J. (1979), Ascribing mental qualities to machines, Computer Science Department, Stanford University, Stanford CA, http://www-formal-stanford.stanford.edu/jmc/ascribing/ascribing.html

Meyer, J.-A. /Wilson, S. (1990) (eds.), Simulation of adaptive behaviour: from animals to animats, Cambridge MA: MIT Press

Milgrom, P. /Roberts, J. (1992), Economics, organization and management, Englewood Cliffs: Prentice Hall

Mill, J. S. (1859/1989), On liberty, Cambridge: Cambridge University Press

Miller, G. (1997), Protean primates: The evolution of adaptive unpredictability in competition and courtship, in: Whiten, A. /Byrne, R. (eds.), Machiavellian Intelligence II, Cambridge: Cambridge University Press, 312-340

Miller, M. / Drexler, K. (1988a), Comparative ecology: A compultional perspective, in: Huberman, B. (ed.), The ecology of computation, Amsterdam: North-Holland, 51-76

Miller, M. / Drexler, K. (1988b), Markets and computation: Agoric open systems, in: Huberman , B. (ed.), The ecology of computation, Amsterdam: North-Holland, 133-176

Miller, M. /Krieger, D. /Hardy, N. /Hibbert, Ch./Tribble, E. (1996), An automated auction in ATM network bandwith, in: Clearwater, E. (ed.), Market based control, Singapore/ New Jersey /London /Hong Kong: World Scientific, 96-125

Moravec, H. (1996), Körper, Roboter und Geist, in: Maar, Chr. /Pöppel, E. /Christaller, T. (Hrsg.), Die Technik auf dem Weg zur Seele -Forschungen an der Schnittstelle Gehirn/Computer, Rowohlt: Reinbeck bei Hamburg, 162-196

Moulin, B. /Chaib-draa, B. (1996), An overview of distributed artificial intelligence, in: O'Hare, G. /Jennings, N. (eds.), Foundations of Distributed artificial intelligence, New York: John Wiley & Sons, 3-56

Mullen, T. /Wellman, M. (1995), Some issues in the design of market oriented agents, in: Wooldridge, M. /Müller, J. /Tambe, M. (eds.), Intelligent Agents II, Agent Theories, Architectures, and Languages, Berlin /Heidelberg /NewYork: Springer, 283-298

Musgrave, R. (1994), Die öffentlichen Finanzen in Theorie und Praxis, Bd. 1, 6. Aufl., Tübingen: J.C.B. Mohr (Paul Siebeck)

Nalebuff, B. /Brandenburger, A. (1996), Co-opetition, London: HarperCollins Business

Nass, C. /Steuer, J. /Tauber, E. (1994), Computers are social actors, in: Proceedings of the International Joint Conference on Human Factors in Computing, 72-77

Negroponte, N. (1997), Agents: From direct manipulation to delegation, in: Bradshaw, J. (ed.), Software agents, Menlo Park CA: AAAI Press / MIT Press, 57-66

Neubauer, H.-J. (1999), Der verdunkelte Blick, in: Frankfurter Allgemeine Zeitung, Nr. 271, I

New Yorker (1993), Cartoon, in: New Yorker, July

Newell, A. (1982), The knowledge level, in: Artificial Intelligence, 18 (1), 87-127

Nonnenmacher, G. (1989), Die Ordnung der Gesellschaft - Mangel und Herrschaft in der politischen Philosophie der Neuzeit: Hobbes, Locke, Adam Smith, Rousseau, Weinheim: VCH Acta Humaniora

Norman, T. /Sierra, C./Jennings, N. (1997); Rights and commitments in multi-agent agreements, working-paper, Dept. of Electronic Engineering, Queen Mary & Westfield College, London

North, A. (1994), Economic performance through time, in: American Economic Review, vol. 84, no.3, 359-368

North, D. (1984), Transaction costs, institutions, and economic history, in: JITE, 140 (1984), 7-17

North, D. (1990/92), Insititutions, institutional change, and economic performance, Cambridge: Cambridge University Press

Nozick, R. (1974), Anarchy, state and utopia, Oxford: Blackwell

Nwana, H. /Lee, L. /Jennings, N. (1995), Coordination in sofware agent systems, working-paper, BT-Laboratories, Ipswich

O'Hare, G. /Jennings, N. (1996) (eds.), Foundations of Distributed Artificial Intelligence, New York: John Wiley & Sons

Oliveira, E. /Fonseca, J. /Jennings, N. (1999), Learning to be competitive in the market, in: Proceedings of the AAAI Workshop on Negotiation: Settling conflicts and identifying opportunities, Orlando

Olson, M. (1965/71), The logic of collective action, Cambridge MA: Havard University Press

Olson, M. (1982), The rise and decline of nations, New Haven: Yale University Press

Ordille, J. (1996), When agents roam, who can you trust?, research-paper, Lucent Technologies, Computing Science Research Center, Murray Hill

Orwell, G. (1949/84), 1984, New York: Penguin

Ostrom, E. (1986), An agenda for the study of institutions, in: Public Choice, 48, 3-25

Panzarasa, P. /Norman, T. /Jennings, N. (1999), Modeling sociality in the BDI framework, working-paper, Department of Electronic Engineering, Queen Mary and Westfield College, London

Parkes, D. /Ungar, L. (1996), The tragedy of the commons: Pricing social welfare in multiagent systems, working-paper, University of Pennsylvania, Philadelphia

Pejovich, S. (1997) (ed.), The economic foundations of property rights, Cheltenham: Edward Elgar Publishers

Polanyi, M. (1951), The logic of liberty, London: Routledge and Kegan Paul

Radnitzky, G. (1996), Mehr Gerechtigkeit für die Freiheit, in: ORDO, Bd. 47, 149-167

183

Rammert, W. (1998), Giddens und die Gesellschaft der Heinzelmännchen. Zur Soziologie technischer Agenten und der Multi-Agenten Systeme, working-paper, Freie Universität, Berlin

Rao, A. /Georgeff, M. (1995), BDI agents: From theory to practice, technical-note 56, Australian Artificial Intelligence Institute, Melbourne

Rawlins, G. (1997), Slaves of the machine - the quickening of computer technology, Cambridge MA: MIT Press

Richter, R. (1990), Sichtweise und Fragestellungen der Neuen Institutionenökonomik, in: ZWS, Jg. 110, 4, 571-591

Richter, R. / Furubotn, E. (1996), Neue Institutionenökonomik, Tübingen: J.C.B. Mohr (Paul Siebeck) (Engl.: Furubotn, E /Richter, R. (1997), Institutions and economic theory, Ann Arbor: University of Michigan Press)

Rosenschein, J. / Genesereth, M. (1985), Deals among rational agents, in: Proceedings (IJCAI-85), Los Angeles CA, 91-99

Rosenschein, J. / Zlotkin, G. (1994), Rules of encounter: designing conventions for automated negotiation Among Computers, Cambridge MA: MIT Press

Roth, A. (1999), Game theory as a tool for market design, working-paper, Havard University, Department of Economics and Graduate Schoold of Business Administration

Rothschild, E. (1994), Adam Smith and the invisible hand, in: American Economic Review, Papers and Proceedings, vol. 84, no. 2, 319-322

Rump, N. (1999), Schlüssel für Noten - Urheberrechte und deren Schutz im Internet, in: NZZ, Nr. 228, 1. Oktober, 77

Russell, S. (1997), Rationality and intelligence, in: Artificial Intelligence, 94, No. 1-2, 57-77

Russell, S. /Norvig, P. (1995), Artificial intelligence: a modern approach, Englewood Cliffs: Prentice-Hall

Saam, N. /Harrer, A. (1999), Simulating norms, social inequality, and functional change in artificial societies, in: JASSS, vol. 2, no. 1, http://www.soc.surrey.ac.uk/JASSS

Sandholm, T.. /Lesser, V. (1995), Equilibrium analysis of the possibilities of unenforced exchange in multiagent systems, working-paper, Computer Science Department, University of Mass., Amherst

Sandholm, T. /Lesser, V. (1995/98), Issues in automated negotiation and electronic commerce: Extending the contract net framework, in: Huhns, M. /Singh, M. (eds.), Readings in Agents, San Francisco: Morgan Kaufmann, 66-76

Sandholm, T. /Lesser, V. (1997), Coalitions among computationally bounded agents, in: Artificial Intelligence, 94, 99-137

Savage, L. (1954/71), Foundations of statistics, New York: John Wiley & Sons

Schiller, T. (1995), Liberalismus, in: Nohlen, D. (Hrsg.), Wörterbuch Staat und Politik, Bonn: Bundeszentrale für Politische Bildung, 393-398

Schillo, M. /Funk, P. / Rovatsos, M. (1999), Who can you trust: Dealing with deception, research-paper, DFKI GmbH, Saarbrücken

Schotter, A. (1981), The economic theory of social institutions, Cambridge: Cambridge University Press

Schwan, A. (1993), Politische Theorien des Rationalismus und der Aufklärung, in: Lieber, H.-J. (Hrsg.), Politische Theorien von der Antike bis zur Gegenwart, Bonn: Bundeszentrale für Politische Bildung, 157-258

Shafer, G. (1986/90), Savage revisited, in: Shafer, G. /Pearl, J. (eds.) Readings in Uncertain Reasoning, San Mateo: Morgan Kaufmann, 122-144

Shapiro, C. /Varian, H. (1998), Information rules: A strategic guide to the network economy, Cambridge MA: Havard Business School Press

Shneiderman, B. (1997), Direct manipulation versus agents: Paths to predictable, controllable, and comprehensible interfaces, in: Bradshaw, J. (ed.), Software agents, Menlo Park CA: AAAI Press /MIT Press, 97-108

Shoham, Y. (1996), The open scientific borders of AI and the case of economics, in: ACM Computing Surveys 28A (4)

Shoham, Y. (1997), An overview of agent-oriented programming, in: Bradshaw, J. (ed.), Software agents, Menlo Park CA: AAAI Press /MIT Press, 271-290

Shoham Y. /Tanaka, K. (1997), A dynamic theory of incentives in multi-agent systems, working-paper, Stanford University, Stanford

Shoham, Y. /Tennenholtz, M. (1995), On laws for artificial agent societies: off-line design, in: Artificial Intelligence, 73, 231-252

Shoham, Y. /Tennenholtz, M. (1997), On the emergence of social conventions: modeling analysis, and simulations, in: Artificial Intelligence, 94, 139-166

Simon, H. (1996), The sciences of the artificial, Cambridge MA: MIT Press

Singh, M. (1996), A conceptual analysis of commitments in multiagent systems, technical-report, Department of Computer Science, North Carolina State University, Raleigh

Singh, M. (1997), An ontology for commitments in multiagent systems: Toward a unification of normative concepts, technical-report, Department of Computer Science, North Carolina State University, Raleigh

Singh, M. (1998), Agent communication languages: Rethinking the principles, in: IEEE Computer, December, 40-47

Singh, M. /Huhns, M. (1999), Principles of agents and multiagent systems: Social, ethical, and legal abstractions and reasoning, Tutorial at the 16th International Joint Conference on Artificial Intelligence (IJCAI-99), Stockholm

Smith, A. (1776/1976), An inquiry into the nature and the causes of the wealth of nations, Cambell, R. /Skinner, A. /Todd, W. (eds.), vol. I & II, Oxford: Clarendon Press

Smith, M. /Bailey, J. /Brynjolfsson, E. (1999), Understanding digital markets: Review and assessment, in: Brynjolfsson, E. /Kahin, B. (eds.), Understanding the digital economy, Cambridge MA: MIT Press

Smith, R. (1980), The contract net protocol: High-level communication ad control in a distributed problem solver, in: IEEE Transactions on Computers, C-29 (12), 1104-1113

Stone P. / Veloso, M. (1997), Multi-agent systems: A survey from a machine learning perspective, working-paper, Computer Science Department, Carnegie Mellon University, Pittsburgh

Stork, D. (1996) (ed.), Hal's legacy, Cambridge MA: MIT Press

Streit, M. (1995), Ordnungsökonomik - Versuch einer Standortbestimmung, Diskussionsbeitrag 04-95, MPI zur Erforschung von Wirtschaftssystemen, Jena

Streit, M. /Wohlgemuth, M. (1997), The market economy and the state - Hayekian and ordoliberal conceptions, Diskussionsbeitrag 06-97, MPI zur Erforschung von Wirtschaftssystemen, Jena

Sugden, R. (1986), The economics of rights, co-operation and welfare, Oxford: Basil Blackwell

Sutton, R. /Barto, A. (1998), Reinforcement learning: An introduction, Cambridge MA: MIT Press, http://envy.cs.umass.edu/~rich/book/the-book.html

Sycara, K. (1989), Argumentation: planning other agent's plans, in: Proceedings of the 11th International Joint Conference on Artificial Intelligence (IJCAI-89), Detroit, 517-523

Tesauro, G. /Kephart, J. (1998), Foresight-based pricing algorithms in an economy of software-agents, working-paper, IBM T.J. Watson Research Center, Hawthorne NY

Tesauro, G. /Kephart, J. (1999), Pricing in agent economies using multi-agent Q-learning, working-paper, IBM T.J. Watson Research Center, Hawthorne NY

Thearling, K. /Ray, Th. (1997), Evolving parallel computation, in: Complex Systems, vol. 10, no. 3, 229-237

Tokoro, M. (1993/98), The society of objects, in: Huhns, M. / Singh, M. (eds.), Readings in agents, San Francisco: Morgan Kaufmann, 421-429

Tokoro, M. (1994), Agents: Towards a society in which humans and computers cohabitate, Perran, J. W. / Müller, J. P. (eds.), Distributed Software Agents and Applications, Berlin /Heidelberg /New York: Springer

Tullock, G. (1985), Adam Smith and the prisoner's dilemma, in: Quarterly Journal of Economics, 100, 1073-1081

Tullock, G. (1987), Rent seeking, in: The New Palgrave: A Dictionary of Economics, vol. IV, London and Basingstoke: Macmillan Press, 147-149

Vanberg, V. (1998), Hayek's constitutional political economy, in: Ama-Gi, vol. 1, no.1, http://www.lse.ac.uk/clubs/hayek/ama-gi/ama-gi.htm

Varian, H. (2000), Market structure in the network age, in: Brynjolfsson, E. /Kahin, B. (eds.), Understanding the digital economy, in press, Cambridge MA: MIT Press

Vaughn, K. (1989), Invisible hand, in: Eatwell, J. / Newman, P. /Milgate, M. (eds.), General Equilibrium, New York: Norton

Vaughn, K. (1999), Hayek's theory of the market order as an instance of the theory of complex, adaptive systems, Working-paper, George Mason University, Fairfax

Vidal, J. /Durfee, E. (1998), Learning nested agent models in an information economy, working-paper, Artificial Intelligence Laboratory, University of Michigan, Ann Arbor

Vigna, G. (1998) (ed.), Mobile agents and security, Berlin/ Heidelberg/ NewYork: Springer

Voigt, S. (1997), Breaking with the notion of social contract: Constitutions as based on spontaneously arisen institutions, Diskussionsbeitrag 01-97, MPI zur Erforschung von Wirtschaftssystemen, Jena

Vriend, N. (1996), Rational behavior and economic theory, Journal of Economic Behavior and Organization, vol. 29 (1996), 263-285

Vriend, N. (1999), Was Hayek an Ace?, working-paper, Queen Mary and Westfield College, University of London

Walsh, W. / Wellman, M. / Wurman, P./ MacKie-Mason, J. (1997), Some economics of market-based distributed scheduling, working-paper, University of Michigan, Ann Arbor

Walsh, W. /Wellman, M. (1999), Modeling supply chain formation in multiagent systems, paper presented at the workshop on agent mediated electronic commerce (IJCAI '99), Stockholm

Ward, M. (1998), There's an ant in my phone..., in: New Scientist, no. 2118, 24 Januar, 32-35

Weiss, G. (1997), Distributed artificial intelligence meets machine learning – Learning in multi-agent environments, Berlin /Heidelberg /New York: Springer

Weld, D. /Etzioni, O. (1994), The first law of robotics (a call to arms), working-paper, Department of Computer Science and Engineering, University of Washington, Seattle

Wellman, M. (1996), Market-oriented programming: Some early lessons, in: Clearwater, S. (ed.) Market based control, Singapore/ New Jersey /London /Hong Kong: World Scientific, 74-95

Wellman, M. (1998), Multiagent systems, in: MIT Encyclopedia of the Cognitive Sciences, Cambridge MA: MIT Press, http://cognet.mit.edu/MITECS

Wellman, M. /Wurman, P. (1997), Market-aware agents for a multiagent world, working-paper, Artificial Intelligence Laboratory, University of Michigan, Ann Arbor

Wiener, L. (1994), Digitales Verhängnis: Gefahren der Abhängigkeit von Computern und Programmen, Bonn: Addison Wesley

Williamson, O. (1985), The economic institutions of capitalism, New York and London: Free Press

Williamson, O. (1986), The economics of governance: Framework and implications, in: Langlois, R. (Hrsg.) (1986), Economics as a process, Cambridge: Cambridge University Press, 171-202

Willmott, S. /Calisti, M. (2000), An agent future for network control?, in: Informatik-Informatique, Nr. 1, 25-32

Wooldridge, M./Jennings, N. (1995) (eds.), Intelligent agents, agent theories, architectures, and languages: A survey, Berlin/ Heidelberg/ New York: Springer, 1-21

Ygge, F. /Akkermans, H. (1999), Decentralized markets versus central control: A comparative study, in: Journal of Artificial Intelligence Research, 11, 301-333

Zacharia, G. /Moukas, A. /Maes, P. (1998), Collaborative reputation mechanisms in electronic marketplaces, working-paper, MIT Media Laboratory, Cambridge MA

Zakaria, F. (1997), Ein beunruhigender Trend – Die Demokratie blüht, nicht jedoch der konstitutionelle Liberalismus, Frankfurter Allgemeine Zeitung, Nr. 288, 15

Zimmermann, H. (1994), Die Rolle von Prinzipien in der Theorie der Wirtschaftspolitik, in: ORDO, 45, 137-145

About the author

Dirk Wagner obtained a Licentiate in Economics from the University of Fribourg (CH) in 1996 and a MBA in International Management from the Royal Holloway College of the University of London (UK) in 1997. Between 1997 and 2000 he was dedicated to an interdisciplinary research project of the Centre of Public Choice and the Institute for Informatics at the University of Fribourg under the supervision of Prof. Guy Kirsch and Prof. Jürg Kohlas. The present study summarises the outcome of this project. Next to his academic work Dirk Wagner worked for a management consultant firm and in the corporate strategy department of an industrial corporation. Meanwhile his professional interests and activities focus on the development of electronic marketplaces on the Internet.